WRITING MUSIC FOR TELEVISION AND RADIO COMMERCIALS (and More)

A Manual for Composers and Students

2nd Edition

Michael Zager

The Scarecrow Press, Inc.
Lanham, Maryland • Toronto • Plymouth, UK
2008

SCARECROW PRESS, INC.

Published in the United States of America by Scarecrow Press, Inc.
A wholly owned subsidary of
The Rowman & Littlefield Publishing Group, Inc.
4501 Forbes Boulevard, Suite 200, Lanham, Maryland 20706
www.scarecrowpress.com

Estover Road
Plymouth PL6 7PY
United Kingdom

Copyright © 2008 by Michael Zager

British Library Cataloguing in Publication Information Available

Library of Congress Cataloging-in-Publication Data

Zager, Michael.
  Writing music for television and radio commercials (and more) : a manual for composers and students / Michael Zager.—2nd ed.
      p.   cm.
  Includes index.
  ISBN-13: 978-0-8108-6139-8 (pbk. : alk. paper)
  ISBN-10: 0-8108-6139-9 (pbk. : alk. paper)
  eISBN-13: 978-0-8108-6219-7
  eISBN-10: 0-8108-6219-0
  1. Music in advertising—Instruction and study.   2. Television advertising.
3. Radio advertising.   I. Title.
  MT67.Z34   2008
  781.5'413—dc22
                                                                2008009184

To my wife, Jane; our children, Jonathan, Allison, Stephen,
and Nicholas; our grandchildren, Jack and Lily;
and my mother, Frances.
Thank you for your love, support, and patience.

Contents

Preface

This second edition of *Writing Music for Television and Radio Commercials (and More)* is intended to be an overview of the creative process of composing music for commercials and other related compositional genres. (Separate books could be written about several of the subjects covered.) The tools of composition and arranging and how to approach and analyze creative situations *can* be taught, but talent *cannot* be taught. Applying the analytical and creative methods suggested in this book will assist composers in achieving their creative goals. When interacting with advertising agencies, composers are immersed in a surreal mixture of music and business. The goal of advertising agencies is to please clients by creating viable and successful advertising campaigns, which helps to sell products or to create images for their products and/or their overall brand(s). It is a composer's job to compose music that best suits commercials, not to necessarily write music that satisfies him or her personally. The ideal solution is to compose music that satisfies both the creative needs of composers and the business objectives of agencies and their clients.

To gain the most from this book, it is advisable but not necessary to have a basic knowledge of theory, harmony, and orchestration. Many successful jingle writers lack a formal music education. It is unusual for composers who specialize in traditional underscoring (background music) not to have a formal music education. The book will also be helpful to students interested in film scoring. Composing commercials is a unique craft and should be studied as a separate discipline. Advertising writers, art directors, and music producers can also read sections of this book to understand the creative process from a composer's viewpoint.

Please note that the CD included with the book contains examples of various musical genres and sound effects discussed in the text. When a CD track applies directly to the subject matter, you will be directed to listen to a specific track.

Acknowledgments

Without the mentoring, teaching, and friendship of David Tcimpidis of the Mannes College of Music, a division of New School University, this book would not have been written. Thank you for making my dream of becoming an educator a reality.

I would like to thank my friends whose knowledge and expertise contributed to the information contained in this book. Robert Rainier—thank you for your guidance and for sharing your vast knowledge of music book publishing. Thanks also to my colleagues and business associates Alfred Brown, Patricia Fleitas, Fookloy Ford, Stuart Glazer, Marshall Grantham, Cissy Houston, Joel Harrison, Dale Johnson, Lisa Kalb, Christopher Lennertz, Mark Mayhew, Arthur Meranus, Raul Murciano, Dennis Powers, John Russo, Steve Schnur, Kevin Teasley, Jack Wall, and Alejandro Sanchez-Samper.

I would like to thank my publisher, Scarecrow Press, and my editors, Kellie Hagan and Renée Camus.

Introduction

A study by the *Harvard Business Review* concluded that people remember 20 percent of what they hear and 30 percent of what they hear and see.

While the process of composing involves numerous steps and skills, the composer's goal is to elicit an emotional response from the audience. Therefore, when composing music for television and radio commercials, composers must focus on receiving the proper reaction from the audience. Sometimes the reaction to the score is subliminal; however, without music, some commercials might not be as effective. The composer's objective should be to achieve the reaction that the creative team (writer, art director, and producer) wants to elicit. The music must enhance the scenes and add "feeling" to the messages behind the concept of the commercials. *The music must help "tell the story."*

It is the emotional reaction of hearing music that creates a lasting impression. For example, a song on the radio usually triggers a memory of an event or time period in the listener's life. In the film *Jaws*, the two-note bass theme played when the shark was near a potential victim created an anticipation of danger. Within Intel commercials, the musical logo (theme) at the end of the spots is anticipated since viewers have frequently heard the theme because of repeated airplay. During the television program *The X-Files*, the short musical theme played with an unusual synthesizer sound creates an emotional response and also musically telegraphs (to the audience) the general concept of the series.

> ♫ Throughout the decades, music has always held a special place among the arts because of the emotional response it creates. Various cultures have banned music and thought of it as evil. People have been jailed for listening to and playing unacceptable music; instruments have been burned. Songs have always reflected the attitudes and mores of society.
>
> In Plato's *Republic*, Socrates wanted to ban the musical modes (specific scales) "because more than anything else rhythm and harmony find their way to the inmost soul and take strongest hold upon it, bringing with them an imparting grace, if one is rightly trained, and otherwise the contrary."

Music can evoke any mood imaginable. The composer's choice of instruments, harmonic structure, compositional structure, recording techniques, and synthesizer effects all evoke a response from the audience.

The subtlest compositional device can affect an audience's visceral response to a commercial. For instance, if the composer uses a "negative-sounding" musical sound effect within a scene that is intended to provoke a positive response, the audience might have a negative reaction to the entire commercial. This is a frequent compositional problem; therefore, the composer must have a clear understanding of the musical mood expected by the creatives. An additional problem is that musical effects and moods are subjective. The music might sound interesting and or positive to the composer but generate a negative response from the audience.

In contemporary society, virtually all forms of entertainment and informative presentations use music: commercials, motion pictures, television programs, industrial films, corporate events, electronic games, recordings, and more. The emotional mood that music creates is of the utmost importance. For instance, a specific style of music is often heard when a telephone caller is put on hold. Airlines usually play "middle-of-the-road" music (sometimes with voice-over announcements) since the music has to appeal to a sizable demographic. A record label will often use the label's most recent releases as the "on-hold message."

Choosing the most appropriate musical style can make the difference between success or failure for a commercial. It is advisable to conduct in-depth discussions with the creative team at the advertising agency so that everyone has a clear understanding of the assignment and the function of the music. Even though most creatives have a specific vision of their creative goal(s), it is advisable for composers to contribute additional suggestions. Composers are the musical experts, and experienced creatives will generally value a composer's input.

1

Advertising Agency and Process Structure

Developing Commercials for Television

The creative people (referred to as the "creatives") at advertising agencies hire composers to write music for commercials. Clients hire agencies to plan, design, place, and supervise their advertisements or advertising campaigns. Not all agencies perform all functions; some agencies only buy the media placement, while others only create and execute print, television, and radio commercials. Major agencies are generally full-service agencies.

Most global agencies provide ancillary services related to advertising. These services include public relations, direct marketing, sales promotion, and media buying. In order to be competitive, large agencies must be full-service providers.

Since large agencies usually service international accounts, they must consider the local or regional culture of their consumers. This affects both the advertising and the music. Global agencies are concerned with obtaining international accounts since they can be lucrative and also aid in attracting additional local clients. To remain competitive, they strive to maintain both types of accounts.

For example, when analyzing the global music charts, the top 10 singles are rarely the same in each country or territory. If an agency decides to create original advertising music to be used globally and the assignment is to reflect the current, popular, worldwide musical culture, the agency creatives and the composer should research international hits and incorporate the feel and structure of the music in the newly composed music.

Since cultures vary, agencies might use the same music on various commercials that have been specifically designed for local or regional cultures. Sometimes, the agencies will use different music on each commercial because they want the music to reflect local or regional musical tastes.

Agencies are concerned about building a brand for their clients. The advertising must either help to achieve product sales or to successfully build a brand or company image (also called institutional advertising). The music serves as a significant contribution to the creative process.

In general, after months of market research, clients provide advertising agencies with a list (referred to as a "laundry list") of marketing objectives. The clients want their objectives integrated in the advertising. Agencies are often involved in choosing the objectives. In most agencies, the key creative, research, and account people work with clients to plan creative strategies that will best accomplish their business objectives. Composers must understand the business of advertising in order to create music that accommodates the business strategies of specific products. Composers have to work within that structure, which varies between agencies.

The following is a creative brief (laundry list) for a beauty product. The name of the product has been withheld.

Creative Brief for Television

Advertising Objective

1. To generate awareness and promote trial of (product name)
2. To drive the customer to the counter to purchase the product and/ or receive a complimentary sample with a consultation on how to use the product

Target Audience

1. Forty-plus female users of facial treatment products who are concerned about the signs of aging
2. Women who want to reduce wrinkles

Customer Benefit

1. The product is a unique formula designed to reduce and correct the appearance of wrinkles.

Reason to Believe

1. The formula is patented by the manufacturer and delivers powerful, full-strength, antiwrinkle benefits within the skin's surface layers. The targeted formula is time released to fight wrinkles continuously for 16 hours.
2. After two weeks: Fine lines begin to disappear, and smoother skin is revealed.
3. After four weeks: Surface wrinkles are reduced, age spots fade, and skin is visibly resurfaced.

Tone

1. Breakthrough, contemporary
2. Efficacious, scientific, and technological
3. 30-second television spot

Timing

Spot begins to air on November 19. (Tapes due to accounts beginning on October 19.)

This brief was given to the creatives and the account personnel working on the account. It served as a guide for the writer, the composer, the director, the editor, the producer, and the account people. Although the product description is thorough, it is still a difficult task for the creatives to develop advertising that will project an image for the product and also keep the audience's attention. Composers have the same mission. These challenges make advertising fascinating.

Demographics

Demographics is the study of human population. There are usually choices when determining the potential marketing and advertising strategies for products. One choice is to gear the advertising toward a particular demographic. Agencies and clients perform extensive research to determine their target market. A carefully planned strategy exposes products to new markets.

Research consists of random phone calls, normally the first step. The purpose is to determine the demographics of their potential consumers, the magazines they read, their income average, the vehicles they drive, their musical taste, and supplementary information that will provide a profile of potential buyers. If an individual seems to fit the proper profile, they might be asked to attend a *focus group* for which they are paid a fee. People are selected at shopping centers, church groups, or other appropriate locations. Focus groups help provide agencies with relevant information, and this affects their advertising strategy.

Focus groups are held for the purpose of research before a creative strategy is developed. (Focus groups are also conducted after a commercial has been completed.) Commercial ideas are sometimes tested prior to final production. Groups are of varying sizes and usually consist of 2 to 10 participants. In a large group, some attendees might dominate the conversation, causing relevant information from the other participants to be missed. The agency might construct a list of 20 or 30 potential "taglines" (slogans) or show pictures that create visual images of the product. Their goal is to determine the viability of the product(s) being tested. The information from the various focus groups is compiled and a report submitted to the agency and client. Campaigns have been canceled and/or changed after studying the results. The information is used as a guide to determine strategically viable advertising and marketing that could appeal to their current or potential consumers.

Example of a demographic: Women between the ages of 18 and 22 or ambitious women who have careers in business, denoting that they are generally intelligent and educated people.

Psychographics

Psychographics is the study of psychological reasons for consumers' behaviors. Research can determine the influences of lifestyle and the psychological traits that motivate them to purchase certain products. There are many products for which demographics do not necessarily affect sales. For instance, consumers' ages for many products might range from 20 to 75, and their gender is irrelevant. The product claims to solve a problem or concern of the purchaser. For example, consumers frequent health food stores to acquire special vitamins that claim to help their memories. The advertising is geared toward health issues or emotional needs rather than catering to a specific age or income demographic.

Example of Psychographics

For many years, Clairol (the beauty care company) used the popular slogan "Does she . . . or doesn't she?" In 2002, they changed their entire focus and used the slogan "A beauty all your own" for all of their hair color products. The intention was to convey the message that beauty comes in all forms. They were not targeting consumers of a specific age or weight or folks who belong to a specific group. The message is that beauty is individual; there is not just one standard. This was the first time in 50 years that Clairol focused on overall image rather than on individual products.

The results of their research showed that women rejected one beauty standard that is conveyed primarily through advertising; in addition, attitudes toward aging and multiculturalism have changed. One of their print ads showed a picture of eleven happy-looking women of various ages, ethnicities, and hair colors with the printed slogan "a beauty all their own."

Although Clairol's products are geared toward women, this is a good example of psychographic advertising. (Arguably, Clairol could be considered a cross between psychographic and demographic advertising since it appeals to women of all ages.)

View their current website at www.clairol.com. They are using long-form video commercials designed for the Internet called "Welcome to Shade Aid." The videos are designed to help women decide on the proper color for their hair. Internet advertising has proven effective.

Sociographics

Sociographics is the study of a consumer's social status, such as consumers who can afford to purchase a new S-Class Mercedes-Benz, which has a minimum price of almost $90,000.

Research Affects Music

The results from demographic, psychographic, and sociographic research affect the style of music composed for commercials. In the case of a demographic, if the research shows that the average consumers are 20- to 30-year-old females, agencies would most likely suggest music that appeals to that age-group.

With psychographic and sociographic research, the music must not "offend" any of the many groups that might purchase a product. Therefore, the agency would probably request music that is not intrusive or identifiable with a specific group. This is a generalization; creatives might experiment with numerous musical approaches and select a musical direction opposite the genre that would be most acceptable by traditional standards. For instance, there are styles of contemporary music that appeal to a diverse demographic. It is advisable for composers to make creative suggestions.

Developing Advertising

After analyzing the results of the research, the creative department introduces numerous ideas for advertising campaigns or individual commercials. The creative director generally selects several compelling ideas for further development and eventual presentation to the client.

After a client has selected the campaign or individual commercials that will best portray the client's message, the agency will generally test the ideas and/or commercials with focus groups. Focus groups are made up of average people considered to be members of a selected demographic and who are paid to view a presentation of a commercial(s), provide feedback, and are willing to be interviewed.

Most creative ideas for television commercials are presented to clients and focus groups (following the initial focus group sessions, which concentrate on exploratory questions) either in storyboard form or through the use of animatics or steal-o-matics.

A *storyboard* consists of a group of photographs or cartoon-type drawings with dialogue and/or voice-over copy written under each frame; visual instructions, such as camera angles, lighting, and any other essential descriptive information, are also included. The "story" of the commercial is displayed.

An *animatic* is a "moving" storyboard. The board is usually shot on video, with dialogue or voice-over added. Music is often added. Most animatics present a feeling of movement.

A *steal-o-matic* is made up of a series of scenes taken from film libraries, television programs, commercials, and other sources that contain appropriate footage. The scenes are edited together in such a way that they replicate the commercial the agency proposes to film or videotape. This is the most realistic manner to demonstrate a commercial(s). Many times, when the audio, including the music, is synchronized to a steal-o-matic, it appears complete. The rights to most of the footage are not available; consequently, the steal-o-matic cannot be used. The agency takes the risk of making a steal-o-matic that looks *too* complete because some of the scenes are too costly to film within the proposed budget. Therefore, it is possible that the final agency film might look inferior to the steal-o-matic.

Limited productions: In rare instances, agencies produce limited productions, which are scaled-down versions of commercials. They use actors, music, announcers, graphics, and other elements that make the commercial appear complete. The production cost is considerably less than the budget for the final production. Usually, the commercials that obtain the highest focus group scores and/or that test well on television are produced and aired. Some agencies allocate great importance to focus group scores and/or television tests, while others use the results as a part of a comprehensive evaluation process. The winning presentation(s) is given to the director to use as a guide for filming the final production.

Focus groups: Focus group participants are asked many questions concerning the commercial(s), including their reaction to the music. The composer may be asked to rewrite the music if the reaction is poor.

During the initial research phase, focus groups are also used. The focus group participants are asked questions that will help the researchers develop a profile of their potential consumers. The agency might present a series of taglines, which could eventually become the most identifiable slogan connecting the public to the product, or visual images may be presented and explored. This could help the creatives take the proper approach to developing a campaign and image for the product.

Television tests: Many products and commercials are tested on television in a specific region(s) of the United States. If the product sells, the commercial or campaign is considered successful, and airtime is bought on a national basis (assuming the product is sold nationally) or a regional basis.

Some products, although sold nationally, sell the majority of their projects regionally. In this situation, the greatest share of the media buying takes place regionally. For example, the majority of sales for the soft drink Dr Pepper are in the western and southwestern regions of the United

States. Therefore, most of the commercials are aired in the applicable regions.

Testing ideas: Companies spend substantial research and development monies testing ideas and campaign concepts before most commercials are completed. The client and the agency must feel relatively secure that the basic concept and message of the commercial(s) will be successful.

Agency executives, both creative and business, make certain that each frame of picture, dialogue, and/or voice-over that was approved after the test presentation is replicated by the director and editor in the final film.

Sometimes, the process of planning advertising involves months of presentations and revisions before the commercial is broadcast. Most often, the radio commercials of the same product mirror the television commercials. (Radio commercials do not usually receive the same amount of preparation and investigation as television commercials because they are normally extensions of the television commercials or advertising campaigns.)

The Function of Music in Advertising

Music provides an important ingredient in the creative process. A well-crafted composition can create an identity for a product. Some of the most memorable advertising slogans are used as lyrics in advertising jingles (short songs).

Examples of advertising slogans used as lyrics in jingles are, "G.E., we bring good things to life," "The Pepsi generation," and "Come see the softer side of Sears."

Advertising Age, a leading trade magazine, listed their choices for the 10 most effective slogans of the twentieth century. Many have been the basis for jingles and multiple campaigns:

1. Diamonds are forever (DeBeers)
2. Just do it (Nike)
3. The pause that refreshes (Coca-Cola)
4. Tastes great, less filling (Miller Lite)
5. We try harder (Avis)
6. Good to the last drop (Maxwell House)
7. Breakfast of champions (Wheaties)
8. Does she . . . or doesn't she? (Clairol)
9. When it rains it pours (Morton Salt)
10. Where's the beef? (Wendy's)

The following are honorable mentions:

1. Look Ma, no cavities! (Crest toothpaste)
2. Let your fingers do the walking (Yellow Pages)

3. Loose lips sink ships (Public Service)
4. M&Ms melt in your mouth, not in your hand (M&M candies)
5. We bring good things to life (General Electric)

Musical logos are identifiable short melodies usually played at the end of commercials or used as a symbol for products or companies. Arguably, the most recognizable musical logo is for NBC Television; just three notes created a network identity that has lasted for many years.

When an agency makes a ''pitch'' to a client for a campaign or individual commercial(s), a creative strategy is presented, and within that strategy is a reference to music. The agency might suggest that the music be fun, authoritative, serious, or warm and that it evoke an emotion that supports the message of the advertising. Sometimes, musical examples are played at strategy meetings. A composer might be asked to record a demo in a certain style, or music from a commercially released CD might be presented as an example. *There are no rules!*

The Music Producer's Role

Because of the important role that music plays in commercials, agencies scrutinize the content and the production of the music. Some agencies (mainly major companies) have staff music producers whose job is to produce advertising music.

Music production in advertising is similar to producing records or producing music for motion pictures. The best analogy is to compare it to the process of film direction. The film director is responsible for the creative quality of the final film, and the music supervisor is responsible

♩♩ Most television networks and individual stations hire advertising agencies to create the promotions for their shows (television, print, and radio) and to help create images for individual stations and networks. A musical example is the use of the John Williams's theme for all NBC News events. When audiences hear the NBC News theme—arranged in multiple variations—there is an automatic subliminal reaction that informs them that they are going to view a program or special announcement associated with NBC News. (*Underscoring* is the background music used behind dialogue, voice-overs, film, or video. This musical form can provide the ambience for a commercial. Some commercials have no dialogue and use only pictures and music.)

for the production and quality of the music. In advertising, the music producer is responsible for the final music presentation. The job requires the music producer to make sure that the following is achieved.

1. The music meets the needs of the creative team. The creative team is generally specific about the musical goals for a commercial(s). (The advertising producer is responsible for the entire production.)

2. The sound quality and musicianship are of the highest standard.

3. The synchronization of the music to the film is correct. If during the recording session the music producer wants to revise the music track, it is his or her responsibility to communicate with the composer.

4. The utmost technical industry standards are achieved.

The music producer also helps select the composer. Demonstration reels from various composers are presented to the creatives, who are usually searching for a certain style of music. In most instances, a composer who has written compositions in that musical style receives the assignment. Additionally, a music producer assembles music production budgets and residual payment estimates.

Residuals and Buyouts

Musicians and singers receive recording session fees for the initial recording. *Residual payments* are additional fees paid to musicians and singers (actors and announcers) based on the amount of airplay a commercial receives and on the number of markets in which it is shown. The residual payment scale is negotiated among the musicians' and singers' unions and representatives from the advertising industry.

Residuals are not required to be paid in all states of the United States. For example, Texas and Florida are considered right-to-work states and are nonunion states. The payments paid to musicians and singers in nonunion states are called "buyouts." A buyout is a one-time payment for services, and the performers do not receive residual payments or additional union benefits. Unions exist in some right-to-work states, but musicians and singers (actors, announcers, and so on) are permitted to work without joining a union.

Sometimes, the account supervisor, or account executive, will attend the music recording session to "hand-hold" the clients, who usually do not understand the recording process. A composer should be thoroughly prepared before a session. To lower the risk of encountering problems while in the recording studio, a music demonstration of the music, known as a demo, is almost always requested by agencies and susequently approved by clients prior to the final music session.

The Composer's Role

The composer is, typically, the last creative person to be hired during the production of a commercial. When music is added as an underscoring (background music), it is essential that the composer view the final, edited picture—referred to as a *final cut*—in order to write music that will properly enhance the picture. Unless the client has approved the final edit, the music will most likely have to be rewritten if the film is reedited; revising the edit will change the placement of the music. It is also possible that the revised edit could change the message of the commercial. This could affect the style of the music.

Example of a typical problem in television commercials: If the music is building to a powerful musical "hit" (music and picture happening simultaneously) and the section of film has been delayed by four frames, the audience will hear the "hit" too early. The audience can hear and see a variable of two frames of picture. If the section of film is varied more than that, not only will the "hit" be perceived as being early, but also the music following the "hit" will not be in sync. This is why it is essential that the composer writes to the final edited film. In reality, clients request editing changes numerous times before the final edit is approved.

Sometimes, a composer is asked to write music prior to filming. The following are some of the reasons.

1. If singing or dancing is shown on camera, it is best to write and record the music prior to production. The music track can be used on the film set to help the singers and dancers achieve exact synchronization with the music. Suggestion: In the situation described in number 1, it is advisable for the composer to *suggest* that music be written and recorded before filming. The potential technical pitfalls might not occur to the creatives. It is not uncommon to notice poor lip-synching (singers moving their lips to a prerecorded track) and dancers not dancing in time with the music. There are several reasons:

- The singers did not lip-synch to the final music track during filming.
- The director was not paying attention to the lip-synching.
- The director did not notice that the dancers were not in time with the music during filming.
- Poor editing. Most scenes are filmed numerous times, using various camera angles. If the film is not edited properly and some of the selected scenes have synchronization problems, the final result is not acceptable.

2. An alternative to the method described in number 1 is to record a simple melody with a click track tempo (a metronome click, e.g., 100 beats per minute) and play that music track on the set while filming. This gives the singers and dancers the correct tempo. After the film has been edited and approved by the client, the final musical arrangement can then be completed. Sometimes, this is a preferred working method because if changes are made during the filming, it is easier for the composer to adjust the final music track.

If the director wants the singers to sing live on the set, the music should be prerecorded as a "scratch track" sans vocals. (A scratch track is a simple track, e.g., piano or guitar only. The scratch track provides a tempo and feel for the singers.) This gives the singers the ability to create a more spontaneous, live performance. The sound engineer cannot play the music track too loudly on the set, or the music will bleed onto the vocal track and cause technical problems when mixing the music track; this is called *leakage*. After the film has been completed, the composer receives a copy of the vocal track and creates the final arrangement based on the performance of the vocals sung during the filming.

Unusual experience: The agency creatives decided that they wanted the actress in their commercial to sing the musical "tag" (an identifiable singing logo at the end of the spot). They wanted her to sing "wild," meaning without any musical track to guide her. This could have resulted in multiple problems:

- There was a specific number of seconds allowed for the singing, and if the actress extended that time, the music would not have fit in the commercial.
- The key had to match the rest of the underscoring, so there would be a smooth transition into the vocal tag.
- Without guidance, the actress might not have sung the melody accurately. Because of logistical problems, the singer could not attend a separate recording session, so the tag had to be recorded on the set. A temporary piano track was looped (repeated) numerous times on a DAT (digital audiotape), allowing the vocalist to sing and record the tag numerous times. The vocal was isolated from the piano track and added to the final music. The result was perfect, but the client decided to change the ending, so the actress eventually had to rerecord the vocal.

3. Music is played on the set to help create an appropriate mood for the actors. Even with a storyboard presentation, a musical background can help sell an idea to a client.

Structure of a Creative Team

Composers work directly with the creatives: producers, writers, and art directors. The creatives are usually specific about the musical direction of an individual commercial or a commercial campaign. The following are their job descriptions.

Advertising Producer

There are two categories of advertising producers. One is an administrative producer, and the other is both administrative and creative. Producers calculate budgets and help find and hire directors, composers, editors, announcers, and actors in addition to other personnel and/or companies necessary to accomplish an assignment. Important decisions need approval by the writer, the art director, the group creative director (the immediate supervisor of the writer and art director), and the agency creative director (the paramount creative job at an agency); agencies make recommendations to their clients and seek their approval before proceeding. While on location, the producers and the creative team supervise and are responsible for the entire production. The following is my interview with Lisa Kalb, advertising producer:

MZ: What does an advertising producer do?

Lisa: A producer works with the creative team, the copywriter, and the art director in making their storyboard come to life, assisting them both creatively and financially—they are 100 percent responsible for the budget. The producer will help them find the director, the editor, the music company, the right casting director, and the right talent; does talent negotiating (negotiates rights maybe with a business manager) and is the liaison to the account team, the client, and the creative team; and really works in consort with all of the players that I mentioned to make a commercial happen. From the minute a storyboard is handed to them to the moment it gets on the air, the producer is in charge of every stage of development.

MZ: Do you usually supervise more than one job at a time?

Lisa: Not usually. Usually there is one big job and maybe five small jobs. There are a lot of commercials that music is redone for, reedited, or there are radio spots that need to be done, or there is bidding out many other jobs for future work, so there are always a number of other projects happening simultaneously, but some producers are fortunate enough to have assistants, some producers are unfortunate enough to have five big jobs going at the same time, so it varies.

MZ: Whom does a producer report to?

Lisa: It could be the head of production for the agency, or it could be the creative directors.

MZ: How much input does the average producer have on who gets hired to work on a commercial?

Lisa: If it is a good experienced producer who has a good track record with the agency and specifically with the creatives, the producer might have a great relationship with the creative director or just with the art director on the team. If that is all in place, I would say my input is pretty well accepted and important, and I would say anywhere between 50 and 75 percent in my particular case. The norm is that the producer is not part of the creative team. The more unusual situation is when the producer is brought in to offer creative solutions. I have been asked to devise storyboards based on how it will affect production.

MZ: I have worked with producers who have no creative input. Is that unusual?

Lisa: I would say it's common. I'd say it's 50-50. For example, it depends upon how strongly a copywriter or an art director feels about an area of expertise in a commercial. In the area of music, the copywriter or the art director more often than not have a specific point of view. I would say music is the area in which—for myself—my opinion might be less taken. In the area of music, I'd say the creative teams really rule.

MZ: Do producers specialize in certain types of productions?

Lisa: Absolutely. I am beauty [production]. There are producers who just work on cars. Retail is an area, knowing how to tag [change endings] hundreds and hundreds of versions a year . . . that's a specialty, and there are many nuances involved with that . . . in just cranking out and knowing how to get the best prices.

MZ: Do freelance producers usually market themselves in one area?

Lisa: No, they shouldn't. It's too limiting. There are so few jobs out there, and if you are lucky, you are going to be able to be working on many different things, so that you can have a number of different types of works on your reel and you can keep selling yourself in any area.

MZ: How often does the style of the final music end up being what the creatives first envisioned?

Lisa: I'd say 25 percent of the time the original style of music, as directed, is accepted in the end.

MZ: What advice can you give to composers who want to compose advertising music?

Lisa: Versatility is really great or just being really fabulous doing one particular style of music. That way you can freelance and work for a number of different music companies, with them knowing that you are an expert in one particular style of music. If you want to have your own music company, you do need to be versatile. Work for someone for a number of years is the best advice because it's really hard.

Not all agencies afford the producer the same responsibilities and authority. At some agencies the producers are part of a production department, and at other agencies the producers are part of the creative department. If problems occur, the producer consults with the head of production. At some agencies the producers report to the production head, while at other agencies they work directly for the creative director. Let us assume that the filming is running over budget and the creative team wants to continue shooting because the director has not captured their vision. The final decision is made based on the hierarchy at an agency. At some agencies the head of production has the ultimate power, and at others the creative director makes all final decisions. A representative from the client is always at a filming and will ultimately give permission—or not—to exceed the budget.

> ♩♩ Example (television commercials): Many directors think that they can improve a commercial that the client has approved for filming. Savvy directors film the "board" (storyboard) that has been approved by the agency and the client and then ask permission to shoot an alternative version. The key word is *ask*. Many directors will not be rehired by agencies because they refuse to shoot the approved commercial.

Copywriter

Copywriters and art directors usually work as a "team" to create and develop advertising concepts and commercials. The creative director gives the copywriter and art director specific instructions as to the objectives of the client. A copywriter's primary job is to write scripts, announcers' copy, and print copy. The following is my interview with copywriter and creative director Joel Harrison:

MZ: What does a copywriter do?

Joel: The basic job of a copywriter is to communicate the benefits of a product or service to the prospective buyer—the viewer on television, the reader of any printed material, the listener of the radio—and to do it in a creative, compelling, riveting way so it's not boring. The worst thing a copywriter can do in advertising is to write boring copy.

MZ: When an agency hires a copywriter, are they expected to write print as well as broadcasting, or are some copywriters specialists?

Joel: These days since there is so much television, you get into the advertising business as even a cub copywriter, you'll write television as well as print—moreover, more and more advertising is over the Internet, so there are even more kinds of media these days for copywriters to get involved with.

MZ: Do you think that the Internet will become a major source of sales as a result of advertising on the Internet?

Joel: It's really the future. I think there will be new forms of advertising. I think that over time, we will be seeing less and less advertising on television, certainly network television and even cable television. I think there is going to be more one-on-one—a certain advertiser will find out where they can reach his or her main prospect for buying a product, and they will try and get that message to that person. A lot is going to be done on the Internet. I can see more and more of an advertiser's message being directed that way.

MZ: How are commercials created?

Joel: It is almost always a team effort—a writer and an art director working together on an assignment. I as a creative director will decide who I want working on it, depending upon the importance of the project, we would all sit down in a room—the account people, strategic planners [and the creative team]—they will have found out who the target audience is, what the benefit of the product or service is, and key consumer insight—where our head should be in trying to come up with some successful and compelling copy to sell the product. That's the way it is done—give the assignment to a team or several teams, set up a timetable, probably work backwards from when the advertising has to air or be in print. . . . Any good creative director won't just say they don't like the work; they will say, "Hey, you've got a great selling line here, why don't you try it this way? Why don't you try doing it with music? Try doing it with a testimonial approach." That's what a creative director does—gives creative direction. I know plenty of creative directors who just look at work and say this stinks. You've got to tell them why you don't think it is hitting the mark, why you don't think it's a bull's-eye, what's wrong with it, what can be right with it.

MZ: How many campaigns do you develop for a presentation?

Joel: I always have had a rule of thumb. I would never show too much or too little. I usually try to show two or three different ideas, and sometimes those two or three ideas may have several executions in them.

MZ: When you are working at a large agency and you have two or three ideas, what is the next step?

Joel: In a large agency, more times than not, you would then go to the executive creative director and then share it with the top account person. It's very important for the agency to have everybody on the same page so you don't go to a client and there are any internal disagreements.

MZ: How much does the head account person have to say about the actual creative work as opposed to the content of the work?

Joel: It really varies. I find that really good account people get it. They understand where the creative heads are because they've got a streak of creativity in their bodies themselves. I have had more than a few experiences where I have worked with account people who were so good that they sometimes have either come up with a creative idea or really enhanced it.

MZ: How does a person become a copywriter?

Joel: Put together a portfolio and take it to agencies. That will be your proof to them that "I can do stuff, and I'm pretty good."

MZ: How do you decide on the genre of music you want for a commercial?

Joel: I can only speak for myself, but I think that whenever I have done something and I think it requires music, I've just come up with—in my head—what I think the music should be. But it is never that definitive because I am not a musical expert—you or people like you are the music mavens. I would sit down and share ideas with you, give you input on how I hear it, and sometimes you would say, "That won't work," or you'd say, "That's a terrific approach, let me mull that over and come up with a couple of ideas." A lot of it is really gut.

MZ: How often do composers suggest a style of music that is in a different direction than what you asked for?

Joel: Probably half of the time—a music person who just executes what I have in my head without coming up with something else is not really doing their job.

MZ: What percentage of copywriters know how to write lyrics, and how open are they to having the music company edit a lyric given to them by the copywriter?

Joel: I have found that most copywriters don't know how to write [lyrics]. They can write lines, they may not scan, they may not work musically. It has been my experience that when you then take it to a good music company, [they] in a very frank, open kind of discussion can point out things, point out ways of making it better. Sometimes they take the lyric and rewrite it. Sometimes they say, "This won't work." I have found that copywriters who write lyrics are not lyricists. They're not paid to be lyricists. Egos should not stand in the way of changing lyrics to make them better.

MZ: What do you do when you are handed a "laundry list" of points to be included in a lyric and there is too much information to fit into the short time span of a commercial?

Joel: The advertising shouldn't start until there is an agreed-upon strategy, and that strategy should be very, very single-minded.

An example is, "Tasty Cakes taste great." The reason for that is they have more butter and they are baked longer. That's a simplified strategy. If account people say that "you have to say that we have been in business since 1923 and our ovens are made of iron and our delivery men have nicer mustaches and our icing has more sugar in it," then you are going to have advertising that is not going to work on any level. I am a big believer in less is more. A simplified strategy, whether you're doing a musical jingle or not, will lead to better, single-minded, stronger, and more successful advertising. If that [the simple strategy] doesn't contain the kitchen sink, you're not going to have to put in a lyric or a print ad.

MZ: What are some of the large national accounts you have worked on?

Joel: Lots of Proctor and Gamble business, Crest toothpaste, Bounce, Dawn, Charmin, Ivory Snow, Zest, Kraft General Foods, Cool Whip, Post Raisin Bran, Crystal Light, Texaco.

MZ: Do you find that copywriters specialize in categories?

Joel: I think these days that's true. The best example I can give you is Business to Business and the Internet. There are people who have training in that they started by working on WorldCom or American Express. People like that become well versed in those categories. So I think it's very hard for someone who is working on, say, package goods, for example, to make the jump into something that is highly technical like the Internet and a lot of Business to Business advertising.

MZ: The advertising business is interesting because it is as much business as it is creative. When you are creating an ad, are you thinking as a creative writer, or are you thinking as a business-person? What goes through your mind?

Joel: Yes, yes. More as a creative person because that's what they pay me to do, but I also think of it in terms of the business. I think of the category, I think of the competition, I think of what the competition is doing, how the competition will react to this, how we can beat the competition. I'm a big believer in knowing the business of advertising in addition to the creative side of advertising.

MZ: There are many creative commercials that are not effective advertising. Can you give me some examples?

Joel: In the boom period of the Internet, some of the most creative and entertaining, most clever advertising was done for lots of the Internet companies, but most of them failed. They didn't burst the Internet bubble by themselves, but people were entertained by the advertising but had no idea whose company it was, and this is borne out by research. Any good, successful advertising will really connect the message to the product.

MZ: Is there any advice you would like to give to young composers who want to write for commercials?

Joel: I would say, listen to the creative people when you meet with them, but don't be afraid, don't be intimidated by them. Be strong. If you've got a good idea, don't keep it to yourself, don't be afraid of offending them, because if they have anything going for them, they will listen. These creative people are really not music people; they may have some instincts, as I alluded to before, but when you get into that room, you're going to size up pretty quickly what could be the right and best solution. Don't be afraid for a give-and-take because in so many cases, they listen to you . . . you're the mavens, be strong, be bold, and don't be afraid.

Art Director

Art directors work with copywriters to create advertising concepts and commercials for broadcasting, print, the Internet, and other media. Art directors are responsible for the visual "look" of commercials. Most commercials are first portrayed in a series of drawings called storyboards, which are either drawn or supervised by art directors. Each frame (picture) of a commercial is drawn and has visual and audio instructions (dialogue, camera angle, audio effects, and so on) below each drawing. A well-drawn storyboard is usually a very close visualization of how the final film will look.

After the writer and the art director have presented an idea(s) to their superiors and the idea(s) has been accepted, the art director usually oversees the visual part of the presentation to the client. The following is my interview with art director and creative director Arthur Meranus:

MZ: What does an art director do?

Arthur: An art director usually works with a copywriter. When you are talking about newspaper advertising, the art director actually lays out the ad's position elements, supervises photography and typography, and works with the writer to come up [with] the most cogent advertising possible. In television, the art director works more as a storyboard artist. They work with a writer to develop an idea and then transfer that idea to a storyboard. Most often they will supervise the production of the television commercial. Art directors usually have some graphic design training, go to art school.

MZ: How much influence does the art director have in choosing music for a commercial?

Arthur: Generally, the art director, by definition, would not have a great deal of influence, but in today's business the art director is more of a jack-of-all-trades and is really responsible, with the writer, for the creative product in total. So, his opinion and the writer's opinion weigh about equally in choosing music for commercials.

MZ: How do you choose the style of music for a commercial?

Arthur: If you want to have a continuing theme for the music, then you're dealing with multiple styles, and you pick the styles that seem to fit the situation that you're developing now. When it comes to designing [music] for a campaign, you have to make a decision whether you want it to sound very current or you want it to feel like a period piece or whether you want the music to drive the action or want the music to be a bed for the action—how you deal with lyrics all depends on the message and the tone of the advertising. So, most often you agree in advance what the tone of the advertising should be and then pick music to go with that tone.

MZ: How often does the initial musical direction end up being the musical style?

Arthur: Most often a good creative team will go to a music company with a tone and a feeling that they want to achieve, and then they will ask the music company if they have any ideas that fit their basic direction, and if the music people come up with a better idea, a smart creative team will go along with that. I would say that happens one-third to one-half of the time.

Structure of an Account Team

Account Directors, Account Supervisors, and Account Executives

The account people are the direct liaisons from agencies to clients and are involved in all aspects of client services. They are the liaison to the media buying department (assuming that the agency buys the media for clients), which includes television, radio, newspaper, print, the Internet, billboards, and other forms of advertising and marketing. The agency receives commissions or fees for their services. Media placement is one of the most crucial functions of an agency. The wrong strategy can mean failure. Some agencies provide only the creative work, while others solely provide the media buying. Most large agencies offer both services.

Researchers

Researchers help clients research the best advertising strategies that will help to achieve their business goals. This involves extensive research.

Agencies are asked to help clients "invent" new product ideas. The research involves trying to determine what consumers need, or want, that is not available; clients then develop a product(s) to fit that need(s).

Assignments

1. Select a product that has a demographic audience. State the name of the product and the target audience. Suggest several musical styles that would appeal to that audience and the reasons for choosing the musical styles. Compose two 30-second pieces (instrumental) of music in the appropriate style.
2. Select a product that has a psychographic audience. State the name of the product and the target audience. Suggest several musical styles that would appeal to that audience and the reasons for choosing the musical styles. Compose two 30-second pieces (instrumental) of music in the appropriate style.
3. Select a product that has a sociographic audience. State the name of the product and the target audience. Suggest several musical styles that would appeal to that audience and the reasons for choosing the musical styles. Compose two 30-second pieces (instrumental) of music in the appropriate style.
4. Refer to the briefing ("Creative Brief for Television") earlier in this chapter. Write two 30-second instrumental pieces, in different styles, that will accomplish the objectives. Explain the reasoning behind each approach.

> ♩♪ I have written music for fictional products; the product labels and commercials have been developed as if the products existed. Sometimes, this work is tested to see if it is prudent to spend considerable resourses for product development. Until the recent past, prescription drugs were not advertised to the public. The purpose of the advertising is for patients to ask doctors to prescribe them. Prescription drugs are heavily advertised on broadcast television and radio, cable and satellite outlets, on the Internet, and in print advertising. The general public is now aware of many prescription drugs.

2

Composing for Television and Radio Commercials versus Composing for Films

Let me begin by saying this: Some commercials would not work if they contained music. Especially spots that depend on drama and tension—or are intended to be very serious. Other spots call for sound design, which is not really music per se. But it's been my experience over the years that music can really be a driving force in making commercials work.

For years I created vignette commercials and used whimsical music tracks to "tie the spots together," which kept the musical momentum. They were usually instrumental tracks but sometimes lyrics were incorporated. Good, strong, stirring anthem-type spots—usually corporate in nature—can elevate a client's message, make it memorable and give viewers chills up and down their spine, which is a very good thing to happen!

Many highly successful spots don't contain one word of copy (incidentally, I as a copywriter, created such spots and didn't feel left out because it's really the idea that counts)—but rather, rely solely on great, mind-sticking music.

Bottom line: Music, when used well, written by composers who understand the role of advertising, can make a good spot better and turn a great spot into an award winner—and quite possibly a classic. I cannot emphasize enough the role music plays in broadcast advertising. So much so that sometimes the element people remember about a commercial is the music. Not the idea. But I guess, even then, if the music helps them remember the product—and they go out and buy the product—the clients haven't wasted their advertising dollars.

—Joel Harrison, former senior vice president
and group creative director at DMB&B

The crafts of composing, orchestrating, and arranging commercials differ from scoring films, although the musical elements are basically the same.

21

Commercials are minifilms. Consequently, a musical assignment must be accomplished in a much shorter time span. The average film score contains approximately 40 minutes of music; the average television commercial lasts 30 seconds. Composers who specialize in writing music for commercials must have the ability to compose music that sounds unified while working within severe time restrictions.

Some composers who compose music primarily for commercials find it challenging to write expanded compositions because they have developed an unusual compositional skill. The opposite is true of film composers. They find it challenging to compose in short forms.

The following are some of the differences between the two diciplines.

Films: The director is the creative force. A film director usually hires the composer and provides the creative direction for the musical score. Most directors or editors will include temporary music to the film while editing. This music is referred to as a ''temp track (score).'' The music for temp scores can be extracted from any source, such as CDs, music from other films, symphony recordings, and so on. The purpose of a temp score is to provide the director, producer, and composer with a sense of the style of music that the director feels will enhance the film. The composer is given the film with the temp score so that he or she can reference the temp music while composing.

Some directors want the original music to be in the exact style as the temp score, whereas others direct the composer to use the temp score only as a guide; all directors work differently. Most directors want to hear a demo of each film cue (music section), which is usually accomplished by scoring the cues on synthesizers and samplers. The director usually asks for revisions, and the composer rewrites the music before the final recording session.

Commercials: The copywriter, the art director, and some producers are the creative forces. Composers are normally guided by a committee. They usually work directly with a creative team. The creative team, plus the agency creative director and the client, must approve the final music. Sometimes this structure creates problems. The creative team might not agree with the creative director and/or the client as to the musical style that works best for the project. When disagreements occur, it is usually the executive creative director of the agency who makes the final decision, unless the client insists on using an alternate composition.

Commercials: The final approval comes from the client. Usually, the success of a commercial or a commercial campaign is measured by increased sales and/or the public's awareness of a product. Clients want final approval on all aspects of a production. If a difference of opinion occurs between the client and the

> ♩♪ Some large agencies have music departments. The music producers guide the composers and act as the intermediary between the music department and the creative department.

agency, the agency usually substantiates their suggestions on the basis of research. They present their final recommendations to the client.

Some prominant clients hire only global agencies (with worldwide offices) because they would like their advertising to have a universal and coordinated effort. (This strategy is not always successful since cultures differ and a campaign that achieves results in one territory might not attain success in another.) Some clients also want to hire an agency that is experienced in media buying. Placing advertising (broadcasting, print, Internet, and so on) is a crucial business decision. Clients often hire one agency to produce the creative work and another agency to buy the media. Some clients purchase their own media, but this is rare.

Films: Studio heads make the final decisions. Success is measured at the box office. Very few directors have the right to select the "final cut" (final edit). Major films are tested with audiences in much the same manner that commercials are tested with focus groups. If the test results are unsatisfactory, a director may reshoot or reedit scenes; some directors shoot two endings and test both versions. Studios will financially support a director's vision if the budget allows and the studio feels that the film is worthy of further investment.

In both films and commercials, music and sound (sound effects and dialogue) serve a vital function. If the music and sound are removed from a film, most films lose a vital part of their effectiveness. Music and effects are crucial to the emotional content of most films.

As previously stated, the main difference between television and radio commercials and film writing is the length of the compositions. A commercial music writer composes pieces that run between 10 seconds and 1 minute. Within that time period, there can be many visual and emotional changes that have to be addressed within the composition. There may be one theme with a varied orchestration that conforms to the changes in the pictures. Changes can occur within a second or two. In other instances, one commercial might require numerous musical styles and themes; for instance, a commercial showing a cruise ship's ports of call may require music indigenous to each country referenced.

Composing for Unity

It is common for commercials to have a completely different mood in the first half than in the second half. A typical example would be a commercial for a pain reliever, such as aspirin. The beginning of the commercial might depict someone with a headache. After taking the product, the character becomes pain free. Most often, the music must enhance each emotion portrayed throughout the commercial. Be careful not to musically overemphasize certain sections, or the music becomes cliché.

The most difficult skill to master is to write a composition that sounds cohesive rather than divided into numerous disjointed musical sections sewed together "with the wrong colors." This skill is developed through the use of compositional and arranging techniques. (These topics are described in detail later in the book.)

Conclusion

The most important aspect of a composer's job, in both mediums, is to musically capture the essence of a film. Film composers must understand the emotions a director is trying to communicate with the music. Some directors may want scenes scored to reflect the literal action (e.g., fight scene) or obvious emotional aspect (e.g., romantic) of a film; others may have a completely different view of the emotional influence the music should evoke. Reaction to music is subjective, making it difficult for composers to always satisfy directors.

♩♩ If clients do not receive tangible results from an agency's work, the account is "put up for review." The client invites several agencies to "pitch" the account. Each agency is given a budget and a date to present their creative work, and in some instances a media buying plan is included in the presentation. (Not all agencies perform both functions.)

The same criterion applies to the advertising creatives. Five directors working on a project bring five different viewpoints to a project. The same applies to creative teams working on the same commercial. It is a composer's job to uncover the essence of what is wanted and to achieve that goal.

Assignments

1. Videotape a scene from a motion picture. Analyze the musical composition and its relationship to the scene. What does the music accomplish? Would the scene be just as effective without the music? Why or why not?
2. Videotape a commercial. Analyze the musical composition and its relationship to the scene. What does the music accomplish? Would the scene be just as effective without the music? Why or why not?

3

Musical Skills

Approaching Composition for Commercials

> Music is a unifying and liberating campaign element. I helped create the "Best Part of Wakin' Up" campaign for Folgers Coffee. The signature music gave us flexibility and infinite variety, and it allowed us to immediately own the advertising in any media.
>
> —Arthur Meranus, former creative director of Cunningham & Walsh, former creative director of N. W. Ayer, and former global creative director of DMB&B

Musical styles have been associated with creative and sociological aspects of society throughout most historical periods. Musical periods are usually referred to by the same names given to art, architecture, and other defining elements; the classical, baroque, and romantic periods or the music of the 1950s and 1960s are several examples. Popular song lyrics reflect the times. During wars, patriotic songs and antiwar songs define generations; for example, songs about drugs define much of the 1960s and 1970s. Dances also reflect the times; for example, swing music and the Lindy Hop characterize World War II, and the trend continued into the 1950s with the founding of rock and roll. In the 1960s, the tremendous influence of the Beatles was not limited to their music. The Beatles were equally influential in shaping the youth culture of the Western world. These musical examples are used by advertising agencies to generate ideas for commercials. *Saturday Night Fever* defined not only the disco era of the middle 1970s but also a specific lifestyle—that of a working-class family in New York. A majority of commercials depict contemporary society as the focal point of the advertising. This is reflected in the musical, cinematic, and sociological content of a commercial.

It is advantageous for commercial composers to have a thorough knowledge of popular music as well as traditional "classical" training (historic periods) and also ethnic music of various cultures. Understanding music history helps composers guide advertising agencies in the selection of musical genres that will enhance their advertising campaigns. Story lines might reflect a specific historic period. If a composer has musical knowledge of the period, his or her musical suggestions might help guide the creatives in new directions. Knowing various styles makes it easier for a composer to emulate a musical style.

Listening to the radio, purchasing music in various styles, listening to film and television scores, attending concerts, and analyzing scores helps composers familiarize themselves with various music genres. Commercial composers must be aware of musical trends and styles. Listen to the sonic qualities of the drums, basses, guitars, unusual synthesizer sounds, and other instruments. Sounds, especially in contemporary popular musical styles, become trends, as do unique musical patterns. For example, in dance music (club music) the 909 drum machine, in combination with new samples and drum modules, has produced popular drum sounds for many years. In addition to sounds, musical patterns can define a style. Producers must be aware of the market since popular sounds and patterns change quickly.

A pulsating repetitive synthesizer line, usually with a sixteenth-note delay (repeated notes), is an example of a rhythmic trend that defines a genre. One example is *Trance*, a style of dance music. Many Trance arrangements have one vocal phrase, which is usually a memorable phrase that is intermittently repeated throughout the song.

In some dance music, the bass drum (kick) sound is long and deep, usually played with an 808 drum machine bass drum that contains a long delay mixed with a more defining 909 kick sound. The bass is normally coupled with a sub-bass and consists of muted-sounding indefinable notes that are not "heard" but felt. The sound creates a low rhythmic thumping groove that fits with the more definitive kick drums. The sub-bass sound is used because dance clubs have sub-bass speakers. The sub-bass creates a pounding low end that adds to the excitement of the music.

There are also trends in the sound of mixes (final recordings). Bass and drums may be emphasized, or a guitar(s) is the most prominent instrument. The use of unusual effects, such as reverbs and special effects, also define trends. For this reason, music is categorized in historical periods. For instance, the "sound of the fifties," the classical period, swing, and other musical eras all have identifying musical elements.

Audio effects can contribute to a commercially successful record as exemplified by Cher's hit "Believe," in which an unusual effect is used on her lead vocal. It almost sounds as if she is yodeling. The same effect was used on many recordings after the worldwide success of Cher's record. (This effect was created with the Antares Auto Tune computer plug-in.)

Phil Spector, a highly successful producer in the 1960s, developed a musical environment referred to as the "Wall of Sound." Excessive reverberation (or echo) and a definitive "soundscape," combined with unique arrangement techniques, became the signature of Spector's productions.

This is a superlative model of production techniques establishing a trend. Many producers tried to emulate his sound.

The Internet is an excellent research tool for composers. Information concerning any musical genre can be found. Stylistic recordings, tuning parameters of unusual instruments, and esoteric recordings (difficult to locate in record stores) are examples of information that is easily accessible on the Internet. Specialty record stores—both brick and mortar and Internet stores—are also valuable sources for researching obscure music. For example, stores specialize in selling world music, dance music, and old vinyl records. The stores stock recordings that cannot be found in the average retail outlet; the same applies to sheet music. It is crucial to learn certain musical and technical skills. Included in these skills are the following:

1. Musical authenticity
2. MIDI (Musical Instrument Digital Interface)
3. Digital audio
4. Technical studio knowledge as it applies to music production (e.g., use of effects, reverbs, and so on)
5. Arranging and orchestration (discussed in a separate chapter)

Modern popular composition is directly linked to this knowledge. The following is a discussion of these skills.

Authenticity

The creatives often request that the music emulate a specified time period or a specific style. One of the key problems encountered by composers is how to achieve stylistic authenticity. It is apparent when this goal is not achieved; unfortunately, music that sounds contrived is common in commercials.

Creatives often play composers musical examples from commercials, motion picture sound tracks, CDs, or other sources. The copyright laws protect the sounds of records (or other forms of recorded music) as well as the actual notation of songs or instrumental compositions; these are called "soundalikes." If a recording is re-created, it is also considered a soundalike. If the composer decides to use a sample (recording and playing back a section of an existing recording, sound, or effects), sample clearance rights must be obtained. Usually this requires paying a fee and/or additional compensations; the negotiations should be handled through an attorney or a sample clearance company.

A landmark case involved a singer who imitated Bette Midler on a music track for a Ford commercial. Midler sued and was awarded a substantial settlement.

I arranged a series of commercials for Burlington Coat Factory for which the client licensed the song "Shop Around," which was originally recorded by Smokey Robinson and the Miracles. The client obtained the rights to the song, which did not include the right to copy the original arrangement; in addition, the singers could not imitate the sound of the original singers. Before the commercial was broadcast, a musicologist was hired to analyze the recordings. Her mission was to examine the new recording for possible plagiarism. A male and a female lead singer were recorded, and the agency opted to air the female version so there could be no claim that the singer sounded like Smokey Robinson. Although composers have to be cautious, they can replicate a sound without committing plagiarism.

Analyze arranging (orchestration) and compositional styles and observe patterns and musical rules that identify musical styles within historical time periods. The following section contains specific examples of music styles.

Throughout his career, Johann Sebastian Bach, one of the world's great composers, copied and arranged other composers' works as a learning exercise. This should be periodically practiced with all styles of music. Many stylistic elements become easily recognizable when composers and arrangers study music in detail; it becomes easier to duplicate a style. The harmonic structure, voicings, instrumentation, and musical form, along with additional elements of a musical style, can be learned through this teaching method.

In the study of Western music history, from the beginning of codified music, musical "rules" were strictly followed. From the Gregorian chants and the music of the Renaissance to the baroque, classical, romantic, and twentieth-century styles, harmonic and rhythmic conventions have been adhered to. Combinations of instruments became identified with musical periods. For example, the basso continuo, also called thoroughbass, is a notational system developed during the baroque period. The bass part and treble part, which made up the melody, are the only written notes. The continuo was used at a time when music was beginning to be conceived as consisting of a melody and a harmony. A harmonic code, called figured bass, was placed above or below the bass line, and the harmonies were defined through musical symbols. The part was played by a keyboard or lute and improvised by the musicians. The bass part, called a continuo, was played by a harpsichord, clavier, or lute along with a violoncello, bass gamba, or bassoon.

If an assignment is to write in the baroque style, that does not necessarily indicate composing a continuo with figured bass. The baroque period lasted from 1600 until 1750 and incorporated many styles of music. Play several styles for the creatives so that they can choose the appropriate approach for the commercial.

If the assignment is to compose a piece that is in a contemporary popular style, does that denote rock, rhythm and blues, jazz, or dance? The musical direction should be well defined.

Often, the creatives listen to music to help spawn musical ideas for commercials. A group of Spanish monks recorded an album of Gregorian chants that became a popular hit. The album inspired the creatives to use a Gregorian chant on what would become a very successful wine commercial.

Gregorian chant dates back to Pope Gregory I (Gregory the Great), who was pope from 590 to 604. To achieve musical authenticity, the following rules have to be observed:

- An unaccompanied men's chorus—usually sung by monks—singing in Latin
- A single line melody with no harmony
- Music that was unemotional in attitude because the music served the religious text rather than the beauty of the singing
- A scale system that was neither major nor minor

Gregorian chant is written in various formats. It can be sung in the *antiphonal* (two choirs with alternating lines), *responsorial* (the soloist sings and the congregants respond), or *direct* (sung without alternation) performance styles. Ask the creatives which format is most appropriate for their project.

In addition to the three performance styles mentioned (antiphonal, responsorial, and direct), follow the compositional rules. Study the written music (which has been converted to modern notation) and listen to well-performed recordings, which will help composers and arrangers understand the style. Listening can be especially helpful while in the recording studio since it provides a reference point for the singers. Hire singers who perform in this genre; they are versed in the nuances and texture of the music.

The same general approach should be adapted to jazz, rhythm and blues, hip-hop, gospel, country, ethnic, and popular music. There are elements in all musical periods that define a style.

Jazz

Jazz is America's music. Started in New Orleans, the basic elements are derived from the slaves who sang music while working in the fields. The music developed into an extraordinarily intricate and unique form of American music and produced some of the greatest instrumentalists and singers of any genre of music. There is no other current style of Western music that has its basis in improvisation. The harmonic jazz language, which developed from this music, has been the inspiration for most other forms of American music. This includes the music of George Gershwin, Duke Ellington, Aaron Copland, Steely Dan, B. B. King, Kenny G, and many other musicians and composers. Different styles of jazz are associated with various time periods.

The Middle Ages is a significant period in Western musical history. Although notation systems existed prior to the Middle Ages, musical notation underwent rapid development during this period, making it possible for music to be notated and enabling musicians other than the composer to perform it. Musical rules were invented that included modes (eight musical scales) as well as rhythmic and harmonic rules.

Jazz combines improvisation and musical notation with rhythm and harmony. A jazz composition varies each time it is played because of the improvised solos. The melody is always the same because the underlying rhythmic and harmonic structure does not change. The basic harmonic structure for most jazz compositions has been documented in written form, with a combination of notation and identification of the harmonic structure (chord changes) along with an indication of the number of measures, the tempo, and the time signature.

Dixieland jazz is associated with New Orleans, and the genre has been used on many commercials that are associated with that city. Most commercials promoting Mardi Gras contain Dixieland scores and New Orleans funeral band music, which is also unique to the region and, therefore, creates an instant identity.

Become familiar with the instrumentation that denotes specific styles. For example, if an assignment is to create a Dixieland piece, in addition to understanding the style, an authentic instrumental combination is a cornet (not a trumpet), a clarinet or soprano saxophone, a piano, a banjo (optional), a trombone, and drums. The size of the ensemble can vary, but the basic performance style cannot change.

Swing music was most popular in the late 1930s and 1940s. There have been numerous films depicting World War II, and the music featured is swing. The Gap stores re-created the popular dance the Lindy Hop in a series of commercials—called the Gap Khaki Swing—that depicted the predominant dance style of the 1940s and early 1950s. (The dancers and the set look contemporary.) There has been a resurgence of swing music; swing dance clubs have opened throughout the United States and Europe.

Let us assume that the assignment is to create the sound of the Glenn Miller Band. The unique sound of that band came from years of Miller experimenting with instrumental combinations. The final signature sound was that of a clarinet used in place of the traditional alto saxophone as the lead instrument of the saxophone section. The band also had a fluid and polished sound that resulted from Miller's penchant for perfection; the Miller Band was never sloppy.

Assume that a commercial requires vocals depicting the same time period. A vocal group called the Modernaires sang with the Glenn Miller Band. Their lead singer was a female backed by three men, making their musical style distinctive. If this were the assignment, it would behoove the composer to ask the agency to hire a musicologist to determine if there could be a soundalike copyright problem. The agency would most likely have to receive permission from both the Glenn Miller estate and the Modernaires to re-create their sounds.

Re-creating Sounds

If the creatives ask a composer to re-create the sound of a popular vocal or instrumental group, listen only to the artists' popular recordings. The public's perception of a "sound" comes from hearing select recordings repeatedly. Not all songs or instrumentals recorded by groups or soloists have a consistency; therefore, if a composition that does not depict an artist's signature sound is chosen as an example and the composer emulates that piece, the new composition or arrangement will not sound like that artist.

I worked on a campaign for Entenmann's cakes. The music for one of the commercials had to capture the sound and arrangement of a recording that emulated music of the 1930s. To help achieve that goal, the engineer recorded the beginning of a vinyl record (only the scratching noise heard before the music entered) and looped it (repeated it) throughout the track. This technique helped to re-create the ambience of a 78-rpm recording. Several popular records of the 1930s were referenced while mixing. The final product accurately depicted the sound of the 1930s.

It is important to note that if the same assignment were given for a feature film, the composer would have a longer time period to re-create the sound; commercial composers must work within a shorter time frame and with a lesser budget.

In the 1950s, 1960s, and 1970s, the Hammond B3 organ with a Leslie speaker is the organ heard on most recordings. The Hammond has a distinct sound that is difficult to duplicate; it behooves composers who want to re-create the sound to rent a B3 with a Leslie speaker. (New Hammond organs that duplicate the sound of the original B3 with a Leslie speaker are being manufactured.) A typical 1950s-sounding ballad would traditionally incorporate the following:

1. The piano playing triplets
2. Possibly a tenor or baritone saxophone
3. The musical chord progression I, VI, II, V, I
4. Background singers singing typical traditional syllables of the era, such as the doo-wop genre

The purpose of the preceding examples is not to present a tutorial on a specific project but to demonstrate how to research traditional stylistic elements, which will help composers accomplish a musical goal. Listening to examples is the most effective research tool.

The Latin Market

> 102.6 million: The projected Hispanic population of the United States as of July 1, 2050. According to this projection, Hispanics will constitute 24% of the nation's total population by that date.
>
> —U.S. Census Bureau

Most major clients advertise in the Spanish language and steer their commercials to appeal to various Hispanic cultures. Within the Spanish-speaking communities, many subgroups have specific, cultural mores. This directly affects the choice of music used in commercials.

Dr. Raul Murciano Jr. is a professor at the University of Miami's Frost School of Music. He is an expert in writing music for commercials targeted for the Spanish-speaking markets. The following is a synopsis of a discussion on this subject.

In the early 1960s, there was a massive exodus of Cubans who moved to Miami, Florida, as a result of the Cuban Revolution; this exodus continued for many years. In the past 5 to 10 years, other Spanish-speaking people from many countries have also moved to the Miami area (e.g., people from Colombia, Venezuela, Nicaragua, and other Central and South American countries), but the Cuban population still remains in the majority.

This presents a problem for composers: How do they choose the style of music that will appeal to the various cultures and subcultures?

The first concern of the advertising agency is in their choice of voice-over talent. Each culture has its own idioms and pronunciations that are indicated by the announcer and/or actors. This is important for a composer to know because it provides the best indication of the target market. Fortunately, most singers singing in Spanish do not have a specific accent and therefore sound generic; the one exception is the accent from Spain, which has a noticeable lisp sound (most British singers also have a generic accent when singing). What *is* important is the tone of the voice. Various cultures have different styles of singing, which include the tone of voice as well as the use of melismas (decorative phrases). The composer should hire singers who sing with the proper tone and style of the particular country or region being targeted.

The creatives generally specify the rhythm and feel of the music they desire. As is the case with most Anglo commercials, more often than not, creatives in the Hispanic market want music that emulates the music currently being played on Hispanic radio and television stations. If the assignment is to imitate an older style, the creatives will want the music to emulate that style. (They usually provide an example.) As mentioned previously, *do not plagiarize*.

Since Hispanic music varies between countries and regions within countries, the native musicians perform the music in idiosyncratic styles. Even if the rhythms in different countries are basically the same, the performers' interpretations differ. Therefore, hire musicians who will perform in an authentic style. (This concept is discussed in the next section.)

If an assignment is to compose one commercial that will be broadcast in Spanish-speaking countries, how does a composer write generic music that appeals to all of the countries? This can be problematic. Most often, different arrangements of the same music are written in a style that appeals to one nationality. Sometimes only one music track is completed and broadcast in many countries.

For example, Dr. Murciano was asked to write a generic composition for Visa International that would be broadcast throughout South America. The target market was affluent consumers who lived elegant lifestyles. The film did not depict a certain culture and was generic in its visual look—it could have been filmed in any South American country. Dr. Murciano analyzed the film and reached the conclusion that since all their cultures shared a common European heritage, he would give the music a symphonic treatment by incorporating traditional instruments and composing and orchestrating music with an aristocratic texture. He mixed traditional orchestral instruments with instruments such as the guitar, which is used in many South American countries; the instruments were not played in an ethnic style, thereby eliminating the possibility of identifying a specific culture.

Author's Example: While composing and/or arranging a series of commercials for Dr Pepper, I had to adapt one jingle to various Spanish and English styles. Latin house music and hip-hop were the chosen genres. The commercials were various lengths (e.g., 15 or 30 seconds) and performed in Spanish, mostly Spanish, mostly English, and Spanglish, a mixture of Spanish and English. Not only were numerous compositional revisions necessary to accommodate the various versions, but also creative questions had to be answered prior to writing.

Dr. Murciano's musical approach resulted from a conversation with the creatives on how to appeal to all cultures in their target market with one composition. Since it is possible that the creatives might not have been aware of the potential musical problem, they were pleased with Murciano's creative solution.

Composers have to present their ideas with a clear and thoughtful explanation of why they choose to explore a precise musical path. A mistake in solving this musical problem could have caused a decline in sales. If the commercial did not appeal to the target audience in each country, the sales would most likely have declined, and the account might have been put up for review.

The importance of research is once again demonstrated. There are many styles of Spanish music, encompassing the Caribbean, Mexico, South America, Central Amercia, as well as Spain, and within each country or territory the musical styles and pronunciation differ. Therefore, it was important to grasp the target audience. The client did not want the Caribbean sound (e.g., Cuban and Puerto Rican styles). Dr Pepper has a relatively small market share in the northeastern United States, where there is a sizable population of Puerto Rican and Cuban immigrants. They wanted the commercials to appeal to Mexican Americans and the general Hispanic population since Dr Pepper has a considerable market share in the western United States, which has a large Mexican American population. None of the music was arranged in a traditional Mexican musical style because Dr Pepper wanted to appeal to a young audience that does not listen to or identify with traditional forms of Latin music; instead, Latin house music—dance (disco) music with Latin percussion—and hip-hop were chosen.

Hire Musicians and Singers Who Are Specialists

Studio musicians and singers are usually skilled in many styles, but some specialize. Learn their strengths. For example, if the assignment is to write a sonata for violin and piano in the style of the classical period, a violinist familiar with that style knows that certain musical ornamentation was not written down but was expected to be added by the performer. Most country singers and musicians use generic vocal and instrumental ornamentations that clearly characterize a style of music. [Listen to track #8 on the enclosed CD.]

The following is my interview with Alfred Brown, an accomplished studio viola player in New York City. He is a graduate of the Curtis Institute and is a musicians' contractor for commercials, films, television, and records.

MZ: What is the best background for a studio musician?

Alfred: The best studio musicians have eclectic backgrounds. Their ability to read music is well above average . . . not only reading the notes but reading dynamics and knowing styles. You might get someone from the Philharmonic who can read the notes, but they don't necessarily have the feel of a studio musician, because a studio musician knows what goes with a particular kind of music. That can be said for all musicians—for drummers, for guitar players, for saxophone players—they have a feel—the best thing I can say about them is that they have a good sense of music like a chamber music player. They are very sensitive to each other['s playing]. You can come into a room and read the music down once, and by the second time, you've got a very good idea of what the music feels like—what it sounds like—what the nuances are, and what the leader wants. One of the most important things is that we have no time to rehearse, and you have to read it [the parts] almost like a performance. People like David Nadien [past concertmaster of the New York Philharmonic] can read beautiful solos in a way that sounds like a finished performance. There are severe time restrictions [because of budget], so everything has to be done as quickly as possible.

MZ: How does one train to become a studio player?

Alfred: The only training that I know of is by actually doing it. I think that playing chamber music is the best training. They have to feel the other players in the room—to be sensitive to the other players around them. When you are looking at a part, you might hear that part somewhere else in the orchestra, and you listen to the way that person plays it or that person might have heard you playing it earlier—no part in the orchestra is by itself. You always listen very carefully to what is going on around you.

MZ: Do you think that rhythm section players are categorized more than the other sections?

Alfred: I would say yes. [Many section players specialize in a particular style.]

MZ: How about brass players?

Alfred: They tend to be categorized into jazz players or classically trained players, but many of them cross over. Jazz players are not called upon to play strictly classical music, so they can cross over if they are really good.

MZ: How do classically trained players become familiar with popular styles?

Alfred: I think you have to listen to different kinds of music. [In the case of string players,] you have to listen to the articulation of the bowings, for instance, and how a section plays, because sections usually play together—they play pretty much the same feel. Pop phrasing is very often different than classical phrasing.

MZ: Is there any other advice you would like to offer?

Alfred: Be open and play chamber music as much as possible—ensemble playing.

Compose and Arrange in the Generic Style of the Instruments

Many composers (arrangers) compose music using an instrument, such as piano or guitar. One of the dangers of this method is they might not internalize the generic sound of the instruments they are writing for. If they have limited technical ability on their instrument, their writing may be compromised.

While writing for strings, it is imperative that composers (arrangers) understand the various bowing techniques. Bowing cannot be heard on a piano but can be internalized in composers' minds. A legato (smooth) passage requires smooth bowing that is indicated by bow markings in the music and by arco markings. Pizzicato is a plucking of the strings and creates a unique effect. Tremolo is created by the bow moving quickly across the strings, creating a trembling effect. Very high parts written for the violins will sound thin in the studio minus a full complement of violinists playing the same part.

♩ A musicians' contractor (referred to as a "contractor") specializes in hiring the most skilled musicians for an assignment; they also submit the union contracts that are required by the various unions. This is a highly specialized skill. If composers request musicians who play unusual instruments, a competent contractor will know them. For example, the Broadway production of *The Lion King* requires numerous African instrumentalists. Not only do the musicians have to be capable of playing the score, but they must also be "actors" because they are onstage and part of the production.

Internalize the part first and then write the notes. This technique should be applied to all parts that live players will perform. "Hearing" the instrument (internalizing) will enable composers to capture its true essence.

Hire native musicians to perform compositions written in a typical folkloric style. The use of ethnic instruments requires a complete understanding not only of the technical limitations of the instruments but also of the creative playing styles. Characteristic rhythms, patterns, and ornamentations are native to performing styles. If a nonnative musician can play an instrument, the performance will not neccesarily sound authentic if the musician is not involved in the musical culture and customs of the native society.

The Census Bureau requested a commercial campaign comprised of twelve commercials; they required various authentic styles, such as Arabic, Polish, and Russian. (Examples of each genre are available on the Internet.) The commercials stressed the benefits of filling out a census report. This assignment also addressed the problem of changing musical and emotional moods within the same commercial. Each spot opened with scenes of the native country of a family and evolved into that same family living in the United States. Understanding the style and technical limitations of ethnic instruments helped to achieve authenticity. Each composition had to change from a native style into an American jazz arrangement, incorporating the original theme. Because of budget restrictions, the number of musicians was limited. The solution was to hire three or four native musicians and six to eight contemporary musicians and to add synthesizers. This combination achieved a rich sound without destroying the mood.

The commercials aimed at the Russian audience and the Polish audience required the use of an accordion. In most instances, an American composer would request the instrument that is commonly played at social gatherings. This would have been a mistake because generic Polish and Russian accordions differ; each has a distinct sound. The announcers spoke the Russian and Polish languages, as the commercials were directly geared toward an audience that had immigrated to the United States. The agency assigned a Russian creative for the Russian commercials and a Polish creative for the Polish spots. Both executives were detail oriented and focused on achieving an authentic representation of their native music.

The Arabic commercials presented an even more challenging assignment. Four native instruments were used: a nay (a flute made of cane with six finger holes and one thumb hole); an ud (also spelled "oud"—a short-necked, plucked guitar-like instrument); native drums, which included a duff (also spelled "daff"—a one-headed drum that rattles with a tambourine-type sound when struck); and a darabukka (a one-headed drum made of pottery, wood, or metal). In addition, the jazz ensemble included a piano, electric bass, and drums.

The nay player brought nays in all keys. To make the assignment more difficult, one of the commercials used music composed by Mozart. The challenge was to begin the commercial with Mozart arranged in an Aramaic style and transition into a jazz version of the same music.

The arranger had to understand which compositional devices would create an Aramaic sound. Aramaic arrangements usually include the melody performed in unison or octaves. Aramaic music has certain rhythmic patterns that are popular, much in the same manner that Latin music comprises different rhythms, for the mambo, rumba, and the cha-cha. After experimenting, it was decided to play the first part of the music in a traditional, ethnic, rubato, emotional style (the film dictated emotion) and then transition into an upbeat jazz groove with a faster tempo, adding contemporary instruments and rhythms. The piano assumed the melody in a jazz style, and the Aramaic instruments played fills. This musical solution brought the ethnic feeling of the Arabic homeland into a new life in the United States. The music evoked the story of the film.

Because the campaign involved a total of twelve commercials (six for radio and six for television), there was a two-month period to experiment with the music. This is an unusually long time period to work on a commercial. Besides creating authenticity, the most challenging part of the assignment was writing the transitions from the native-sounding sections to the jazz sections. Many hours were spent experimenting with various solutions.

The music used for one of the Polish commercials was a very popular song in Poland. Because most of the audience would recognize the composition, the creative executive in charge had the composer work with the arranger prior to recording. This helped to ensure that the musical interpretation would be accurate. Although this approach could have been uncomfortable, the composer was a knowledgeable musician and cooperative, making for a pleasant collaboration.

Budget restrictions have been a problem throughout music history. The string quartet developed as a result of budget restrictions. Symphonies performed in the late 1700s and 1800s could not always be performed with multiple string players on each part. Therefore, each part was often restricted to one player—thus the evolution of the trio or quartet or sometimes a quintet. Some of the smaller churches could not afford to pay more than one performer; sometimes the number of musicians was limited by choice (H. C. Robbins Landon, editor, *The Mozart Compendium*, Borders Press, 82).

It is conceivable to be asked to compose and arrange music in fifties, hip-hop, Latin, pop, and classical styles in one week. No matter how diverse, the creatives will expect the tracks to sound authentic. It is surprising how many commercials do not contain music that captures the essence of the intended style.

The more varied a composer's ability to write in various genres, the better his or her chance of receiving numerous assignments.

Common Mistakes

Many composers and arrangers write for instruments they are unfamiliar with. When this occurs, the sound will not be authentic, and the part will sound contrived. In writing music for commercials and film, ethnic instruments are sometimes used to achieve a unique feeling or ambience. Become familiar with the native sounds, nuances (playing style), and technical and musical limitations of instruments before writing for them. [Listen to tracks #2–6 on the enclosed CD.]

Ethnomusicology is the study of musical sounds and performance styles of various cultures throughout the world. George Harrison, a member of the Beatles, did more to promote the synthesis of ethnic instruments in traditional pop music than any other musician. He studied the sitar (a guitar-like Indian instrument) with the world-renowned Indian classical sitar performer Ravi Shankar. He then proceeded to use the sitar on albums *Rubber Soul, Sgt. Pepper's Lonely Hearts Club Band,* and several others. This was the beginning of what is now referred to as World Music. *Billboard*, the leading music magazine, publishes a contemporary World Music chart.

Ethnic instruments are played and tuned in a unique manner. Instruments that have the same name (e.g., balaphone, an African xylophone) have dissimilar tunings in different countries. The nuances of the performance style are also unique to certain countries and regions.

Ancient instruments have limitations. For example, most wooden flutists, from different countries, have multiple flutes, each tuned to a different key; contemporary flutes are chromatic instruments, so it is not necessary to have more than one instrument. (This is not a reference to the differences between a piccolo, flute, alto flute, or bass flute.)

The typical performing style of the kora (an African lute harp) incorporates the use of triplets. The kora player has to change tuning (in a manner similar to tuning a guitar) when playing in various keys. The kora is not a chromatic instrument.

Author's Experience: The kora has 21 strings made of fishing line. It can be played only in certain keys and is tuned by moving bundles of line wrapped around pegs that are inserted in the kora's neck. I used the kora in a commercial that required a West African style. The instrument has a unique structure; therefore, understand its limitations before writing. Similar to other instruments, the kora is traditionally played in a very distinct style. Listen to recordings and absorb the generic sounds and performance styles. It is advisable to consult with instrumentalists to question if passages can be performed and if the traditional styles are adaptable. The parts must be written and performed properly, or the performances will sound awkward.

Writing for ethnic instruments requires research and study. It is as important for composers to be familiar with the more common genres, such as rhythm and blues, rock, New Age, jazz, Latin, and pop.

Author's Example: A harp is not a chromatic instrument. Composers must calculate the time it takes for a harpist to manipulate the pedals, or the music will be impossible to perform. Call a harpist and ask questions. It is improbable that composers, orchestrators, and arrangers will know the nuances of every instrument. It

is essential to be familiar with the tessitura (best-sounding range) of each instrument.

Common Problems

Writing in the wrong register. A part might sound suitable on a piano or synthesizer but might not sound appropriate played on the real instrument. Some synthesizers are able to play notes that exceed the registers of the real instruments they are emulating. For the music to sound authentic, study the ranges of the instruments and their tessituras.

Not using the proper voicings or harmonies when composing or arranging in a specific genre. For example, if writing in the classical style, study the harmonic and compositional theoretical practices of the classical period. Follow the same practice when writing music for the baroque period and all other musical time periods. In contemporary popular music, there is extensive use of samples (digital recordings that can be triggered with a keyboard or other instruments using MIDI) and electronic music. Be acquainted with the nuances of the style.

Determining the proper key for singers. The key affects the emotional feeling of a composition. If a key is too high, the voice may sound strained; if it is too low, it can sound lackluster. The key might be physically out of range for a singer. Audition the key with the singer before finalizing the arrangement.

The key of a composition directly affects the mood of the music. Playing a composition in various keys evokes a completely different ambience to the same composition. A high key may sound lively, whereas a lower key may sound too dark.

Utilizing inappropriate instruments. Emulating music written in 1948, using an electric bass guitar would not be appropriate because the instrument was not invented until 1951. If the assignment was to compose music in a traditional symphonic form, the saxophone would, in all probability, not be used, with certain exceptions. Do not let music get in the way of dialogue. If the music is in the same frequency range, the scene will sound too cluttered. [Listen to track #9 on the enclosed CD.]

The foregoing are some of the pitfalls that can be experienced if careful attention is not given to all composing and arranging decisions.

MIDI

MIDI is the acronym for Musical Instrument Digital Interface. Synthesizers are manufactured by many companies, and inputting them through MIDI routers enables the devices to synchronize with each other and to play back simultaneously. Most synthesizers enable the use of 16 MIDI tracks per device, indicating that 16 individual events (channels or sounds) per synthesizer and its associated MIDI-based hardware, such as reverb units, can be triggered on an individual basis. MIDI provides digital data, not sounds; each synthesizer produces the sounds.

Computers have changed the world of music in much the same way as satellites, radio, television, telephones, films, and other forms of communication have. The ability to use MIDI (and samples) is one of the most important technical skills a composer/arranger in any musical idiom can possess. It has revolutionized the way music is written and performed. Composing music for commercials and understanding and having the ability to implement the technical applications are as essential to the completion of the process as writing the music.

Sequencers

Sequencers enable composers to arrange a composition one track at a time and to play back MIDI and audio data, simultaneously triggering various synthesizers and other audio data. They provide a recording platform, nonlinear editing, and performance playback: events such as sustain, velocity, aftertouch (the pressure applied to a note after the initial attack affects the output level), pitch bends, transposition, and other parameters are a sampling of the events that programmers can manipulate. Most sequencers provide detailed editing systems, enabling programmers to accomplish almost any imaginable sound manipulation.

Most sequencers are computer programs; stand-alone hardware sequencers are less popular. Computer-based sequencers can synchronize with digitized video clips, such as Quicktime Movie and video players (not often used), making it possible to play music in synchronization with video. The graphics of most computer sequencers emulate tape recorders, with virtual playback, record, fast-forward, and rewind buttons, and recording consoles, with faders, automation, sends, effects, and so on. Many sequencers display the musical notation that has been played into the system; the notation can be edited and printed. (Programs such as Finale and Sibelius, dedicated notation programs, are more advanced than the notation systems found within sequencer programs. Many professional copyists use this software.)

In any genre of film writing, composers have to time the scenes and choose the tempo(s) before composing. In most instances, since the music has to correspond to the action (both emotional and physical), it is very difficult to conduct live musicians without the aid of a click track (metronome); it is also problematic to play back electronic music in sync with the action without synchronization. After a tempo(s) has been chosen, sequencers instantly provide essential technical information that enables the programs to play in sync. Digitized video clips are loaded into computer programs, and the scenes change according to measure numbers. This enables programmers to work in a nonlinear manner. A video player must roll to chosen sections, which is time consuming. With digitized video clips, a programmer can navigate from measure 3 to measure 24 instantly, and the video follows.

When a sequencer is connected to a video player, the composer can roll the tape to a specific scene, and the computer will display bar numbers and real-time and SMPTE (Society of Motion Picture and Television Engineers) frame numbers (a time code), providing an address for the specific location. For example, if the tempo were 120 beats per minute, the indicator might read that the action takes place on the third beat of measure 15. The composer compiles a list of markers that describe the action, serving as a guide to composing the final composition. Next to the markers is the SMPTE number, bar number, tempo, and real time. (These are discussed in detail in chapter 5.) This system is rarely used since digitized video clips (video) are able to load into sequencing programs.

Electronic music and editing has enabled composer/arrangers to program music that would be impossible for live musicians to perform. The most obvious example is the programming of drums, using very complex rhythms with numerous percussion instruments played simultaneously. Special effects (delays, various reverbs, and so on) are added to the mix, giving the final drum part a unique sound that could not be achieved through traditional methods. The same theory applies to other instruments and audio. Composers have to consider this technology when composing and/or producing music. Virtually any musical ideas can be realized. This is the primary difference between composing for traditional instruments performed by live musicians and using only electronic instruments or in combination with live instrumentalists.

Sequences provide automated recording and automated mixing. A graphic display of a recording console works in the same manner as a hardware version of a recording console and tape recorder. The transport controls display a record button, fast-forward and rewind buttons, and a stop button. As previously mentioned, the measure numbers and beats are displayed in a separate window, enabling the programmer to also read real-time and SMPTE time codes. The mixing console contains channel strips with send knobs, pan knobs, mute buttons, automation buttons, and track assignment buttons. The individual faders, located within each channel, are used to adjust levels. The aux send knobs enable the use of effects such reverb; EQ (equalization), which can alter the frequencies (treble, midrange, bass, and so on); and other parameters that are included within hardware versions of recording consoles. After the music has been programmed, the individual sounds (tracks) are mixed together to form a final musical combination called a *mix*.

Digital Audio

Digital audio has revolutionized recording. With digital audio, the analog sound is converted into a binary code composed of 0s and 1s and then reconverted to analog through the use of digital-to-audio converters. The conversion enables the sound to be heard through a speaker system; digital sound cannot be heard without this conversion. The sound of digital is debatable. Some listeners enjoy the sound because it is pristine—clean and transparent. Others prefer the "warmer" sound of analog tape. Most rock-and-roll bands favor analog recording because they feel it has a "dirtier" sound and a deeper bottom end; most pop and rhythm-and-blues music is recorded in a digital format since producers like the crisp, clear sound. It is a matter of personal choice. Both formats are used in all styles of music, although digital recording has captured the market.

A third option is called Dolby SR (spectral recording), which is a noise-reduction system used with analog tape that improves noise reduction up to 24 decibels over systems without it. The result is a quiet, warm sound. Many producers prefer the Dolby SR format to plain analog or digital recording because of the warmer sound.

The digital format has now become the standard of the global music industry. Some producers mix and record in the digital format and transfer the final mix on analog tape. They prefer the "warmer" sound of tape. (Very few companies manufacture analog or digital tape because of the low demand.) The following are some advantages to digital audio:

The principal advantage of digital technology is the ability to copy and combine information without a loss of quality. With analog recording, the frequency with which tracks are copied and recopied determines the noticeable quantity of hiss and distortion. With digital technology, digital numbers are stored and converted into analog signals, enabling the audio to be heard. Consequently, there is no loss of quality when copying data.

The digital format allows a programmer to perform nonlinear, nondestructive editing on software-based computer systems. Nonlinear editing enables programmers to instantly locate any section of a file without having to fast-forward to a location. Since there is no tape, the computer program memorizes the parameters of the edit, and the edit is performed instantaneously. Most programs work by highlighting specific regions for editing. For example, if the assignment is to delete measures 4 through 27, the programmer highlights the region and pushes delete. Digital technology also allows for multiple mixes and numerous edits without losing any recorded information. The parent files are retained unless deliberately erased. This enables experimentation without a loss of audio quality.

Computer music-sequencing programs contain digital audio (e.g.,

Pro Tools and Digital Performer) and include basic effects plug-ins.
Plug-ins are computer-based digital effects and signal processing virtual
units that perform the same functions as their hardware counterparts.
Effects incorporated with most programs are reverbs, echoes, equalizers,
gates, and compressors. As with hardware units, there are many variations and choices of plug-ins. They all sound different and offer dissimilar
features. Since purchasing third-party effects can be costly, before purchasing it is advisable to listen to the demo CDs provided by most manufacturers. Many manufacturers also offer demonstration downloads from
their websites as a marketing tool. Some of the plug-ins automatically
erase after a predetermined time period.

    Hardware-based digital recorders do not require tape. Much the same
as computer-based recorders, these units provide nondestructive editing
features as well as the same basic functions offered with computer MIDI
audio programs. To a composer/arranger, the advantages of computer-
based digital technology unquestionably have no competition. Digital
technology has transformed the recording industry.

    One of the problems with computer-based digital audio is that it
requires sizable hard-disk memory for storage as well as additional processing power to operate peripheral music software. Digital plug-ins also
require supplementary processing power. Insufficient processing power is
frustrating and hinders programmers from completing their creative
visions. Consider the following advice:

1. Purchase the fastest computer with the most RAM that your budget
   allows.
2. Save digital audio on a separate hard drive. Do not save audio on
   the same hard drive that contains the computer's operating system.
   Many problems can occur because of this practice.
3. Burn a CD or DVD of your files as a safety measure and for future
   reference. Memory is a valuable commodity, and even large storage
   drives eventually fill up. It is wise to save your files on several outboard hard drives.

Samplers

A sampler records audio, converts it to digital audio (stored in RAM), and
plays back through the use of a music-sequencing program. Notes generated from a keyboard controller can trigger the sampled sounds. Many
sampling CDs and CD-ROMs, containing virtually any sounds composers
require (e.g., orchestral instruments, drum loops [grooves], sound effects,
and so on), are sold in retail outlets or can be downloaded.

    Samplers are hardware based and computer based. The sounds can be
edited, which helps to achieve a wide variety of sound manipulation. Filters, velocity, time compression (changing tempo without changing the

pitch of the instrument), and the ability to truncate (erase the unwanted parts), transpose, or normalize (achieve the strongest volume level) sounds are some of the changeable parameters.

Hardware samplers do not deplete the CPU (central processing unit) power, which contains the brains of a computer. When using plug-ins (effects and signal processing) with digital audio, many computers run out of memory. Using hardware-based samplers provide many of the features of computer audio. The sounds of hardware samplers, combined with digital audio in a computer-based system, are a powerful compositional tool.

Studio Technology as It Applies to Music Production

It is not the intention of this book to concentrate on the technical aspects of recording, but composers must have some basic knowledge. The use of recording technology not only affects the overall "sound" of recordings but may also determine how composers conceive their music. For instance, the ambience of a vocal might emulate the accoustics of a church or cathedral, as did the Gregorian chant sung on the wine commercial referred to earlier; a guitar sound can be embellished with numerous delays, echoes, and other effects—guitars used in surfing music have an identifiable delay.

The form of a composition or arrangement written to be recorded is directly related to the effects processors used on voices and instruments. There must be enough space between the notes for effects to be heard. This should be taken into consideration while writing. Not having a thorough understanding of technology can result in "musical confusion." If not used properly, delays and echoes can create a cloudy soundscape, and the final music tends to have no definition of sound. The creative use of technology requires experimentation.

Whereas in the past composers studied traditional composition and orchestration, contemporary composers and arrangers must also have technical knowledge (in addition to traditional training) to survive in the world of commercial music. An understanding of signal processors, audio effects, and recording consoles is of utmost importance.

Signal Processors and Audio Effects

Audio effects are added to the original signal; *signal processors* change signals. The use of signal processors and audio effects has become as important in audio as it has

> ♫ For the purposes of this discussion, the terms *audio effects* and *signal processors* are used interchangeably.

been in film effects processing. Signal processors can change a sound in infinite ways, helping composers achieve unique sounds. The creative use of these devices is determined by the composer, arranger, and/or music producer.

The most commonly used processors are called DSPs (digital signal processors). The same effects that can be programmed into hardware-based processors are available in digital software processors. The software-based virtual processors, which are virtual versions of the same hardware processors, usually look and work almost exactly the same as the hardware versions. The parameters are adjustable, and the computer can store and recall the settings. This saves a substantial amount of time. If a session required 10 hardware signal processors, all 10 devices would have to be reset by hand to revise a mix. With computers, the settings can be stored and recalled.

Most new plug-ins are designed only in software versions. Digital technology has replaced certain audio hardware that is now obsolete. Not only is the software easier to program, but it is also less costly. Virtual signal processors enable users to automate the parameters. If the programmer/engineer wants to increase or decrease the amount of reverb in each measure, the computer automates the changes. Most plug-ins can also be automated. Some hardware consoles include automated processors, whereas almost all software sequencer programs contain this feature.

Computer-based sequencers, which contain digital audio as well as MIDI, include a basic complement of plug-ins. Many third-party manufacturers make plug-ins, but not all plug-ins work with all software programs. Before purchasing third-party plug-ins, ask the manufacturers if they support your software program. Most sequencer manufacturers include a list of supported third-party vendors. This information can also be found on the manufacturers' websites.

One of the major problems encountered with the use of plug-ins is that a computer might run out of memory and not support the number of devices required; plug-ins are memory intensive. The program might crash or inform the user that the computer is out of memory. The response time to each command may become so sluggish that it creates a hindrance to the flow of an ideal creative environment. There are two basic solutions to this problem:

1. Add additional RAM to the computer, which creates more memory.
2. Copy an audio track, including the signal processing, to another audio track. For example, a vocal might have a delay. The vocal, along with the delay, can be bounced (combined) onto a new track, and the delay effect can then be removed from the program, thereby lessening the memory load on the CPU of the computer. This frees up memory so that another effect can be used.

It is conceivable that the final mix will have multiple tracks that contain prerecorded processing; the engineer balances the tracks to achieve a final mixed track. One of the problems with this process is that when the tracks are balanced and a particular effect does not sound appropriate, the only solution is to rerecord that track and adjust the effect. This can be time consuming. The solutions to these problems depend on the budget, but with creative thinking and planning, most technical problems are solvable. The following are some commonly used processors.

Equalization (EQ). Equalizing is the ability to filter sound frequencies by using low-pass, high-pass, and band-pass filters. Recording consoles, real or virtual, offer engineers the ability to alter the sound of the signal flowing through each channel. *EQ* (the industry term) can alter the sound minimally or radically. For example, adding EQ to high frequencies can add clarity to a muffled-sounding vocal, and cutting the low frequencies can delete the "mud" from a bass sound. Engineers are able to boost or cut frequencies and increase or decrease the gain (volume) of selected frequencies. Basic consoles generally contain low-frequency, midrange, and high-frequency equalizers. Sophisticated recording consoles contain more complex EQs and better-quality EQs.

In addition to console equalization, separate hardware units can be patched into the recording. The two most popular types of equalizers are *parametric EQ* and *graphic EQ*.

Parametric equalizer. All frequencies of parametric equalizers can be boosted or attenuated by "smoothly" adjusting the volume levels of selected frequencies. The Q adjustment allows the engineer to select a specific sound and boost or cut the level without affecting surrounding frequencies. They are manufactured with a variety of bands, such as a three-band equalizer or an eight-band equalizer. More precise editing can be accomplished with multiple bands. Parametric equalizers are included with most hardware and software recording consoles.

The frequencies of other types of equalizers can be edited by selecting predetermined steps, called discrete steps, that are changed by clicking a knob.

Graphic equalizer. The frequencies of graphic equalizers are arranged according to musical octaves. In place of knobs, sliders are used. Frequencies are adjusted by moving the sliders in a linear fashion. Many graphic equalizers have up to eight frequency bands.

Equalization is important to the creative process. Only the basics have been covered in these descriptions. Equalizers are complex devices, and using them effectively requires extensive experimentation by engineers and programmers.

Reverberation units. Reverb creates a feeling of space and ambience. The delays mimic sound reflecting from walls, ceilings, and other nonabsorbant surfaces. Delays (a series of repeated echoes) are measured in milliseconds and are changeable. Some reverb units allow complex programming, helping to achieve interesting effects. The parameters of the virtual size and surface material of a room are programmable. Standard presets are small room, large room, auditorium, cathedral, drum rooms, live-sounding rooms, and dead rooms (minimal reverb). In more intricate units, hundreds of programmable combinations are offered. Some reverbs contain presets only. Several reverbs are frequently used to achieve a desired ambience.

The software DSP versions are programmed in the same manner. The sound and programmability vary with the manufacturer. One manufacturer may have multiple delay units with different sounds and editing parameters, while other manufacturers offer fewer choices. Selecting reverb units is a matter of individual preference. Some units sound "warm," while others are more resonant.

Delays. Delays are used to create various effects, the most common of which is adding a feeling of space and depth to a vocal or instrument. By listening closely to most contemporary recordings, a very faint repeating effect can be heard behind the vocals. The length of the delay (e.g., an eighth note, a sixteenth note, a dotted eighth note, or a triplet delay) depends on the desired effect. The gain (volume level) of the delay is adjustable, and proper use of delays adds depth to a mix.

Another use of delays (as described earlier with the Trance music example) is to create a rhythmic, repeated effect on an instrument that creates a rhythm. An eighth-note or sixteenth-note delay is employed. The most obvious question would be, "Why not write two eighth notes or four sixteenth notes for each note rather than use a delay?" The answer is that delay units can be programmed to use additional parameters in combination with the delay (e.g., feedback or repeats). Delays help to create an ambience that cannot be accomplished by merely repeating notes.

A bass part incorporating delays and feedback as part of its basic sound has to be composed with the delay incorporated in the writing process. A composer would almost certainly write a different part if the effect were not an intrinsic part of the basic sound. This is an example of how an effect is directly related to composition.

As previously mentioned, delay units are programmed in milliseconds. A formula can determine the number of milliseconds (at a determined bpm [beats per minute]) that will create a chosen delay. The formula is $1,000/(bpm/60)$ = quarter-note delay in milliseconds. There is also a printed list that supplies this information at various tempos. Sometimes, experimenting with various delays produces the desired effect.

Another common usage is to create a doubling effect. During recording, the backgrounds are usually doubled. The singers record each part two or three times, creating a richer sound. Choosing the proper delay can accomplish a similar effect. When parts are doubled by the singer(s) who sang the original part, the intonation and vibrato vary, making the doubled effect sound more natural than the perfectly processed double. It becomes both a creative and a financial decision whether to double parts.

Session fees and residual payments are higher when performances are doubled.

The expense of doubling should be included in the budget. The agency must know, prior to the session, that you plan to double. Doubling can be costly and will be deducted from the creative fee if it is not approved beforehand.

Delays, analogous to equalization, can be used in creative ways. It is determined by the creator's imagination.

Compressor/limiters. Compressor/limiters automatically attenuate signals that go above a programmed volume level (gain) called a *threshold*. For example, using a compressor/limiter produces essentially the same function as lowering a fader to avoid distortion. If a compressor is set to a 2-to-1 ratio, for every two decibels of sound input, one decibel of output level will occur. If a compressor can be set to very high compression ratios, the effect is called *limiting*. (Not all compressors are also limiters.)

Compressors are commonly used in commercials. By averaging the level between the loudest and softest sections, the overall track becomes louder. If a track has a rhythmic arrangement, compressing the track creates a more powerful result. When used with vocals, instead of a singer sounding too loud and the track too distant, the music track surrounds the vocal.

Compressors are commonly used on individual tracks for the recording of kick drums, snare drums, bass, and additional parts where the dynamic range of the music is relatively equal (e.g., hip-hop rhythmic tracks). If the dynamic range is critical to the effect of the composition, compression should not be used (e.g., classical music), as it changes the dynamics of the music.

A song heard on the radio sounds noticeably different than when it is heard on a CD player because most broadcast stations have *limiters* (compressors with a higher threshold and ratio) that attenuate signals that go above a designated threshold. When the dynamics of a track are compressed, the audio sounds as if the levels are relatively equal; compression can add energy. Many commercials (as well as records) have special radio and television mixes. For example, most commercials are equalized brighter (exaggerating the higher frequencies) than an average record; the higher frequencies are attenuated on the radio and television, and the extra highs compensate for the loss. After the music mix has been completed, the mixed tracks are compressed for the same reasons stated previously.

Expanders increase or decrease the dynamic range. They help restore dynamics in a signal if it has been overcompressed. They are the opposite of compressors and limiters.

Noise gates can mute unwanted material such as noise between recorded information or an open microphone not being used. The parameters are adjustable. Noise gates are exaggerated expanders.

Time compression changes the tempo of a track without changing the key.

Pitch correctors can correct poor intonation.

Transposition changes a key. (The ability to **transpose** is usually found in computer-based sequencing programs and hardware samplers.)

Flanging (flanger) is created by using a 1- to 10-millisecond delay in combination with filtering. It sounds like a "swishing" effect.

Chorus devices are used to create a doubling sound (as well as other effects). For instance, a lead vocal with a chorus effect sounds as if the lead singer overdubbed the original part.

If a singer arrives at a session and the key is wrong, using the **transposition** parameter, included with most software sequencers and samplers (hardware or software), can instantly change the key of a MIDI program. The parameters in sequencers are adjusted by intervals, such as up one whole step or from the key of C to the key of D.

Changing a key by using the audio transposition parameter might sound unnatural—a vocal may sound like Mickey Mouse if the transposition is too excessive. In addition, a change of key might require changing the octaves in which some of the instrumentation is written. For example, a change of key might cause a bass part to sound too high, so it would have to be lowered by one octave. This will, most likely, require rewriting some of the parts because the range of an instrument might not accommodate the new key. For instance, if the lowest note on the new bass part is notated as a low B (below the bass clef), the bass cannot play the note because it is below the range of the instrument. The arranger has to either select another note or play the B one octave higher. (The bass sounds one octave lower than where it is written.)

Filters. Filters are used to eliminate or reduce sections of an audio signal. For example, a high-pass filter allows only frequencies above the designated threshold (which is adjustable) to pass, while the frequencies below are attenuated. Conversely, a low-pass filter allows only the frequencies below the threshold to be heard, and the frequencies above are attenuated. Notch filters attenuate specific frequencies. Filters can be used creatively to help achieve unusual sounds and eliminate unwanted frequencies, such as a low hum.

Only the basics of signal processing have been discussed. Numerous devices can create unusual results. When purchasing gear, cost is a factor. If the budget is low, buy traditional software plug-ins, hardware effects devices, or a combination of both. Equalizers, reverberation units, echo units, compressor/limiters, expanders, gates, delays, and choruses are essential to recorded sound production.

The Recording Console (Mixer)

Many of the physical functions described next can be accomplished with the aid of a computer that is built into some consoles.

The differences between recording consoles and mixing consoles have narrowed. Channels can be assigned to tape recorders or digital audio devices so that the material can be recorded or processed; although mixers can be routed to recording devices, they are usually associated with live sound reinforcement. Recording consoles and mixing consoles are manufactured in both computer-based software and hardware configurations. Most engineer/programmers use a combination of the two. Consoles are either analog, digital, or a combination of the two formats. Digital consoles currently dominate the market and will continue to do so as technology advances.

Digital recording consoles incorporate a computer and an interface; they convert the analog signals into digital signals and route the signals digitally. This enables an engineer to instantly recall the entire signal path since the information has been stored in the computer or on a dedicated hard drive. The most minute changes can be accomplished, saved, and recalled without compromising the quality of the signal; there is no loss of quality because it is digital. This process saves time and money. The digital signal path also can sound cleaner (less distortion) than an analog signal path.

Some **analog consoles** are controlled digitally. The signal path is analog, but all other parameters are controlled digitally. The signal path stays in the analog domain in an analog console. Each time a mix is recalled, all the parameters (EQ, the signal processing devices, and so on) have to be set by hand, but the automation recalls the level changes.

Because audio technology has been moving at such a rapid pace, many affordable digital consoles are available. Purists who do not like the sound of digital use traditional analog consoles, but the majority of recording will continue to be in the digital domain.

An instrument or voice might sound fine soloed but must be adjusted when listening to a full mix. The recording or mixing console enables engineers to equalize the sound of each track by cutting or boosting the frequencies; this enables engineers to blend the instruments more effectively.

Channels enable input signals to enter the console. Recording and mixing consoles have multiple channels. (The number of channels differs between manufacturers and console models.) Microphone-level inputs allow microphone signals to enter the signal path via XLP (three-pin) cables or quarter-inch cables. Line-level inputs allow electric instruments, such as an electric guitar, to enter the signal path via quarter-inch cables or by routing the signal through devices such as a preamplifier. (The instruments can also be inputted into a channel through other devices.) The input levels are adjustable. Engineer/programmers must avoid distortion that will occur if the input signal is too "hot" (loud).

Faders control the volume levels (gain) of each track. (Faders are used to adjust the levels of not only vocals and instruments but also signal processors, groupings, and so on.) As previously discussed, in order to attain the best balance between channels, levels have to be adjusted (along with the signal processing)—faders are used to perform this function. Some consoles are automated, while others must be adjusted manually. Automated faders play back the level changes. Some automation also saves and plays back the signal processing. The number of faders available depends on the console.

Individual faders (with signal processing) can be grouped together and bused (sent) to **group faders**; for example, the drums (snare, kick, hi-hat, toms, cymbals, and so on) can be bused to two group faders, the electric and acoustic pianos can be sent to two group faders, and so on. The level of the group faders can be adjusted to achieve the best balance. For instance, to increase the level of the drums, the engineer/programmer only has to increase the level of two (group) faders rather than alter the individual faders of each drum or cymbal. The balance on the combined tracks can be modified by changing the parameters on the individual faders, which in turn affects the overall balance on the grouped tracks. The individual faders are automated, and automation of both level and signal processing can be adjusted throughout the track.

The master fader is used to adjust the overall output level of the console. The signals from each channel are bused to the master fader. If the levels from the individual faders are too "hot" (loud), distortion occurs. The distortion might not register on the master fader meter. The faders might register acceptable levels, but the overall master fader level still may register too "hot," resulting in a mix that sounds distorted. Listen very closely to the mix since distortion is sometimes difficult to detect.

Depressing a **solo button**, which is located near each fader, allows an individual track or multiple tracks to be soloed without lowering other faders. Soloing is useful when there are many tracks and the engineer or producer wants to listen to one track or a grouping.

Depressing **the mute button**, also located near each fader, mutes an individual track. This function can be programmed with the use of automation. Muting is helpful for mixing and tracking and can be a quick method to experiment with various combinations of tracks.

Panning is the placement of sound in the audio spectrum—left, right, center, and so on. A panning potentiometer (pot) is located near the fader. For example, a hi-hat might be panned to the right, the tom-toms to the left and right (stereo), and the kick drum to the middle. Panning helps to create a soundscape. If too many instruments are panned to the same location, there will be a lack of separation, and the track will sound muddy and cluttered. Panning creates a stereo or surround-sound environment.

Auxiliary sends, located near each fader, bus the output signals of channels to another source; aux sends are used primarily to aid in signal processing (e.g., delays or compression). As the level of the send knob is increased, more of the effect is mixed with the original signal. Aux sends are also used to adjust the level of monitor mixes or headphone mixes.

Singers or instrumentalists request customized balances in their headphones (e.g., more vocal, a louder bass, less drums, and so on).

Engineers and music producers determine the use of the aux sends; many devices and uses can be assigned. Most consoles have eight or more aux sends.

Returns send back the processed signal to the output of the console.

Master aux sends and **master returns** set the overall master output and input levels of the devices (reverbs, delays, and so on) assigned to each send/return. The level of each aux send is changeable.

If the master send level or return level of a reverb unit is too "hot," the reverb, which is used only on the tracks the engineer chooses, will distort. This can be adjusted by lowering the input and/or output level of the device. If the master output level is too low and an individual aux send is turned up, very little effect will be heard. The solution is to increase the level of the master send (to the aux sends) and/or master return.

Limiters, expanders, noise gates, and compressors (previously described) are built into expensive consoles and are included with most sequencing programs. If these devices are not built into the console, outboard gear is used. They are essential to recording and mixing.

The gain / trim knob enables engineers to achieve additional gain to an incoming signal. For instance, many instruments or microphones have a low output signal, and the trim increases the signal to an acceptable level.

When balancing the levels of individual faders, frequently a signal is too weak. The fader might be set to its maximum gain, but the output level remains insufficient. The trim knob increases the level of the signal. (Compressors and expanders might also help solve this problem.)

Channel inputs enable signals to enter a signal path, and **channel outputs** enable the signals to be heard.

The assignment buttons, which are located within each channel strip on a recording console, send a channel's signal to an outside source, such as a tape recorder. If the kick drum is on channel 1, it can be bused to track 5 or another track on a tape recorder by depressing the number 5 button. Many consoles require the engineer to turn a knob to the left to access odd-numbered assignment buttons and to the right to enable even-numbered buttons. (Individual channels can be bused to group faders.)

The monitor section outputs the combined audio signals to the speaker monitors. Some consoles have a separate monitor system that can be used for various purposes, such as a separate headphone mix. The B monitor section allows engineers to adjust the balances without disrupting the overall balance of the A monitor section.

On most consoles, channel strips have VU meters. A meter displays signal strength and distortion. As previously mentioned, distorted signals can be very subtle, and the meter reading will help determine the source of the distortion. The **master fader meter** displays the overall output signal from the console.

In addition to the meters, **clipping lights** are located on most channel strips. When a clipping light is lit, there is normally distortion. Most sequences also have clipping lights.

Amplifiers, preamplifiers (preamps), and phantom power are included in most consoles. Amplifiers boost the gain of the overall audio signal so that the speakers can attain their maximum effectiveness. Pre-amps boost the signal of low-level individual input signals so that they can attain their maximum power; preamps also help avoid distortion. Condenser microphones have a very low level output; the power for the microphone is provided directly from the console with *phantom power*. A button located on each channel strip enables the channel to use the phantom power.

All professional and many project studios have **patch bays**. A patch bay contains all inputs and outputs from the devices in the studio setup, such as synthesizers, reverbs, digital delays, compressor/limiters, and so on. Instead of the output of a synthesizer being routed to the input of a reverb unit and the output of the reverb returning to the recording console, these functions can be activated by plugging in patches within the patch bay.

Automation permits engineers to automate almost all functions of a console, such as level, panning, muting, signal processing, and so on. It is simple to update a file. Not all consoles have partial or complete automation. All computer-sequencing programs contain full automation. Automation is the most essential element in the process of mixing since the most minute detail can be adjusted and recalled.

Conclusion

The basics of a recording console have been discussed. The manner in which a console is implemented is not merely technical but a creative process as well. A creative recording engineer is as essential to the success or failure of a track as musicians and singers. It is analogous to the contribution a film editor makes to a film.

Time Code

Most composers use digitized video clips when composing for film or video. A video is digitized (usually at a low resolution to conserve disk space) and is loaded into a computer-sequencing program using a video capture card. This is a nonlinear method and therefore saves much time. For instance, if bar 4, beat 1, is the desired location, the picture and the audio can be synchronized with a push of a button on the computer keyboard. Composers can make spotting notes in the sequencers while the program runs in sync with the video.

Before digitized video was the industry standard, video was synchronized with a computer-sequencing program by using SMPTE time code. Following is a description of how it is implemented.

SMPTE (Society of Motion Picture and Television Engineers) time code (also called longitudinal time code) is the preferred code for audio and video production. The time code is displayed on the screen (hours, minutes, seconds, and frames) and is burned in. (The code has been added to the video and is permanently on the screen.) For example, a code that reads 05 10 18 27 refers to the video address 5 hours, 10 minutes, 18 seconds, and 27 frames. Let us assume that a car crashed at this video address. Depending on the tempo, composers are able to determine the measure and beat in which an event occurs. The time code is based on a 24-hour cycle. One of the stereo audio tracks generates an audible time code.

Another form of time code is VITC (Vertical Interval Time Code). In this process, the code is recorded on an address track. The advantage of using an address track is that it does not eliminate one of the two stereo audio tracks. This method requires a very expensive professional video player. The visual time code is not necessarily burned in; it can be viewed when necessary and then hidden.

NTSC (National Television Standards Committee) is the American standard for video. Black-and-white video contains 30 frames per second; this is called non–drop-frame code. Color video contains 29.97 frames per second; this is called drop-frame time code, meaning that frames are automatically dropped to make up the difference in time. With drop-frame code, there are 108 frames per hour extra, which translates to 3.6 additional seconds per hour. When using drop-frame code, two frames are dropped at the beginning of each minute, with the exception of every tenth minute. This corrects the timing problem.

Composers must inform editors of the tape format (e.g., VHS) and time code incorporated. (Most commercials are in color and therefore require drop-frame code.) A sequencer must be set to the proper setting of either 30 frames per second or 29.97 frames per second. If the setting is wrong, synchronization will not be accurate.

The European equivalent of NTSC is called PAL/SECAM and runs at 25 frames per second; in this format, black and white and color are the same, and both use non–drop-frame time code. Film runs at 24 frames per second.

Time code is also used to synchronize (lock) several tape recorders together.

Assignments

1. Record examples of studio technology as it applies to music production. Submit song samples or commercials in which technology is

endemic to the sound of the recording (e.g., delays, reverb, filtering, and so on).

2. Submit an example of an older musical style (e.g., swing or early rock and roll) that was recently created but sounds as if it were recorded in the original historical time period. List the reasons why the newly created track sounds authentic.

4

Analyzing Commercials

From a Musical Viewpoint

The first step in the process of developing a musical approach to a commercial is to analyze the storyboard. The storyboard outlines the commercial frame by frame through the use of drawings, dialogue, and camera instructions. All pertinent information, which includes the product name, title, and length of the commercial, is notated.

Sometimes, it is problematic to envision live action when viewing a storyboard because it is difficult to show movement in sketches or still photos. Ask the creatives to explain each frame from both a visual and a psychological perspective.

A storyboard helps the creative team and business team visualize the "look" of the final film. As previously discussed, storyboards are usually tested in focus groups, after which revisions are normally made. The final storyboard becomes the shooting guide for the director. (In some instances, the composer is presented with the final film. This is infrequent because the music is usually a part of the initial creative process. A composer is normally involved before the storyboard is presented to the client.)

The most difficult aspect of analyzing a storyboard is the ability to understand the essence of the commercial. Since the dialogue has not been recorded and the pictures are merely sketches, it is sometimes difficult to understand the intention of the writer, which affects the impact of the music. It is advisable to ask the writer to read and record the dialogue and announcer's copy prior to composing the music. Make certain the designated timing (e.g., 15 seconds or 30 seconds) is not exceeded. If the copy does not fit in the proper time frame, suggest that it be revised before approaching the composition. It will be impossible to structure the music properly without accurate timings. To help achieve the proper mood, listen to the dialogue while composing.

Sometimes, it is not possible to have the copy recorded. In that case, it is essential that every aspect of the writer's intention be clearly explained to the composer. Since the commercial has not yet been filmed, the composer has to determine the timings frame by frame. The best approach is to use a stopwatch.

Read each frame or each section and note the timings on the storyboard.

Record all dialogue onto a CD or audio program. (The timings of cassettes are not accurate.)

Leave space for action that has no dialogue. For instance, if someone is walking up steps and it takes 2 seconds, this timing must be included in the calculations.

If working with a digital audio sequencing program, begin composing while listening to the dialogue. This is an excellent reference tool.

Confirm the timings with the creatives. What seems logical may not be the agency's vision. A professional announcer can read advertising copy quickly and be perfectly understood. As a result, the final timings may change. Most agency producers experiment with actors and announcers while either filming or recording, which could alter the initial script. Make certain to have the final copy (script) before writing the music.

If writing to a completed film, it is advisable to check the timings. Sometimes, the film might be too long. Other than an error, this happens because the editor cannot fit the appropriate frames into the allotted time. The composer is asked to score to this longer time. After the commercial has been edited, the film company electronically compresses the entire film so that it fits the correct time. If the time difference is not too extreme, it will be difficult to notice the compression.

The music should not begin until at least seven frames have passed and should end .05 seconds before the film ends. Time is needed for the video to attain the proper speed at the beginning, and room is needed at the end to cut to another commercial (or program) with a smooth transition. Because of new technology, it might be possible to begin the music on the first frame of the picture. Question the producer prior to composing. Ask questions throughout the initial creative meeting. The following are some suggestions.

Who is the target audience? The answer to this question helps to conjure up musical ideas. For example, if the target audience were 50- to 65-year-old women, most likely, hip-hop would not appeal to most of them; therefore, hip-hop would be an inappropriate musical style.

What are the demographics, psychographics, or sociographics of the audience? The answer helps to narrow musical choices. Within these groups, countless musical styles could succeed; ask the creatives for guidance. It is essential to know which styles are *not* acceptable. This should also be a part of the creative discussion.

What musical styles work best? It is advisable to bring examples of musical directions to a creative meeting. Most likely, the creatives will play an example of what they feel would be the appropriate style. If a musical direction has been chosen, ask if they want the same instrumentation and musical mood heard in the example. Often they will like the general feeling of a piece but want the new music to vary from the example. For instance, they might want the original composition to be slower or faster than the example. Make certain that the original composition and arrangement is not plagiarized. It is common for the creatives to expect composers to make their original compositions sound similar to the example. If this occurs, insist that a musicologist examine the composition prior to the final recording. Many agencies request that composers sign an agreement absolving the agency from any claim of plagiarism. *Do not sign such an agreement!*

Author's Note: While working on a commercial for the CD-ROM game "Elmo's World," based on the Sesame Street character, the creatives played a musical example of a simple jazz composition in which the same musical pattern kept repeating. They liked the tempo and instrumentation but not the monotony of the repeated melodic phrase. The first step in analyzing the music was to determine what the creatives liked about the example; they had already revealed what they did not like. The repeated phrase was catchy, and the instrumentation consisted of a rhythm section; the drummer played with brushes, and a vibraphone performed the melody. This instrumentation provided a lively, mellow sound. If the drummer used sticks and a saxophone played the melody, the entire character of the composition would have been different.

The first approach was to divide the commercial into sections. The film consisted of an introduction, which suggested writing a musical introduction; the heart of the commercial, which suggested a melody; a middle section, which suggested a bridge; and an ending, which implied a musical ending. Dividing the music into this compositional form kept the essence of the demo (the predominant theme was a repeated pattern) but eliminated the boredom of only one repeated passage.

Many commercials are analogous to compositional styles that include an introduction, a middle section, and an ending. This helps composers create a cohesive piece of music.

What tempo is most appropriate? The tempo is directly related to the creation of a musical mood. If the music is too fast or too slow, the entire feeling of the commercial changes.

Does the mood of the music have to change within the commercial? Many commercials change moods, and the music will most likely have to change with it. For example, pain reliever commercials (e.g., aspirin) often start with a problem that is cured after taking the medication. In most instances, the opening music should evoke an uncomfortable feeling and transform into a pleasant section that signifies relief. Even though this seems like an obvious musical choice, the creatives might want only one musical mood. Since musical solutions are subjective, discuss various approaches with the creatives before composing.

Music that is suggested by the agency often differs from a composer's initial "musical impression." Since selecting music is a creative process, many styles will accomplish a musical goal.

Should sound effects be musical or realistic? If a large gun is fired, should the audience hear a deep gunshot or a short blast of timpani and low brass playing fortissimo? Using a combination of real effects mixed with synthesized sounds and/or samples creates many effects. The creatives generally know what they want. Discuss the possible solutions before designing the effects. (Composers of commercials often are responsible for creating sound effects; when composing for feature films, sound designers and Foley artists usually create the sound effects.)

What will be the visual look and style of the film? Will it be grainy, shot in color or black and white, edited with fast cuts, traditional or unusual camera angles, and so on? This is difficult to discern when working with a storyboard. Only the creators can answer these questions.

The agency frequently requests several variations of the same piece of music, or they might approve two separate compositions for the same commercial. After the spot has been filmed, the recorded tracks are synchronized to the video, and the final music is chosen.

After a demo has been approved and the final film has been shot, the composer adjusts the demo to fit the exact timings of the film. After viewing the film, the composer or the creatives might suggest substantial musical changes. Many editors use demos as an editing tool. The ambience of the music helps them "cut the film" (edit). Even after the music has been adjusted, the client might suggest additional edits and/or musical changes. This process usually continues until it is time to send the video to the television stations for airplay.

Analyzing a Storyboard

Let us analyze an actual storyboard as if we were approaching a real assignment. We will determine the timings from the storyboard and compare them to the actual timings of the final film. Refer to the storyboard below.

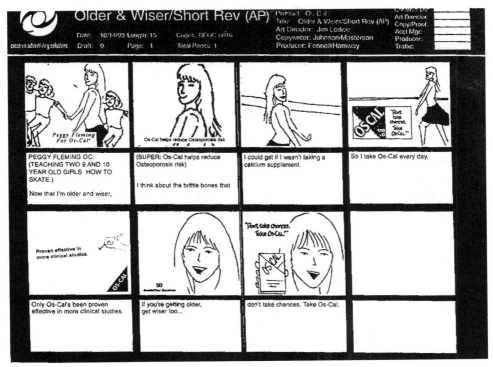

Example 4-1   Os-Cal.

Os-Cal Commercial Campaign

Os-Cal is a calcium supplement. The client chose to design a campaign composed of numerous television commercials. Peggy Fleming, an Olympic gold medalist in ice skating, was chosen as the spokesperson. She was selected because of her age, her fame, and her fitness; she is an ideal role model for the target audience.

The concept of the commercials was for Peggy to skate while telling the audience how Os-Cal has helped her to avoid osteoporosis by providing a calcium supplement.

The title of the commercial is "Older and Wiser," and this version runs 15 seconds (the campaign also included a 30-second version of the same commercial). Each timing is a full sentence.

Frame #1 (two kids on ice, ages 9–12). Peggy Fleming is skating (her name is superimposed on the screen), and she says, "Now that I'm older and wiser,"

Frame #2 (still skating). "I think about the brittle bones that"

Frame #3 "I could get if I wasn't taking a calcium supplement." Storyboard timing: 6 seconds; actual film timing: 5.5 seconds.

Frame #4 (She points to a poster that says "Don't take chances, take Os-Cal.") "So I take Os-Cal every day." Storyboard timing: 2 seconds; actual film timing: 1 second.

Frame #5 (A checkmark is made next to the following text: "Proven effective in more clinical studies.") This sentence was changed for the film. The film dialogue is "Only Os-Cal's been proven effective in more clinical studies." The timing from the storyboard dialogue was 2 seconds. The new dialogue was read in 2 seconds in the final commercial.

Frame #6 (close-up of Peggy's face) "If you're getting older, get wiser too—"

Frame #7 (Superimposed next to Peggy's face is a picture of the Os-Cal bottle with the words "Don't take chances, take Os-Cal.") "Don't take chances. Take Os-Cal." (This is the final frame.) Storyboard timing: 4 seconds; actual film timing: 4 seconds.

The total time of the storyboard reading was 14 seconds; the total time of the final reading on film was 12.5 seconds.

If the composer first had to compose to the storyboard, he might have made the mistake of not figuring in the time it took for Peggy Fleming to skate and pause between lines. In the final film, the extra 2.5 seconds were shots of Peggy skating and Peggy pausing between lines.

For timings to be accurate, always calculate time for action without dialogue.

Assignments

A professional creative director wrote the following exercise. This is typical of instructions given to composers prior to shooting the film. There is no storyboard for this assignment. Complete the project within the time span listed in the instructions:

1. We are shooting a new campaign for XYZ Stores designed to dramatically upgrade the image of the chain.
2. The pictures will be shot by some of the leading fashion photographers, like Helmut Newton and Richard Avedon. The scenes will be shot in New York, London, Paris, and Rome.
3. We will use the best supermodels, like Cindy Crawford and Naomi Campbell.
4. What we need is a piece of music that will capture it all: the pictures, the attitude, and to really upgrade the XYZ image.
5. I would like the music to be truly memorable—it can be hot and sexy, it could be wonderfully beautiful.

6. The assignment is wide open, and I am open to your ideas. Break ground! Break the rules!
7. People who don't currently shop at XYZ should want to from now on.
8. The spots are 30 seconds, but also come up with something for 60 seconds.
9. I want to hear demos in three days.

Additional Exercises

1. Using a storyboard to work from, lay out a score sheet with "hit" points. These hits should either require effects or mood changes in the music. The objective is to write a cohesive piece of music. Each exercise requires a 30-second television score.
2. Write an arrangement of your final composition for a small combo.
3. Compose two or three different pieces of music, in dissimilar styles, for the same commercial. Vary the tempos and moods.

5

Underscoring

Compositional Techniques

Commercials are intended to sell products or create images for companies and/or products. The function of most commercials is to deliver a message explaining why a consumer should purchase a product. Public service commercials provide important information, for example, "All children should receive the polio vaccine." Image advertising creates goodwill for a company (without selling a product). For instance, some General Electric ads inform the public about products that are not sold to average consumers but are sold to hospitals and physicians for use in medical treatments and research. Although some commercials may be creative (with pristine quality film and inspiring music), they may not be effective advertising because they do not present their messages clearly. Most agencies strive to accomplish both objectives by combining creative advertising with a concise message.

Music plays a significant role in conveying a commercial message. Writing music to accompany pictures is analogous to solving a puzzle. *The pieces must fit.* Composers often have to create a labyrinth of sound; the music weaves in and out of a maze until reaching the exit. The difference between a musical puzzle and a conventional puzzle is that the musical puzzle has many ways in which it can be solved. A composer must not only solve the puzzle but also have the solution approved by the client. The most crucial questions that have to be answered by composers are the following:

- How will the audience respond to the emotional content of the music?
- When should the music begin and end?
- What instrumentation is most appropriate for the musical goal? (This depends on the budget and emotional tone of the film.)

These questions have to be answered and approved by the agency creatives as well as by the composer.

Historical Compositional Forms

Music comprises melody, harmony, rhythm, variation, arrangement, and orchestration. *The crucial factor in a well-crafted composition is form.* Unsystematic writing does not create unity or identity. *Repetition and variation are the most used compositional techniques to create form and symmetry.* This is not to intimate that traditional form must be adhered to in modern popular composition. The value of receiving a traditional musical education is that it provides composers with a background, which has a practical purpose when writing commercials and film music.

A comprehensive musical education exposes composers to most forms of traditional music. It also provides an opportunity to learn the harmonic and melodic rules of most historical periods. Just as pianists have to practice to become proficient instrumentalists, composers must compose to develop compositional and arranging skills. Approaching an assignment becomes easier when a variety of musical skills have been developed.

Composition cannot be taught. What *can* be learned are compositional "tools" that, used properly, help develop a composer's basic talent. When master carpenters make furniture, they use a variety of tools. Through years of apprenticeship, they learn how to master the use of a drill, a saw, a hammer, and so on. The same principle applies to well-trained composers; knowledge of harmony, rhythm, melody, and arranging helps to generate and craft a variety of compositional ideas.

Musicians' Brains Wired Differently
By Seth Hettena, Associated Press Writer (2001)

SAN DIEGO (AP)—The brain waves of professional musicians respond to music in a way that suggests they have an intuitive sense of the notes that amateurs lack, researchers said Wednesday. Neuroscientists, using brain-scanning MRI machines to peer inside the minds of professional German violinists, found they could hear the music simply by thinking about it, a skill amateurs in the study were unable to match.

The research offers insight into the inner workings of the brain and shows that musicians' brains are uniquely wired for sound, researchers said at the annual meeting of the Society for Neuroscience.

Neuroscientists often study how we hear and play music because it is one of the few activities that use many functions of the brain, including memory, learning, motor control, emotion, hearing and creativity, said Dr. Robert Zatorre of the Montreal Neurological

Institute. "It offers a window onto the highest levels of human cognition," Zatorre said.

In a study by researchers at the University of Tuebingen, the brains of eight violinists with German orchestras and eight amateurs were analyzed as they silently tapped out the first 16 bars of Mozart's violin concerto in G major. Brain scans showed professionals had significant activity in the part of their brains that controlled hearing, said Dr. Gabriela Scheler of the University of Tuebingen. "When the professionals move their fingers, they are also hearing the music in their heads," Scheler said. Amateurs, by contrast, showed more activity in the motor cortex, the region that controls finger movements, suggesting they were more preoccupied with hitting the correct notes, she said. Scheler, a former violinist with the Nuremberg Philharmonic Orchestra, said the findings suggest that professionals have "liberated" their minds from worrying about hitting the right notes. As a result, they are able to listen, judge and control their play, Scheler said. "Presumably, this enhances the musical performance," she said.

In a second experiment, the violinists were asked to imagine playing the concerto without moving their fingers. Brain scans showed again that the professionals were hearing the music in their heads. Zatorre, who has studied the brain's response to music for two decades, said it was the first time anyone had studied music and its relationship to motor control and imagery.

For example, an assignment might be to compose in a certain historical style. Without knowing the melodic, harmonic, and structural rules of that historic period, it is impossible to complete the assignment. The other advantage of having the knowledge is that it gives the composer a grab bag of ideas to choose from. In modern music, historical musical forms have been expanded.

Well-constructed commercials have form. When a composer writes for film, the form she chooses often results from the requirements of the pictures—the pictures dictate the form. It is the job of the composer to create something that is cohesive, even though it may not be traditional. There are many ways in which this can be accomplished, for example, manipulating a short theme, bridging sections with percussion fills or harp glisses, the use of silence, tempo, and key changes.

Something as simple as a two-measure theme can weave itself into something quite interesting, even though it may not be in a traditional form. Just hearing the theme in unusual places with different instruments can keep the listener's attention. Many film composers base entire scores on one simple theme that is reinvented in various ways. This compositional device is also effectively used in commercials.

Form

All forms of modern popular music have developed from traditional musical forms. The following is a list and description of some traditional forms that have been modified and are still used in most styles of music.

Sonata form originated during the classical period. It contains three sections. The **exposition section,** often repeated, contains themes written in the tonic key. The main theme morphs into a bridge, which in major keys proceeds to the dominant and in minor keys the relative major. The following section contains a new theme and ends with a codetta. This is a simplistic explantion of the basic structure of the exposition. (An **introduction** may precede the exposition.) The **development** section is used to develop and expand the original themes. The use of modulations, themes in retrograde, and inverted and transposed forms are some of the techniques employed. In addition, the use of fragmented themes is common in commercials. (Fragmented themes are frequently used in both commercials and films.) The **recapitulation** is a return of the themes of the exposition with some minor changes. The themes remain in the tonic key rather than the modulating keys previously heard. If the original theme is written in a minor key, the theme might be presented in the major key. The order of the themes usually remains the same as the exposition. Many recapitulations are followed by a **coda** (an additional ending). The first movement of sonatas, called the allegro, uses this form. (This is a general outline of the sonata form. The form varies.)

Recapitulation is used in almost all forms of popular music. The popular song and instrumental compositions usually repeat the chorus numerous times, which helps the audience remember the chorus; in popular music this is referred to as the "hook" of the song. Almost all commercial songs (jingles) have strong, memorable hooks. This helps to create client identity.

Theme and variations is a musical form that dates back to the baroque and classical periods. A theme is stated, followed by numerous variations of the theme. Some commercials and film scores are based on this technique. Varying tempos, keys, time signatures, orchestration, and other compositional devices modify the original theme.

Binary form has two parts, both of which are usually repeated.

Ternary form has three parts and usually has repeated sections.

Rondo form consists of a main theme that repeats between several additional sections that vary from the main theme. The usual classical rondo form is ABACABA. (The A refers to the repeated section. The rondo A section is analogous to the repeated "hook" in most popular music.) This form is often used as the final movement of a sonata.

Modern Popular Compositional Forms

Popular composition is based on traditional forms. As in any historical musical time period, those forms are used as a basis and expanded. Not only is popular recorded music based on composition, but the actual production of the music in the studio (application of reverb, delays, and so on) has become as much a part of the composition as the notation and the arrangement. Aquiring basic knowledge of music production is relevant to a composer's education and success in this field.

These skills apply to writing music for commercials. Since the majority of assignments are to imitate a popular musical style, the composition must contain the same production values as the recorded musical examples referred to by an agency.

It can be advantageous to keep the following production elements in mind when composing.

Listen to the use of reverberation and echo. Is the snare drum dry (without reverb), or does it have a long decay time? Is there a slap echo on the tom-toms (a quick repeat)? Reverberation and echo greatly affect the ambience of a recording.

Listen to the level (volume) of the most prominent instruments. Is the bass prominent in the mix? Is the kick drum as loud as the bass, or is it merely "felt"? Is the overall level of the strings loud or soft in the mix? Certain musical genres have production characteristics; for example, rock and roll has loud guitars, dance music has loud kick drums, and hip-hop has loud bass and drums.

Listen to the equalization of each instrument. Does the piano sound warm, or does it sound thin and percussive? Is the kick drum tubby, or does it have a hard, pointed sound? Is the sound of the bass round and deep, or does the performer use his or her thumb, which creates a percussive effect?

Equalization is a delicate procedure and must be used carefully. Strident, piercing sounds can result from overequalization. Too much low end can cause distortion.

Listen to the sonic quality and level of the vocals. Does the lead singer sound warm and smooth, or does the equalization cause the voice to sound shrill? Is the lead singer doubled in any sections of the song? Are the background singers loud in the mix or much softer than the lead vocal? Are the background vocals doubled or tripled (helping to create a full sound)? Is there more than one person singing the lead? Are the background vocals used as part of the orchestration by singing syllables in place of words?

The sonic quality of the vocals can have much to do with the choice of microphone. Some microphones sound thin and cutting, whereas others sound warm. The same microphone used on different singers will have various sonic results. Experimentation is the only way to determine the appropriate choice.

Listen to the sound of the overall mix. Does the mix have an ambience? Many rhythm-and-blues mixes sound dry (very little reverb) with loud and warm-sounding vocals. Some of the mixes contain layered background vocals (overdubed [recorded] two or three times) that are prominent in the mix. In many rock-and-roll mixes, the guitars are louder than the vocals. In dance music, the kick drum, hi-hat, and snares are usually prominent.

Listen to the overall instrumentation. If the assignment is to imitate the sound of a specific recording, try to use the same instrumentation. For instance, is most of the instrumentation live? It is difficult to program strumming guitars or rock-and-roll guitars that sound live using synthesizers and/or samplers. Some musical styles are almost impossible to create on synthesizers; they require the feel of live musicians. Other instruments sound appropriate on synthesizers. If a string pad is low in the mix, it is difficult to distinguish it from a live string section. The budget for most commercials is not substantial enough to hire a complete string section.

Listen to the elements of the arrangement and the orchestration. Since the goal is to imitate a particular sound, the harmonies and general feel of the orchestration must be similar. For example, are the strings written with closed harmonies, or are the violins playing in a high octave and the remainder of the strings playing a low pad (chords)? Is the guitar playing a rhythm pattern or playing solo fills? Try to follow the basic format of the musical example.

An assignment might be to write in a certain genre without hearing a specific sample. For example, if the assignment is to write a contemporary hip-hop track, listen to the most popular tracks on the music charts and observe the common musical elements. The tempos might range between 95 and 98 beats per minute; the tracks may contain a minimalist approach (sparse instrumentation), and the drum sounds may be sampled from a Roland 909 or 808 drum machine. Observing the most current musical trends will present composers with "musical guidelines" that will help them to complete the assignment successfully.

Underscoring

The term *underscoring* generally refers to instrumental background music that is written to accompany a film. Vocals, usually without words, are often used as a part of the orchestration. Many film scores and commercial scores use vocal choruses to add power and richness. The sound and emotion generated by live singers cannot be replaced by synthesized vocals, although sophisticated vocal samples can produce credible results. (Songs used in commercials are referred to as jingles, even though some songwriters resent the term. Jingles are discussed in chapter 7.)

There is a belief that background music should be "felt and not heard." This means that the score should be unobtrusive and merely accompany the film in such a manner that it provokes the desired emotional response from the audience. If a well-crafted score were removed, the film would lack a key emotional element.

Many commercials contain minimum announcer's copy and/or sparse dialogue. In this scenario, the score is no longer background music but a featured element. This can either help or destroy the effectiveness of the commercial. When the creatives suggest that the composer write a "bed," they are referring to music that is subtle and unobtrusive. If the music is a featured ingredient of the overall commercial, there is usually more time and attention allocated to the composition and production of the music. [Listen to track #9 on the enclosed CD.]

It is obvious when an underscoring does complement the picture. With experience, composers develop a dramatic sense of what works best with a film. A number of musical styles might match the film but may not meet the expectation of the agency. Some creatives are very specific, while others do not know what they want until they hear something that "feels right."

Compositional Techniques

The compositional techniques used for commercials are similar to those used for film scoring. The main differences are the length of the music and a composer's ability to write complete compositions in short formats. Various techniques are discussed in this chapter; it is hoped that this "toolbox" of ideas will be stored in the composer's mind.

One *major* mistake made by composers is to accept assignments they are not qualified to write. Some composers and arrangers are skilled only in certain styles. Accept your limitations and tackle only assignments in those styles. You will most likely not be rehired by an agency that is dissatisfied with a submission.

After analyzing a film, the first step is to decide on the most appropriate style of music and have it approved by the agency. Since the average length of a television commercial is 30 seconds, some of the compositional techniques that might apply to a longer composition might not be relevant to commercials; the time for musical development is shorter and therefore limiting. *Economy is the best compositional "tool" for a commercial composer.* Learn how to expand a flowing composition in a compressed format, which, in many ways, is more challenging than writing an extended composition. The craft can be learned and developed through practice.

The second step is to decide the sections of the film that have to be emphasized ("hit") with either musical accents or effects. Take the video counts in frames (where actions occur) and mark them either on the computer sequencer's "markers" window or on score paper. These counts will determine the measures and beats where the accents have to occur at a particular tempo. A change in tempo, obviously, changes the placement of the hits. It becomes more complicated when there are multiple tempos. With modern technology, a computer sequencer program will automatically convert the timings into the proper measures and beats. Example 5-1 shows hits at different tempos.

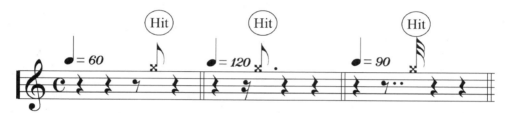

Example 5-1 Tempo hits.

When developing music for a commercial campaign, an agency will often request that a theme be composed, submitted, and approved prior to scoring the film or storyboard. The theme usually must be adaptable to various styles, tempos, and arrangements. Above all, the composition must be a piece of music that has merit without seeing the film. The composer should submit at least three themes. If the client and the agency choose one of the pieces, the theme must be adaptable to various styles. A theme helps to create an identity for a product and, therefore, must become recognizable in its various versions. The following are the most common compositional mistakes and should be avoided.

Beginning or ending the music at the wrong time. When writing for television, always begin the music approximately seven frames into the film and finish the music half a second before the film ends. (At the beginning, it takes time for the video to "roll in" and get up to speed, and at the end, time is needed for a smooth transition from the film to the next event. There are 30 video frames per second.) Current technology might enable the music to begin on the first frame of the picture and end on the last frame. Ask the producer before composing the music.

Composing a theme that is too long to fit into a shorter version of the same commercial. The most common assignment is to write a 30-second theme that can be shortened to 15 seconds. Depending on the musical needs of the film, one suggestion is to write short thematic fragments, which are easily adaptable and lend themselves to modulation, helping to keep the composition interesting. Another suggestion is to write a theme that is no longer than 12 seconds. This leaves room for an introduction and ending within the 15-second commercial and room for expansion in the longer version. (This is based on the tempos of the various versions being the same.) Before writing, experiment with a variety of tempos for the various commercials included in the campaign. It will help determine the flexibility of the theme; not all themes adapt well.

Writing an extended theme that will not work in its original form in all thematic variations. This may be a very difficult assignment. Make certain that the first and/or second part of the theme can be used as independent themes. This is a common problem when compressing the music to fit a 10-second version. The theme might work well in a 30- and 15-second version, but there is not enough time to fit the entire piece into nine seconds. If the theme has identifiable sections that can be lifted (edited), try them—this is usually a satisfactory solution. Most agencies accept this practice because they realize that, otherwise, the original composition would have to be compromised to solve the problem. Since most of the airplay will probably be the 30- and 15-second versions, agencies are willing to compromise.

Writing themes that are not adaptable to different styles and tempos. Some well-constructed themes are not adaptable to different styles and tempos. Although they may fit other styles and tempos, the composition might sound good only in its original form. Make certain that the theme is adaptable. Experiment with the original theme before presenting it to the agency. Once the theme has been approved, the integrity of the composition must remain. The agency and client will certainly notice that the theme is missing or incomplete. If the theme has to be edited for other versions, inform the creatives prior to composing.

After approving the theme and discussing the various versions, the agency might decide to add an additional version. If the theme does not fit the new version in its entirety, present the best solution possible and explain the problem to the creatives. Most often there is an acceptable solution.

Writing compositions that contain odd time signatures, which could make the rhythm and/or melody feel unnatural. (Rhythm, in this context, does not necessarily refer to drums and percussion but to the flow of the composition.) This normally occurs if the composer wants to start a new musical statement during a different section of the film. For example, if a scene changes from pictures of mountains to the inside of a department store, the composer will most likely want to start a new musical idea over this scene rather than continue the previous thematic material. The measure prior to the scene change might require an odd time signature so that the timing is correct. Additional compositional devices that help composers make compositions sound smooth may include a harp gliss, a tempo change, a new lead instrument, and so on.

Writing in the same frequency range as the actors or the announcer. When scoring to film, listen closely to the frequency range of the actors' and/or announcer's voices. Frequently, the composition will sound busy and cluttered. One solution is to choose octaves that will not conflict with the frequency range of the voices. Think of the dialogue as a part of the orchestration. This also has to be taken into account when writing a theme that continues throughout a commercial. Sometimes sparse writing can be very effective, but there are no rules. Whatever technique solves the problem should be used. (The same principle applies when creating arrangements for vocals.)

Inexperienced composers often write compositions that are too loud and powerful to sit under dialogue without masking the actors and/or announcer. The mixing engineer will lower the music track during the mixing process to achieve the correct balance. The problem with this solution is that, in most instances, the music will be too low to be effective. The most effectual solution is to write the music in a less obtrusive manner so that an acceptable balance can be achieved.

Compositional Problems

Let us assume that an assignment is to compose a melody, a rhythmic groove, and to musically accent the product each time it appears. Musically accenting specific events (called "hits") is the most common compositional restriction. For example, let us assume that the picture of the product being advertised instantly appears on the screen in exactly 6.5 seconds, lasts 4 seconds, and disappears and that the film continues with new scenes. Depending on the tempo—referred to as beats per minute—the 6.5-second mark will appear in different measures and on different beats. For instance, if the tempo is 130 beats per minute, the time signature is 4/4, and the hit is at 6.5 seconds, the hit will apppear on the fourth measure, a fraction *after* the third beat. If the tempo is 120 beats per minute, then the 6.5-second hit would appear on the fourth measure, directly *on* the second beat.

Let us also assume that the composition is in 4/4 time, which equals four beats per measure, with the quarter note equaling one beat. It is possible that the measure that contains the hit might require a time signature of 3/4 (three beats per measure), followed by a 2/4 measure (two beats per measure) and return to a consistent 4/4 feel, or four beats per measure.

The next information needed is: In what measure and on what beat does the composition resume? For this exercise, let us assume that it continues on the upbeat of the first beat following a 2/4 measure. Example 5-2 shows multiple meter changes.

Example 5-2 Multiple meter changes

This scenario presents a creative problem. What devices can the composer use to make the composition flow instead of sounding choppy and unnatural? The answer depends on the nature of the composition prior to the hit. We know (from the assignment) that there must be a flowing melody and that it has to lead into the product shot, which will require an effect. We also know that the composition has a percussive engine propelling the track. One solution might be to keep the percussive pattern throughout the hit and have the melody end just before the hit and then lead into the next section with a percussion fill, which is a common connective device. When a groove is continuous, even though the time signature might vary, the groove will, most likely, continue to sound natural. Another solution may be to merely have a sudden stop where the hit occurs and play the effect for the product shot, followed by a drum pickup, which leads back into the groove.

Depending on the melodic structure, it is sometimes possible to add extended note durations or subtract durations in order to meet the needs of the film. For instance, if the time signature did not change and the melody note was a quarter note, one beat short of the following hit, try extending the quarter note to a half note, which allows the next section of the melody to begin on the hit. This solution does not always create a flowing melody that sounds natural. It sometimes requires a restructuring of the melody.

There are many possible solutions to this problem and similar compositional problems. These examples are offered so that students can understand how to approach a similar situation. Experimentation will generally bring a satisfactory solution.

Compositional Techniques

There are certain techniques that can help determine an initial compositional style for a commercial. With experience, composers develop many "tools" that help generate compositional ideas.

Choose a theme for each character. Some commercials have several actors. If time permits, a short motif can be written for each character. This creates a musical identity. One the most commonly used commercial formats is the vignette. In the first vignette, a woman standing in her kitchen says, ''I have been getting headaches for years.'' In the second vignette, a man sitting at his desk says, ''The stress of my job gives me headaches.'' In the third vignette, a college student in his dorm room says, ''Exams give me a headache.''

Let us assume that it takes each actor 4 seconds to say his or her line. If there is a short musical theme that modulates (a new key) each time a line is spoken, the audience will subconsciously relate the theme to each situation. Repeating the theme, modulated, prevents the motif from becoming boring. This is a commonly used device and can be effective.

Generally, the theme has to be simple to prevent a conflict with the voices. A short theme at the end of each line—which bridges with the next vignette—works well. How well it works depends on the amount of dialogue in each vignette. Experiment! Many film composers use this technique; it is more easily applied to longer commercials.

Example 5-3   Excerpt from the Piano Concerto in A minor by Grieg.

Silence is a compositional technique. Inexperienced composers tend to overwrite. They think that the music must be constant, or there will be a lull. This is not accurate. Silence can be one of the most effective compositional techniques; it can create a dramatic mood or merely a surprise, in any genre.

Let us assume that a commercial depicts the horrors of drugs. The last scene is a picture of a dead body, the result of a drug overdose. If the music stops on the shot of a casket, silence will create a dramatic moment.

Not starting the music on the first frame of film can also be effective. Get approval from the creatives before choosing which scene to score first. The creatives are usually quite specific about where they want the music to begin and end.

Ostinatos create tension. Ostinatos (repeated musical patterns), with various sounds weaving in and out, tend to create a feeling of tension. Ostinatos are frequently heard in pain reliever commercials. At the beginning, the patient has a headache, and after she consumes the product, the pain disappears. The patient is then portrayed as living an active life. Many scores accompanying headache scenes contain ostinatos with dark-sounding elements that contribute to a feeling of discomfort; when relief occurs, the ostinatos are replaced with uplifting, pleasant music.

Musical patterns help to create different emotions. One of the advantages of using some of these patterns is that, if used properly, the patterns become "catchy" (memorable), which increases audience identity. There is a short time to establish an identity that these "tools" (e.g., catchy bass patterns, repeated guitar, and piano riffs) are worth investigating.

A nontraditional approach to the music can be interesting. This is usually referred to as "going against the picture"—writing music that is unexpected.

Author's Note: I worked on a commercial for Master Lock that was filmed for the Super Bowl. The picture shows a burglar trying to break a lock without success. The traditional approach would have been to write something dark, electronic, or cinematic; actually, many styles would have complemented the picture. Instead, the agency wanted a calm piece of classical music. The final choice was to use a mellow, vocal serenade sung in German and composed by Mozart; it was a totally unexpected marriage of film and music. The commercial was hailed as one of the outstanding commercials on the Super Bowl and received acclaim within the advertising community; one of the main reasons for the success of the commercial was that the music plays "against the picture."

It was a difficult assignment from several viewpoints. The first concern was to not destroy a great piece of music by having to fit it into a 30-second commercial format. The solution was to find a harmonically acceptable edit point that would make the composition sound as if it had not been edited. After much experimentation with the orchestration, a smooth transition was accomplished.

The second concern was to hire an orchestra that would play Mozart in an authentic style. A third concern was to hire an opera singer who was familiar with singing in the style of Mozart. All items were accomplished. This is an example of how to approach period music.

The musical approach is usually suggested by the agency and is an intrinsic part of the original concept of a commercial. Never "go against the picture" without approval from the agency. If warranted, make a specific suggestion to the creatives; it might spur some creative thinking.

Since contemporary popular music is mostly rhythmically based, it can be advantageous to approach a composition by developing a rhythm pattern as the first step. Understand the style of music before writing a rhythm pattern. Let us assume that the agency wanted a Latin pop rhythm. The next question would be, "There are many styles of Latin-Hispanic rhythms. What Latin style would you like?—Caribbean (denotes congas), maracas playing Afro-Cuban rhythms (denotes a mixture of African and Cuban rhythms), traditional Mexican (requires mariachi trumpets and acoustic guitars, including the Mexican bass guitar, which looks like an oversized guitar)," and so on. Once the desired style has been determined, try writing a two- or four-measure loop (repeated pattern) and play it against the film. Even without hearing a melodic structure, it will be easy to determine if the rhythm is suitable. The next step could be to try developing a rhythm pattern with appropriate breaks and fills to fit the different sections of the film. Then try experimenting with melodic lines, a bass or piano part, or merely experiment until a kernel of an idea feels good; continue developing and adjusting all the elements. Eventually, you will have an interesting piece of music.

Working with a rhythm pattern does not necessarily mean that the rhythm has to be played by percussion instruments. Orchestras can play rhythm patterns without traditional percussive instruments; brass, strings, and woodwinds can play rhythm patterns. For example, ostinatos are rhythmic patterns and can be played by most orchestral sections.

An interesting approach to rhythm-based composition is to notate rhythm patterns without filling in the notes or the instruments that would play them—just write Xs. Then begin experimenting with instruments and notes playing the patterns. Some interesting compositions have been created using this technique.

Try experimenting with instruments other than drums to begin a composition. For example, start with only a piano, which helps to define the harmony. Listen to the piano against the film. If the mood is appropriate, add parts and develop the composition and the arrangement. One of the dangers of using this technique is not being able to expand the orchestration; instruments other than the piano might sound better on a part that had been originally played on the piano. Whenever composing on an instrument (e.g., piano), be very careful not to limit the composition by the inherent limitations of that instrument or the technical limitations that a composer might have in his or her ability to play that instrument proficiently. Try to internalize the composition and orchestration before assigning it to the appropriate instrumentation. Although this concept was discussed previously, it is worth mentioning once again because many inexperienced composers limit their compositional skills because of unnecessary technical limitations.

One of the advantages of working with synthesizers is that it is possible to hear real (sampled) instruments playing a composition without the expense of paying musicians. Once the piece has been demonstrated on synthesizers (samplers) to the agency and received approval, hire musicians—if needed—to replace some or all of the synthesized parts. Synthesized guitars and horns do not generally sound real. If the budget is small and the desired sound is a horn section, add one real horn to the synthesized or sampled section; it is surprising how authentic one live player can make a synthesized or sampled part sound. This technique also works well with strings. (It is always desirable to hire musicians to play traditional instrumental parts. Samples cannot replace the feel of live performers.)

Synthesized sounds are popular, and many of them are not intended to sound real; these are referred to as analog sounds. A synthesizer programmer, through experimentation, usually programs algorithms, which create inventive sounds. The sounds that can be generated are infinite. Genres, such as Trance, most dance music, and electronica, are examples of musical styles that usually do not require live musicians; in addition, most electronic effects are created with analog sounds. Because analog sounds are acceptable to the audience, it behooves composers to learn how to program or hire programmers.

Electronics has changed the manner in which commercial composers conceive of music. Most compositions used in commercials are played by a combination of live musicians and synthesizers. Electronic music not only samples (digitally records) and plays back real instruments (samples) but also has a musical language of its own (as previously described in the explanation of analog synthesis). Because of the available technology, composers are able to conceive of and hear almost any sound imaginable.

If a "musical bed" (sustained chords) is desired, one of the traditional orchestral approaches is to use a string section. With the availablility of synthesizers, composers can combine three or four richly textured sounds to replace a traditional string section; not only will the part sound rich and full, but it will also have a texture different from that of a real string section.

Creating an ostinato with an analog sound is very effective. Ostinatos can create musical tension or provide a beautiful underlying counterpart to a floating melody.

Generating a bass part using an analog bass sound is common in contemporary recordings. Sounds can be edited and/or created using synthesis, offering an infinite variety of sounds. Because of continuous musical trends in commercial music (as previously stated), "sounds" also become trends. Be aware of the current contemporary music markets and stay familiar with the latest technology. After becoming familiar with synthesis, composers begin to conceive of abstract sounds as an intrinsic part of composition.

Computers have changed the manner in which music is conceived and composed. Aside from the popularity and listeners' acceptability of synthesis, the major contribution to the music industry has been the flexibility that computer-sequencing programs have provided. Numerous edits and experimentation can easily be accomplished. Before computers, this process would have been time consuming and costly.

One of the problems that arise as a result of the computer's flexibility is that the agencies sometimes take advantage of composers by asking for numerous edited versions of a composition. Editing does not simply require cutting and pasting. For a composition to sound cohesive musically and technically, most changes require rewriting and restructuring. Even if only one measure has to be adjusted, it is time consuming for several reasons. Because of the many effects that can be applied during programming, editing may create technical problems. For example, if a sustain pedal is open on the last note of the measure where an edit is going to take place, after the new section is spliced to that measure, the sustain pedal would still be open, causing a hodgepodge of sound. The programmer has to determine the problem and solve it by adjusting the length of time the sustain pedal remains open. Similar problems occur with reverbs and other effects. These adjustments can be time consuming without the benefit of additional financial compensation. Unfortunately, this problem cannot be solved because of the competition to be awarded jobs. There will always be composers who are willing to perform extra work without additional remuneration.

The use of effects (whether real sound effects or abstract sounds created with synthesizers or samples) has become a major compositional technique since the advent of synthesizers. Before the common use of synthesizers, specialists, called Foley artists, created sound effects; in addition to the creation of effects by Foley artists, many sound effects have been recorded onto CDs and then matched to a specific action and transferred to film. Today, it is rare to have a Foley artist work on a commercial—composers are expected to add the sound effects. Foley artists are still used in motion pictures. Foley stages at motion picture studios are designed to have Foley artists create live effects, such as footsteps, clothes rubbing together, and so on. Foleying helps to add the ambient sounds of a scene that were not recorded by the live microphones on the set.

Using synthesized sound effects has helped to create a form of composition known as sound design. (In films, sound design refers to sound effects specialists, not music.) Sound design is generally defined as a composition that does not have a melody, contains numerous synthesized and/or real effects, and, more often than not, has a complex rhythm track. Some commercials include only effects and no music. Although there is no music, this form of sound design can create a specific rhythm but not in the traditional sense; the cumulative effect is a rhythmic pace. A dance genre called *industrial* is based on this premise. Sound design can be one of the most creative tools for a composer. Incorporating sound design offers composers an opportunity to work without creative restrictions. Sound design may be created in any genre of music, not just the most current trends.

Sound design is also popular in film scoring. The primary difference between commercials and films is that most films employ Foley artists and composers do not usually design the real sound effects. Big-budget films generally employ sound designers who use both synthesized and Foley effects. Sound design is especially prevalent in theatrical trailers. In almost any action movie, sound design is a major element in the film. Sometimes, well-produced sound design contributes to the ultimate success of a film. For example, in the film *Pearl Harbor*, if the attack had not been accompanied by exciting sound design, the motion picture might not have been as successful as it was. With the sophisticated sound systems that are in most movie theaters (surround sound), the dialogue, music, and effects are as important as the acting, writing, direction, and the cinematic quality of the film. [Listen to tracks #1 and #10 on the enclosed CD.]

When composing and arranging in modern forms of popular music, composers must be aware of the changing sounds used primarily in the drum, bass, and keyboard parts. Because of the popularity of synthesizers and samplers in records, sounds of various instruments become trendy. For example, the most trendy sounds for drums in dance music have emanated from two vintage drum machines—the Roland 808 and the Roland 909. Many manufacturers have sampled the sounds, edited them, and included them on sampling CDs and as part of a collection of sounds included in synthesizers that contain samples. For many years, the Moog synthesizer has been a staple in creating very deep and rich bass sounds. There are many variations of Moog bass sounds. A Wurlitzer electric piano sound, as opposed to a Rhodes electric sound, has become the standard electric piano in chill-out music, also known as down-tempo music. Software synthesizers and software samplers are a member of a programmer's creative palette. Many of these devices contain the most current sounds, which can be edited. This enables composers and engineers to create inventive sounds.

Commonly used phrases and rhythms, in certain styles of music, also become trends. For example, a sixteenth-note drum fill that crescendos at the end of an eight-bar phrase has become a signature in various styles of dance music. A kick drum that plays four quarter notes in each measure (called four-on-the-floor) is the standard pattern for house dance music.

Composers working in popular music must keep abreast of technical and instrumental trends. Composers will be considered musically obsolete if they do not employ the latest sounds and technology.

Musical logos are designed as a form of product identity. Most commercials end with a product shot. It is often helpful to suggest that a musical logo be played over this shot. The logo is especially effective if there is a campaign and the logo is used at the end of each commercial. This technique establishes a musical thread throughout the campaign. Sometimes agencies ask for logos to be sung. (This subject is discussed in chapter 7.)

Featuring a solo instrument (traditional or ethnic) can sometimes bring an immediate identity to a commercial. Before using this technique, discuss it with the creatives; play a recorded sample of the instrument before writing. This is a specific concept and must be approved.

An example of a unique, identifiable sound is the synthesized sound used for the theme of the television program *The X-Files*. The composer experimented extensively before choosing that sound. The theme has a unique and memorable quality. The use of unusual instruments, such as panpipes and ethnic instruments, also helps to achieve unique sounds.

When the story of a commercial requires a change in the musical mood, it is sometimes effective to change the music before a new scene appears. The audience will subliminally anticipate a mood change. Let us assume that the beginning of a film shows a new car sitting in traffic with horns honking, drivers with road rage, and pedestrians crossing the street in front of cars. The car then reaches the open highway, and a feeling of freedom occurs. If the music evokes the confusion at the beginning and the mood shifts to a feeling of freedom, one technique is to start the change of music one or two beats before the change of scene. This method is commonly used in film music.

A suitable piece of music with no hits may be the correct choice. The musical mood can be sufficient to create the correct emotional response to the film. Composers can write without restrictions. This is a common technique in writing film music.

Music Demos

Many agencies hire several individual composers or music houses (comprised of multiple composers) to submit demos for a commercial or a commercial campaign. The success of the demos determines who gets the assignment. Try to submit three pieces of music:

1. Write what the creatives ask for.
2. Write what *you* want to write (assuming you have a different conception than the creatives).
3. Write additional music that is in a different musical direction than the previous compositions.

There are several reasons for submitting a minimum of three demos:

1. The agency will request several demos.
2. A composer has a better opportunity to satisfy the creatives by sub-

mitting various styles. One of the submissions might be unexpected and may be chosen.

3. Submitting more than one example improves the chances of being selected for the assignment.

Submitting too many demos, however, can work against a composer. Some music companies submit six or seven demos. This can be perceived as the composer or music house not fully understanding the assignment and, therefore, fishing for the right result. The best strategy is to submit the most appropriate three compositions.

Demo Production

In general, the musical and technical quality of demos has to be that of a finished track. Before the advent of synthesizers and project studios, composers generally performed the compostion(s) live or recorded a demo on the piano or guitar, which was usually a sufficient presentation. Synthesizers enable composers to present completed or almost completed tracks without having to hire too many musicians, which is costly. Because of this practice, agencies expect master quality demos while paying only minimum demo fees.

To achieve success in writing music for commercials, composers must develop an expertise in the use of synthesizers and samplers. Most composers own project studios and have become, out of necessity, competent engineers. A majority of music houses do not hire composers who cannot submit a complete demo.

Usually, the winning composition requires revisions. The following are some of the reasons revisions might be needed.

Sometimes demos are written to "work prints." A work print is not the final film but, usually, a work in progress. A work print is almost always revised, which also requires a revision of the music.

The agency might suggest adding or deleting "hits." If the hits are in the form of effects, they can sometimes be added to the mixed music track; if the hits are in the form of composition, the piece has to be revised and rerecorded.

It is always advisable to ask the creatives if they want realistic effects added. Do not assume anything.

There are some exceptions with regard to how complete a demo has to sound.

Sometimes the director wants a

> ♩♩ Many hours were spent adding sound effects to a commercial for *Elmo's World* (a computer game for children). However, the effects had to be deleted because it is illegal to create effects that are not included on the game's sound track. The law states that there must be truth in advertising.

rhythmic groove to play on the film set; it helps to create a mood for the actors. In this scenario, a complete track is not necessary. It is advisable to create several grooves, which enables the director to experiment on the set.

An editor may request a rhythm track for editing; it creates a pace or mood. There can be a danger in submitting a rhythm track that is used in editing the final track. If the agency or composer wants to change the tempo or feel, there could be creative problems. For example, the track may lose its feel at a new tempo. Most often, there are solutions.

Some commercials only run approximately 25 seconds, and 4-second local tags are added (at the end) at a later time. Ask the creatives if they want a full 29.5 seconds of music or if they want the music to end with the film. Sometimes, they will ask for a separate musical tag (musical ending). The tag might be used on numerous spots of the same advertising campaign. An example of a singing tag/logo is "G.E., We Bring Good Things to Life."

A simple piano or guitar track might be adequate for a first submission. This is ordinarily acceptable when an agency is exploring ideas and the budget is modest. Once a musical direction has been chosen, an ample demo budget is usually available.

A simple demo is not recommended if there is an option. It is likely that even at the initial stage of selecting music, there will be competition. Most music companies present complete demos.

Conclusion

Compositional "tools" are merely aids. The most important element is creativity, which cannot be taught. Initially, always write what you feel. If the agency disagrees with your musical approach, they will tell you. Most composers cannot explain why they have written a certain piece of music. They usually say, "It just feels right."

Assignment

Tape a commercial and erase the music and dialogue. Transcribe the dialogue, rerecord it with your voice, and view the picture with the new dialogue track. Choose a musical mood (e.g., gentle, high energy, and so on) and write three demos with different musical styles. Experiment by completing several mixes of each composition, trying to create different moods by incorporating technology in an inventive setting, such as phasing, delays, reverb, and so on. [Listen to track #12 on the enclosed CD.]

6

Arranging and Orchestration Concepts

Including Sound Effects and Sound Design

The music, however great or small, is what there is to say. The orchestration is how you say it.

—Robert Russell Bennett

---⚬⚬⚬---

Author's Note: The words *arranger* and *orchestrator* are used interchangeably in this chapter.

---⚬⚬⚬---

This section is devoted not to basic arranging and basic orchestration but rather to a discussion of how to achieve an overall instrumental texture. It is assumed that students have a basic knowledge of arranging. Even if a student lacks this knowledge, an understanding of the concepts is essential in order to guide arrangers or orchestrators in achieving their musical goals. Furthermore, since we are dealing primarily in commercial music, we will focus more on the use of synthesizers than orchestral instruments. Most commercial productions use a combination of synthesizers and live musicians. Rock-and-roll, gospel, and jazz pieces consist primarily of live musicians using synthesizers as one adjunct.

Arranging is the art providing a musical setting for a composition. This includes the harmonies, the basic rhythmic feel (which is usually indicated), and the notation. **Orchestration** is the art of assigning instruments to each note. (The term *orchestration* is most often used when

85

describing the process of assigning the notes to the instruments in an orchestra or additional instrumental combinations.)

Arranging and orchestrating are analogous to painting. A painter has a palette containing paints from which he or she chooses and mixes colors. Arrangers/orchestrators have palettes on which they store notes, harmonies, rhythms, instruments, and dynamics. Painters and arrangers/orchestrators mix colors and use different brushes and strokes to produce a final result. Talent and taste determine the quality of their work.

The twentieth-century English composer Vaughan Williams studied with the great romantic composer Ravel. Ravel's main contribution to Vaughan Williams's style was teaching him orchestration. He taught him "how to orchestrate in points of color rather than lines" (Grout, *A History of Western Music*, 695). This was also Debussy's philosophy.

Film orchestrators use this concept. Composers have to be cautious not to allow the music to interfere with the dialogue. The orchestration has to complement the film through tonal colors.

Analyzing the work of the masters adds knowledge to one's creative "toolbox." Studying their orchestrations and compositions generates ideas.

In most commercial music (excluding motion pictures and Broadway shows), the arranger is also the orchestrator. In film scores and Broadway shows, there is usually a separate orchestrator because of time restrictions.

Most film composers write their scores on six to ten staves (such as an expanded piano part) with instrumental indications, such as "flutes play _____, violins play_____," and so on. Most Broadway scores are detailed, two-stave piano parts and in some instances contain orchestral indications, such as "trumpets play_____," and so on.

Many orchestrators of commercial music not only assign the notes to instruments but also enhance the arrangements. Because of time restrictions, composers indicate additions to be made by the orchestrator, such as "add a jazz drum part," or only the lead saxophone part is written and the indication is to "complete the harmonies with the remainder of the saxophone section."

Arranging and orchestrating for the studio is more complex than writing for a live performance. The main difference is the manner in which the sound can be manipulated. Arrangers have time to address minute details that are inherent to the recording process. Each recorded track can be assigned its own automated equalization and effects. Throughout a recording, the parameters of the sound can continually change through the use of automation. In addition, because of the control over instrumental balance, unusual instruments can be featured. Many of the instruments would not be heard in a traditional live acoustical setting without painstaking manipulation.

Approaching the Score

Begin by writing a simple sketch of an arrangement; include chord symbols and notate the harmonic structure, including inner melodic lines. It is helpful to use the top line of the score paper as an overall guide. Write the melody, chord symbols, and lyrics and/or dialogue on the top line. Once this has been completed, begin writing the arrangement. Use the following outline as a guide.

Organize the score paper with the proper name and key signature for each instrument. (Follow this procedure whether working with traditional score paper or with a computer notation program such as Finale or Sibelius.) If writing a transposed score, change the key signature for each instrument; if writing in concert key, each instrument should have the same key signature. If the score is for a traditional orchestra or band, some score paper manufacturers provide paper with the names of the instruments printed. It is best to use paper that has eight measures per page. Score paper that has only four measures per page can become bulky and difficult for a conductor to follow.

Some composers write sketches and an orchestrator completes the arrangement. Composers work in different ways. Some write detailed sketches using eight or more staves, while others only use two to four staves. They usually indicate the suggested instrumentation for the orchestrator to follow. Many composers record the composition using synthesizers; this serves as a detailed guide for the orchestrator. Some composers watch a MIDI notation computer program while recording an orchestra. (The notation program displays the MIDI notes as regular notation manuscript.) The composer can make certain that the orchestration is accurate by following the MIDI notation. This process also saves time in the recording studio. It is easier to detect errors and correct them.

Some arrangers write a full sketch of the arrangement and then orchestrate it themselves. This generally depends on the amount of time they have to complete the project. Traditionally, arranging commercials has a quick turnaround period, and there is not enough time to notate an entire sketch. Most arrangers who write on synthesizers program the arrangement rather than write it out. They print the notation program that is included with most MIDI sequencer programs.

Some arrangers write in concert key. I prefer writing in concert, especially for a large orchestra. It is easier to "see" the harmonies and quickly find mistakes. If writing in concert, be familiar with the proper transpositions. In the studio, transposition problems must be addressed and solved instantly.

Some arrangers prefer transposing while writing. They think that by seeing the same notes the players read, it is easier to determine if the parts are generic to the instrument—not consistently too high or too low for a particular instrument.

Each section should have traditional rehearsal markings. Mark each main section with a letter, such as A, B, and C, and each measure with a number, such as 1, 2, and 3. This saves time in the studio because the conductor can quickly communicate with the musicians by referring to the rehearsal markings.

Be precise with dynamic markings and other musical indications. The cost of being in the studio prohibits wasting unnecessary time. Plan your modus operandi prior to the session. For instance, if you are recording an orchestra, are you going to record the rhythm section first? Are you planning to double the strings? Are you going to give the editor "stems"? (Stems are sections of your mix, such as stereo brass on one stereo track, strings on another, a rhythm section track, and so on.)

Technological advances have enabled live performances to emulate recordings. This is accomplished in several ways:

1. Some artists play prerecorded tracks in synchronization with their live performance. This enhances the fullness and ambience of the sound. Frequently, they play the tracks used on the original recording.
2. Individual parts are preprogrammed on a computer-sequencing program and played in synchronization with the live performance. The drummer wears headsets and hears a metronome-like "click track," along with the music, which aids in keeping time with the computer tracks.
3. Small-scale productions of Broadway shows sometimes have additional parts programmed on synthesizers or prerecorded; for example, the horns and strings are programmed. This technique is frequently used in shows on cruise ships and in live pop concerts.

Elements to be considered when creating an arrangement follow.

Format and rhythm: Are the verses and choruses in the proper order? This is the responsibility of the composer (jingle writer) and the music producer. The lyricist usually determines the format. (Often,

> ♩♩ If the parts are prerecorded, two Pro Tools rigs (or other programs) are locked together in case one malfunctions.

the lyricist at an advertising agency is also the copywriter.) Determining the basic rhythm feel, the arranger should play a sample for the creatives. The "feel" of the composition is the first element of the arrangement. This is usually predetermined, but there are still creative choices that will vary between arrangers. If it does not seem musical, offer suggestions on how to improve it.

Harmony: Some composers submit only a lead sheet to an arranger. A standard lead sheet consists of a melody, lyrics, and chord symbols. The arranger has many options when choosing how to harmonize the arrangement. Some arrangers add chord substitutions in order to add variety to an arrangement. Do not do this without permission. Some substitutions can change the character of the composition, and the creatives will not "hear" the composition they approved. Play examples for the creatives before completing the arrangement.

Instrumentation: This is generally determined before the arrangement is written. Since the arranger usually has some fresh ideas once the creative process begins, they should be discussed with the creative people. Budget is always a consideration.

The arrangement and orchestration create the mood and musical colors of the composition. The texture of the entire composition is the arranger's responsibility once the composition has been approved. Conduct specific conversations concerning this issue.

The key contributes to the ambience of the composition. Different keys evoke diverse moods. In the key of C major, the first note may be an E above middle C (a major third higher than the tonic); in the key of G major, the first note may be a B above G (a major third higher than the tonic)—a perfect fifth higher than E. This will obviously change the tessitura, which will affect the entire ambience of the composition. The key is crucial and should be considered an important factor while creating an arrangement. Discuss this with the composer.

When arranging vocals, make certain the key is correct before arranging. Call the singers and confirm that the key is within their tessitura. If they arrive at the session and the key is wrong, it might be too late to make adjustments. When the entire arrangement is synthesized, changing the key is simple; if there is a live orchestra, it will be very difficult, unless the transposition is simple, for example, performing the arrangement one full step higher or lower.

Ensuring that the key is correct for the singers is the composer's responsibility. If a rerecording is necessary because of key problems, the additional expense will be deducted from the music company's and/or composer's fee. Since recording the music for commercials is usually the last element before the final film mix, there will be time problems if the music has to be rerecorded. An error such as this, which is easily avoidable, can ruin the relationship between a composer and a music house and between the music house and an agency.

Keys affect voicings. If a key is changed after the arrangement has been completed, pay particular attention to the transposed voicings. Some notes may sound too high, other notes may sound too low and muddy, and some notes will be out of the range of an instrument(s). Usually, a change in key requires harmonic or melodic inversions or restructuring. For instance, after a change in key, if the violins are supposed to play an E below middle C, it cannot be played because the lowest note on a violin is G below middle C. The part has to be rewritten.

Tempo helps to establish a mood. A change of merely two metronome markings can transform the entire mood of a composition. Sometimes, for technical reasons, the original tempo marking has to change. For instance, the piece might not fit the newly edited film when played at the original tempo. If the creatives do not want to change the film edit so that the original tempo works with the film, play the music at a new tempo prior to the recording session. Minute tempo changes may cause some of the creatives to ask for adjustments.

Sound effects. Both musical and real sound effects can add an interesting and unique sound to the music. Consider the sound effects a part of a composition; otherwise, the effects can sometimes mask the music if the music is not written to accommodate the effects. [Listen to track #7 on the enclosed CD.]

Overbearing sound effects can be a problem for composers. Since film composers do not create the effects, they sometimes do not get to hear them until the film has been mixed. Loud effects can mask the music. Unfortunately, this is the director's choice, and a composer can only voice an objection.

Modulation affects the mood of an arrangement. Modulating the key, either up or down, can greatly enhance or detract from the feel of the music. Many jingles contain a chorus that repeats twice. If the chorus modulates up a half step during the repeat, the audience experiences a feeling of being musically "lifted" to a new musical home. If the music is upbeat, modulating can cause excitement; if the music is a ballad, modulating can create a more powerful feeling.

Vocalists singing syllables (vocalize) in place of words create a unique sonority when used as a part of an orchestration. As in the scores to *Star Wars* and *Spider Man*, large choruses are frequently used in film scores. Used properly, the overall sound of the orchestration is enhanced. (The use of choruses in commercials is rare because it is costly.)

Solo instruments can add interest and variety to a composition. The score to *Schindler's List*, composed by John Williams, features a solo violin, performed by Itzhak Perlman. Composer Tan Dun featured solo cello, played by Yo-Yo Ma, in the sound track to *Crouching Tiger, Hidden Dragon*.

Unusual instruments create timbres that draw attention to the music. For example, the Arabic ud (similar to a mandolin) or a nay (an Arabic wooden flute that projects a beautiful expressive sound) will transport the audience to a chosen locale.

Some dance music arrangers record looped tracks (repeated patterns). During the mix, the tracks are muted and unmuted using automation, thereby creating an arrangement. This concept can be applied to certain styles of music—mainly groove oriented.

Approaching an Arrangement

Most composers envision an arrangement and express their concept to the arranger. Become familiar with the genre of music being written. Listen to the radio and to CDs that contain music with a similar arranging concept. The Internet is also a source for research. Most Internet record stores (e.g., iTunes) allow consumers to preview 30-second samples of songs.

If the assignment is to compose and arrange a hip-hop track, it might be beneficial to listen to a hip-hop drum loop while composing. This helps to create the proper ambience and form a foundation for the arrangement. The arranger has a certain goal, and the more specific the assignment, the better chance he or she has of pleasing the creative team.

If the arranger is not the composer, the arranger probably will be communicating directly not with the agency but with the composer. This makes it easier because the composer can converse in specific musical terms. The arranger should ask questions before beginning to work. The following is a list of suggested questions.

Do the creatives want the same instrumentation as the instrumentation used in the example or demo? For instance, if the example is orchestral, the budget may not allow for the same number of musicians heard on the example. Any problems similar to this should be explained to the creatives prior to working.

How many musicians can be hired within the allotted budget? Be certain to allow for the proper number of musicians in the initial budget proposal. Once a budget is approved, it is difficult to increase it.

Will the arrangement require editing to fit versions of a commercial that are either longer or shorter than the original? Agencies often request a 15- and/or a 10-second version of a 30-second arrangement. This affects the creation of the original arrangement. If the arranger has prior knowledge that the arrangement will require a longer or shorter version, create the arrangement with natural edit points. Sometimes it is necessary to rewrite and rerecord the music because the edited version will not properly synchronize with the picture.

Using Technology

There are numerous ways to accomplish a desired "sound." In the section titled "Studio Technology as It Applies to Music Production" in chapter 3 of the first edition of this book, the importance of using technology in creative ways was discussed. In all genres of commercial music, technology is involved in the creation of an arrangement and an orchestration. The use of equalization, as well as effects such as reverberation, echo, delays, flangers, choruses, compressors, limiters, and variations of these devices, applies to the creative process.

If an arrangement requires a rhythm section, a string section, and a horn section (performed by live musicians), internalize the sound and style of the arrangement. Do not rely on an instrument, such as a keyboard or a guitar, to aid in the writing process. A composer's limited technique might hinder the creative process because composers might write only what they are able to perform.

Considerations

Is an acoustic bass (double bass) or an electric bass most appropriate for an arrangement? If the choice is an electric bass, is a fretted bass or a fretless bass most conducive to the arrangement? The sounds differ. Most jazz bassists use a fretless bass, whereas most rock bassists prefer a bass with frets.

There are many electric guitar configurations; hiring a guitarist specifies the mood that will best suit the track. If an acoustic guitar is preferred, should the sound be that of nylon strings or steel strings? Should the guitar have twelve strings or six strings? These factors affect the overall sound of an arrangement.

How should the drums be tuned? For example, should the snare drum have a tight, high sound or a deep sound? Should the bass drum sound tight and dead or have a deep thump?

String Section

The size of a string section depends on the constraints of the budget. The choice of instrumentation depends on the desired sound. The number of violins, violas, celli, and basses will affect the sonic image. The larger the section, the richer the sound.

Assuming that the budget allows for six string players, arrangers use different combinations, depending on the needs of the arrangement. If the section is small, some arrangers might use only violins; others might use three violins, two violas, and one cello, while others may hire four violas, one cello, and one double bass. There are no rules. Creative arrangers know the best instrumental combinations that will help to accomplish their creative goals.

Horn Section

The instrumentation depends on the desired sound of an arrangement. Let us assume that the budget allows for six performers. If the intention is to create power and excitement, the arranger might write for two trumpets, one tenor trombone, and one alto saxophone, one tenor saxophone, and one baritone saxophone. Multiple instrumental combinations will produce a satisfactory result. Let the arranger determine the most appropriate combination.

Rhythm Section

The rhythm section is the backbone of most popular music arrangements. Generally, the rhythm section consists of keyboards, guitar, bass, drums, and percussion. The arranger must become familiar with the various choices of instruments offered in each category. The instruments are discussed in more detail later in this chapter.

One of the main differences between traditional arranging and arranging in a popular musical style is that most arrangers want the rhythm section to sound spontaneous and expressive instead of simply playing a part exactly as written. For this reason, arrangers usually use rhythm section parts as guides and instruct the players to "open up the parts" by adding their individual creative impetus. If musicians did not bring a unique element to their playing, an arranger could hire almost any player who can read music. This is not acceptable in popular music. The same principle applies to synthesizer programmers. Programmers bring individualism to their programming and develop trademarks in precisely the same manner as musicians such as Herbie Hancock and Chris Botti. Many programmers spend as much time programming and developing sounds as they do working on an arrangement. The *creative use of technology* is essential to success in commercial music.

One of the most frequently used features of sequencing programs is quantizing. Quantizing corrects the timing of a MIDI part that is played or programmed into a sequencing program. For example, the notes can be quantized, which moves them to the closest eighth note or sixteenth note and so on. The result could be a precise but rigid part. A swing feel can be added, or the snare drum can be placed behind the beat—"laid back." Most programmers place some tracks either before or after the beat. This helps to achieve a more human feeling. Creating a specific feel might require that some of the parts be precisely quantized and other parts be moved before or after the beat. Experimentation is the only method of achieving the proper overall feel.

The rhythm section should be heard as a tightly knit unit. This can be accomplished in several ways.

If the parts are synthesized, solo each instrument and listen closely for mistakes. Make certain that the parts have been properly quantized. Quantizing a part does not necessarily mean that a quantized setting (eighth note, sixteenth note, swing feel, and so on) is the most appropriate for the composition. For example, an arranger might decide to quantize an entire track with a swing feel; within the "swing feel" programming option, there are suboptions. In addition, check for notation mistakes within the MIDI program. Extreme velocity changes within a MIDI program can make it difficult to hear mistakes unless the tracks are soloed.

Most sequencer programs offer numerous choices within most editing parameters. Through the use of automation, parts can be edited throughout a composition. This helps to accomplish the best feel for each section. Contemporary popular music has no rules. Experimentation is essential.

Solo each section and solo various instrumental and vocal combinations. If each part does not project the proper rhythmic or emotional feeling as an individual component or as an element within a section, either edit the part or compose a new part. When listening to the complete arrangement, the parts may seem to interconnect, but with closer scrutiny, certain elements might disrupt the overall feeling of the track. Making certain that the track "feels good" is rule number one.

If acoustic instruments are recorded into a digital audio program, solo each instrument and verify that there are no mistakes. Since the parts appear as acoustic waveforms, the waveforms can be edited. Digital editing is advantageous not only because parts can be corrected and effects added (noise gates, reverberation, compression, and so on) but also because unlimited editing is available without any loss of audio quality. As a safety precaution, solo each track before releasing the musicians from the recording session. Even though editing waveforms can repair some mistakes, many cannot be corrected. Solo each section and make certain that the "feel" of the track fits with the other parts.

Experiment with writing notation patterns or rhythmic patterns for each part. In popular music, individual parts that have a sequential pattern tend to make a groove more cohesive and memorable. (This approach is not appropriate for all styles of popular music.) For example, if a chord pattern is C major, F major, and G major and the pattern keeps repeating, instead of the bassist merely outlining the chords at random, each time the pattern is repeated, he or she plays four eighth notes, a quarter note, and rest on the fourth beat; continuously repeat the rhythm pattern by transposing it so that it fits each chord (see example 6-1).

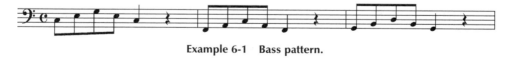

Example 6-1   Bass pattern.

Even if this technique does not work with certain musical styles, creating symmetry within parts results in a more unified arrangement. It is the same approach used by composers. Composition without form may cause musical chaos.

Writing patterns also applies to live drumming or drum programming. Drums (percussion) are the basic foundation of a rhythm section. If the drummer does not create a solid groove, the rhythm section will not establish a proper musical environment. This is accomplished by playing repeated patterns that are interspersed with interesting fills and unexpected rhythmic elements. This approach keeps the drum part interesting.

One technique that helps avoid monotony is to change patterns between sections. For example, if the bridge has a different pattern than the main groove of the track and the bridge is repeated a second time, repeat the same bridge pattern that was used in the first bridge and then return to the original groove; the goal is to create symmetry.

When composing popular music grooves, one effective tool is to write numerous one- or two-bar drum and percussion patterns that complement each other when played simultaneously. After recording the parts, start eliminating individual instruments and selected patterns. This helps to create variety without losing the rhythmic feel. A boring drum or percussion part will ruin a track. There is a fine line between a drum part that has a groove and one that is monotonous.

When adding percussion, apply the same concept used to write rhythmic grooves. Create repeated patterns and keep the parts simple. A percussionist or programmer can be inventive when creating fills but not while establishing basic grooves. Creating a good feel is the objective (not necessarily showcasing technique) when working in popular music. A listener might think that the percussion sounds complex, but what he or she really is experiencing is a combination of parts. Several parts played simultaneously create rhythmic syncopation. The individual parts are not necessarily complicated.

One of the advantages of using a computer-based recording program is having the ability to view the waveforms and ensure that all the parts are aligned properly.

As previously stated, listen to each section individually and then listen to several parts simultaneously; each part should "fit the puzzle." If a part feels awkward, experiment by moving the waveform (forward or backward) until it is in sync with the other parts.

Since analog synthesis is frequently used in popular music, an arranger must think in terms of frequency range in order to place the parts properly within the arrangement. Mentally envision each part as an acoustic instrument. For instance, a high part might take the place of a flute, while a mellow midrange sound might "play the part" of a French horn. Since analog synthesis is usually combined with either realistic samples or acoustic instruments, programmers must be concerned with the potential physical problems that can occur with a mixture of sonorities. The overtones heard in synthesis can sometimes be more complex than those of acoustic instruments and may create either a muddled or an unpleasant sound if combined with other instruments. It is the same concern that an orchestrator has when deciding which instrumental combinations will be the most effectual within sections of an orchestration. When new analog sounds are created, they must be considered new instruments and be added to the orchestrator's musical palette.

The Orchestra and Band

The traditional orchestra is divided into four basic sections: strings, wood-winds, brass, and percussion. The modern commercial orchestra contains synthesizers, flügelhorns, saxophones, trumpets (with effects), electric guitars (with effects), synthesized drums, and electric drums, along with an array of additional instruments and effects.

Popular touring bands employ an engineer who mixes their live sound. (This is referred to as live sound reinforcement.) When using electric instruments with acoustic instruments, it is crucial that the sound engineer be familiar with the proper balance. Electric instruments can obliterate the sound of a band or orchestra. The objective is to re-create the sound of their recordings during a live performance. Sophisticated sound systems enable engineers to closely re-create the sound of a recording.

The same theory of balance applies to the mixing process in the recording studio. It is more easily achieved in the studio because of the control of the mixing environment. Automation gives engineers and producers total control over the soundscape.

Keyboards

Keyboard is a general term for any instrument that has a keyboard: synthesizer, piano, organ, and so on. Before the invention and general use of synthesizers, a keyboardist played acoustic piano, electric piano, and/or organ.

The keyboard synthesizer contains editing parameters in one unit. Keyboards referred to as workstations or MIDI controllers trigger rack-mounted or virtual (software) synthesizers that do not have keyboards but generate the same sounds as the keyboard versions of the same instruments. They are called rack mounted because they can be housed in a rack that holds numerous devices. The advantage of rack-mounted sound modules is that they save space and simplify the task of simultaneously generating sounds from a multitude of devices. One keyboard can control myriad rack-mounted devices. This adds to the creative process because combining synthesizers and samplers to create inventive sounds expands a composer's sound palette. (A synthesizer keyboard can also act as a controller for other devices.)

Some programmers bounce combined sounds to one audio track. For instance, a combination of three sounds can create a smooth, chorale-like background (also referred to as a bed). Creating a combined track allows programmers to use the same synthesizers to create additional sounds.

If digital audio is used in creative ways, several synthesizers (samplers) can create almost any sound. Understand the capabilities of a device before purchasing it. If your budget allows for the purchase of several synthesizers and/or samplers, a variety of sounds should be the main criterion. Do not purchase either hardware or software devices that essentially have the same sounds.

Arranging for Keyboards

Keyboards are used in various ways: to accompany other instruments, to play samples of real instruments and solos, and to create effects and mellow analog sounds, such as pads or beds (held chords that create a silky background). Most synthesizers are equipped with adjustable sound parameters and effects, such as reverb, delays, filters, and oscillators. For example, a vocal track can be completely altered by inputting the vocal through a synthesizer or sampler and editing the parameters. This is generally called a *vocoder*; not all synthesizers or samplers have one.

The arranger determines how the keyboards will be incorporated into an arrangement. Because programming keyboards is complex, it behooves an arranger to consult with the performer as to the various sounds and effects that can be created. If a special sound or effect is required, it is best for the arranger to contact the programmer (performer) prior to the session since programming is time consuming and the sounds should be created prior to the session.

Traditional piano parts (in popular music) are usually notated by using a combination of chord symbols and notation. If an arranger writes a specific pattern, the part will indicate where it begins and ends, followed by chord symbols and the word *simile* (meaning similar); this indicates that the player should improvise using a similar pattern.

The following are descriptions of some popular keyboards.

Electric pianos. Rhodes and Wurlitzer are the most popular brands of electric pianos. The sounds on both keyboards can be edited. The most noticeable feature of electric pianos is the vibrato. When recorded in stereo, the electric piano creates a soothing bed.

Electric pianos, combined with a variety of additional sounds, can create interesting and unusual sonorities. A popular combination is an electric piano and an acoustic piano playing the same part. It sounds both rich and soothing. Another effective combination is electric piano and strings. The combination can create a beautiful and mellow or a powerful sound. Experimenting with additional combinations creates interesting and unique sonorities.

Synthesized electric pianos. Most synthesizers and samplers include a number of electric piano samples in the general MIDI patches that are included with most instruments. An infinite number of variations and combinations can be achieved through editing. Numerous edited versions of the Rhodes and Wurlitzer, as well as less popular electric pianos, are available as samples.

Most programmers who work for synthesizer manufacturers begin with a basic electric piano sound and then proceed to perform a variety of edits, creating new sounds. Each edited version is given a new name and listed separately. One piano might sound mellow, while another may sound bell-like or percussive. A variety of electric piano sounds to choose from saves time for keyboard players.

Many performers create additional edits, enabling them to customize sounds. Most professional musicians create unique sound palettes. When working in the competitive world of commercial music, performers and arrangers try to present an exclusive variety of sounds.

Analog sounds. Sounds programmed on analog synthesizers that cannot be created by conventional instruments are generally referred to as analog sounds. (Editing the VCO [voltage-controlled oscillator], VCA [voltage-controlled amplifier], and the VCF [voltage-controlled filter] creates the sounds.) Most analog and digital synthesizers contain analog sounds in the general MIDI patches that are included with most synthesizers and samplers. An infinite number of variations and combinations can be edited to create an infinite number of sounds. The sampled analog sounds cannot be edited in exactly the same manner as on an analog synthesizer, even though the editing parameters are similar. Analog synthesis was the original format of synthetic music. For a time, not many new analog synthesizers were being developed, but some manufacturers continue to make analog modeling synthesizers, such as Virus and Nord synthesizers. (Analog synthesizers are also available as virtual instruments.) The sounds are popular in all forms of commercial music.

Acoustic pianos. Yamaha, Baldwin, Bösendorfer, and Steinway pianos—among additional manufacturers—have varied timbres and keyboard action. (Each instrument within the same brand varies in sound.) Yamaha is the most accepted acoustic piano in popular music since it has a "cutting" sound when recorded. This said, all pianos have individual characteristics; therefore, choosing a piano becomes a matter of taste.

Synthesized acoustic pianos. Most synthesizers and samplers include various acoustic piano samples in the general MIDI patches that are included with most instruments. An infinite number of variations and combinations can be achieved through editing. Some of the samples tend to sound thin and percussive, whereas others are quite realistic. Combining an acoustic piano with a variety of analog sounds creates interesting timbres. When combining sounds, keep the individual sounds on separate tracks so that the balance can be adjusted during the mixing process.

Digital samples are samples of real acoustic and/or electric instruments, such as acoustic guitars, drums, percussion, strings, or unique sounds. The samples are played on a keyboard, and many emulate the real instruments. The quality of the samples varies greatly between manufacturers. Since purchasing sounds can be costly, listen to the sample CD or to the samples usually available for listening on the manufacturer's website.

Organs. The Hammond B3 organ, with a Leslie speaker, has been the standard organ sound used in all forms of popular music. There are also smaller reproductions of the original organ available for purchase. Virtual synthesizer software replicas of many organs, including the Hammond, are also available. They can be edited basically the same as their hardware counterparts. Organs other than the sound of the B3 might be more appropriate for some arrangements.

Synthesized organs. Most synthesizers and samplers include a number of organ samples in their general MIDI patches. An infinite number of variations and combinations of sounds can be achieved through editing. (Combining an organ sound one octave above a bass can be very effective in certain styles of music, such as dance music.)

Effects generated by keyboards. Keyboards can be used to trigger MIDI effects. For example, each time a keyboard is struck, a delay occurs on the vocal track. The track is bused to an effect in the synthesizer, which generates the delay. Almost any parameter can be MIDIed.

Electric Guitar

The electric guitar is one of the most popular rhythm and solo instruments in popular music. It has line-level outputs that either route the signal through a direct box that converts the signal for optimum signal input into the console or go directly into the recording console, into an amplifier, or to both inputs simultaneously. (All recording consoles have line-level inputs.) A combination of direct and live sounds gives the engineer/producer a choice and offers a safety factor; if one signal is not usable, the other, it is hoped, will be free of distortion or digital error.

Because technology provides numerous options, some engineers always want to have at least one "clean" (no effects) signal that can be channeled through effects during the mixing process. If an effect is recorded on the same track as the original signal, the effect cannot be deleted without rerecording the guitar.

Many rhythm sections have both a lead and a rhythm guitarist. When recording, it is common practice to double the rhythm guitar part, creating a wider, more enriched sound (when desired). (This is a creative decision, not a "rule.")

Rhythmic strumming is an integral part of the sound of a rhythm section. Most commercial guitarists consider themselves either rhythm or lead guitarists. In the same manner that a drummer and bassist have to sound like one unit, the rhythm guitar player has to join the drummer and bassist and "lock" into the groove.

As in other styles of music, rhythm guitarists specialize in certain musical genres. Some are skillful rhythm-and-blues players, while others are accomplished rock or jazz performers. Their styles differ, and so do their choices of instruments. Certain manufacturers make guitars that sound appropriate for rock and roll but may not sound suitable for jazz and so on. Very few guitarists play multiple styles well. Most accomplished studio musicians are versatile, but it is usually prudent to hire a specialist.

Guitar solos are a staple in all styles of popular music. Lead guitarists are similar to lead singers—the "stars" have their own "voice" (individuality). Each genre of popular music has certain characteristics that define its style. Rock-and-roll players generally use distortion, whereas traditional jazz players have a clean, undistorted sound. Other genres have unique characteristics as well. Guitar solos generally have certain musical elements that define the style of the genre, just as the characteristics of a violin solo from the classical period differ from the performance style of a violin solo from the baroque period. A violinist is expected to know and perform the unwritten characteristics and ornamentations of a specific musical period. The same concept applies to performers of popular music.

Within each genre exist subgenres. As previously stated, if a guitarist is instructed to play a jazz solo, does that mean jazz in the style of the 1940s, the 1960s, or another musical period? Be specific when writing an arrangement and hire an expert to perform the part.

A variety of electric guitars are manufactured. Solid-body and hollow-body electric guitars have different sounds, and each brand has a distinct sound. Fender Stratocaster guitars and Les Paul guitars, for example, are among the most popular brands. Guitars are manufactured with an assortment of pickups, which affect the sound. Arrangers must become familiar with the different sounds since the choice of guitar will affect the sound of an arrangement.

An infinite number of effects can be applied to a basic guitar sound. Studio players bring effects racks to recording sessions, and producers and arrangers usually experiment to find the most suitable sound for an arrangement. Most effects can be edited and, therefore, offer a performer numerous choices.

Strumming with a pick as well as finger picking are the most common techniques used to produce a guitar sound. In addition, a metal finger slide, held by a finger of the left hand (by right-handed players), slides across the frets to produce a unique sound, similar to that of a pedal steel guitar. Some guitars have a lever (handle) that, when lowered or raised, results in smooth pitch changing, not unlike using portamento on a synthesizer.

Amplifiers differ in sound quality. Jazz players use different amplifiers than rock players and so on. Distortion is the most prevalent guitar sound in rock and roll, while a clean sound (no distortion), played on an open-bodied guitar, is the most common sound used by jazz guitarists. Amplifiers have distinct sounds. Know the differences in sound so that the proper amplifier can be selected for a recording session.

Most engineers prefer to "take the guitar direct" (into the console) rather than miking an amplifier. The guitar is plugged directly into the recording console and bused to a track. Since guitar effects can simulate almost any amplified sound, often there is no need to use an amplifier. Most rock-and-roll bands prefer to use amplifiers in the studio in order to capture their live sound. Some engineers simultaneously record a direct sound and a live sound and mix the two sounds together. This technique is customary when recording acoustic guitars.

Acoustic Guitar

Acoustic guitars have either nylon or steel strings. The playing style is the same as for the electric guitar, except that finger picking is used more often with acoustic guitars. The sound is usually pure and not "effected" (e.g., delays, choruses, and so on) in the same manner as that of an electric guitar. Reverb is generally added to give the instrument some ambience.

A number of acoustic guitars are manufactured with microphone pickups. A quarter-inch cable (guitar cable) is plugged into the recording console, and the signal is recorded directly. Some engineers mix a direct signal with a microphone signal that is recorded by placing the microphone in front of the guitar. They also want the room sound to be blended in the overall ambience of the sound. Engineers use microphones that are placed far from an instrument to record the ambience of the room.

Most commercial music guitar parts are written with chord symbols and rhythmic indications within each bar; the rhythm notation indicates where to change the chords. Specific parts are notated. Arrangers indicate if the part should be arpeggiated, strummed, or plucked.

Guitar players are hired because of their individuality, which includes their feel, sense of time, technical ability, and musicality. (Some guitar players specialize in either acoustic or electric guitar.)

Range: Electric and acoustic guitar parts are written in the treble clef and sound one octave below where they are written. The guitar is built in C. The lowest string is E, below the treble clef, followed by A, D, G, B, and E (see examples 6-2 and 6-3).

Example 6-2   Guitar open strings.

Banjo, pedal steel guitar, mandolin, lute, ukulele, and other stringed guitar-like instruments are used in various genres of music. Almost all

Example 6-3 Guitar range: staff indicates where the parts are written.

World Music cultures have stringed instruments. The sounds of the various guitar-like instruments can be a welcome addition to an arrangement when played in conjunction with a traditional guitar part.

Basses

The bass (a.k.a. contrabass or double bass) is a unique instrument in popular music because it is used in two completely different settings: 1) as a part of the rhythm section and 2) as the low end of a string section. Some orchestral arrangements contain two distinct parts: an electric or acoustic bass playing with the rhythm section and the double basses playing with the string section.

Since the bass is a significant part of an arrangement, address the intrinsic role it plays not only in sonority but also in creating rhythm. In commercial music, the bassist and the drummer perform as a unit. If there is a lack of synergy, there will be no rhythmic groove. When bass and drums are programmed (synthesized), the bass drum (a.k.a. kick drum) and the bass often play the same rhythm patterns. This creates a deep, rhythmic "bottom end" to the track.

In most traditional symphonic orchestrations, the double basses read the same notes as the celli but sound one octave lower. This combination creates a deep, resonant sound. In commercial music, the bass helps to create a foundation for the rhythm section by playing rhythmic patterns that usually form an inseparable combination with the drums.

In all forms of popular music, the use of the bass continues to evolve. (Synthesizers and samplers contain myriad unique bass sounds that can be edited.) Arrangers have to be concerned that the low frequencies of the bass and drums do not sound muddy. It could be a problem if the notes for the electric rhythm bass are written in the same range as the double basses, which are the lowest member of the string section.

Contrabass

A contrabass, also called a double bass or bass, is pitched an octave below the basses (celli are technically considered the basses) and is the instrument most commonly used in a symphony orchestra.

Electric Bass

Electric basses are used in almost all forms of contemporary music. Some bassists specialize in rock and roll, while others only play jazz, rhythm and blues, pop, and so on. (Not all jazz electric bassists play upright acoustic bass.)

There are primarily two types of electric basses: one has four strings (the standard), and the other has six strings (rare). Several custom-made electric basses have five strings, the lowest note being a B (written below the bass clef) rather than an E (written below the bass clef) found on four-string basses.

In popular music, bass parts are usually written with chord symbols above the notes so that the bassist can improvise using the written part as a guide. Traditional orchestral contrabass parts are always notated.

Bassists (in popular music) are hired because of their individuality, feel for the style of music, sense of time, technical ability, and musicality. Most studio bass players can read music. Commercials are recorded during one-hour recording sessions; therefore, the performers must work quickly and accurately.

Range: Parts are written primarily in the bass clef and sound one octave below where they are written. The lowest string is E, written on the first leger line below the bass clef, followed by A, D, and G. The highest written note is B-flat, above middle C. (The open strings and the bass range are the same as the contrabass.)

Range: The six-string electric bass is rarely used. The notes are written in the bass clef, tenor clef, and treble clef and sound an octave lower than written. The lowest string is B, written directly below the bass clef, followed by E, A, D, G, and C. The highest written note is C, two octaves above middle C (see examples 6-4 and 6-5).

Example 6-4   Six-string electric bass open strings (lowest note is E and highest note is G).

Example 6-5   Six-string electric bass range: staff indicates where the parts are written (four-string range: lowest note is E and highest note is G).

Synthesized Bass

Synthesized basses are extensively used on recordings and in live performances. Some arrangers incorporate several synthesized bass parts, with different sounds, within one arrangement. When a synthesized or sampled
bass is programmed, an infinite number of usable sounds are available.
Editing filters, oscillators, and effects help to create almost any sound.
Arrangers must be aware of the trends in popular bass sounds. This information will be valuable in choosing a bass sound(s) for an assignment. In
popular music, "sounds" (sonorities) become trends, as do rhythm patterns. This generally evolves because producers hear a hit record that has
a distinct bass pattern and/or sound, and they emulate it. The "domino
effect" occurs, and similar patterns are frequently heard on commercials
and records. Commercial arrangers must be aware of trends because they
are frequently asked to imitate current musical styles.

Drums

In popular music, drummers are the backbone of the rhythm section; they
create the basic groove, (with the bassist). In orchestral music, drums (percussion in an orchestral context) contribute rhythm, effects, and colors to
orchestrations.

A traditional acoustic drum set (used in popular music) is made up of
various percussive instruments that are referred to as a drum kit or trap
drums. Most kits are played with a variety of drumsticks, brushes, and
different-sized mallets (used mainly for cymbals and tom-toms); each
instrument creates a unique sound. In commercial music, drummers are
hired for their individuality, feel, and technique. The average drum kit
consists of the following:

1. Snare drum
2. Bass drum (a.k.a. kick drum)
3. Hi-hat cymbals, which open and close with a foot pedal
4. Crash cymbals (used for accents)
5. Ride cymbals (an open, ringing sound, used mostly for rhythm patterns)
6. A variety of additional cymbals of various sizes
7. Large and small tom-toms
8. Some drummers also combine electric drums with acoustic drums
   or only play an electric drum set. Electric drums can either be triggered by an attachment that is connected to an acoustic drum or
   by directly striking pads, producing various programmable electric
   drum sounds.

Range: Drum parts are written in the bass clef, with the lowest space indicating the bass drum, the third space from the bottom indicating the snare drum, Xs above the top line indicating the hi-hat, and other spaces indicating tom-toms, which are usually marked "tom-toms" above the notes; additional cymbals are usually marked with the name of the instrument next to the note (see example 6-6).

Example 6-6   Drum pattern.

Drum Kit

An acoustic drum part can be recorded and then used as a triggering device to generate electric drum samples that can either replace the original part or simultaneously play with the original part. (This technique is frequently utilized in country music.)

Since the groove is of utmost importance in popular music, it is crucial that arrangers be aware of current trends in both rhythmic grooves and sounds. Some genres of music, such as rock, use primarily live drummers; other genres, such as hip-hop, use primarily drum programmers. Many tracks include a combination of a live drummer and synthesized drums and percussion.

It is not unusual for arrangers or music producers to record live drums onto analog tape and transfer them to a computer audio program (e.g., Pro-Tools or Digital Performer) for editing. This is done because they favor what they perceive to be the warm sound of analog tape as opposed to the sound of digital audio.

The advantage of transferring tape to a digital computer program is the ability to manipulate and edit the sounds, using a fast, nondestructive editing process. This enables music producers to present numerous variations of a recording and also to make changes quickly. They have the ability to revert back to the original program since even though the program can be edited numerous times, the original waveforms are never erased. (The waveforms will be permanently erased only if the programmer chooses to erase the parent [original] file.)

> ♩♩ Some engineers think that transferring analog recording to digital audio (for mixing and editing) defeats the purpose of analog recording because the original recorded sound changes when it is transferred. This is a matter of personal preference.

The same recording process is used for percussion, such as congas, bongos, shakers, and tambourines. Many arrangers create synthesized percussion sounds by editing and adding effects to existing sounds. The sounds are not an attempt to duplicate the sound of real instruments but rather an effort to create new sounds that achieve the same rhythmic result as traditional percussion instruments.

Synthesizer manufacturers make *dedicated* (contains only drum sounds) drum machines, some of which contain hundreds of sounds that can be edited, helping to achieve a unique sound quality. Third-party manufacturers also sell myriad sounds. Some drum machines have sophisticated editing parameters and allow programmers great creativity. This is also true of virtual (software) drum machines.

Professional drum programmers spend endless hours creating and editing drum and percussive sounds. It is their "feel" along with their individual pallet of sounds that makes them unique. Drummers, percussionists, and drum programmers (in popular music) are hired because of their individuality, which includes their feel for a musical style, their sense of time, and their technical ability.

Timpani

Timpani (also called kettledrums) are standard drums in symphony orchestras as well as in popular music orchestras. They are usually made of copper covered with a skin. If not overused, the sound of timpani can make a distinct statement within an arrangement. Timpani produce a unique deep, percussive sound. When combined with the basses, a rich low end is created. Timpani are played with mallets.

Range: There are four basic timpani drums. The notation is written in the bass clef. Their tones are adjusted through the use of a foot pedal—the lower the pedal is pushed, the higher the tone. The notes sound where they are written. The range of the lowest drum is from D, below the bass clef, to A, on the lowest space of the bass clef; the second drum from F to C; the third drum from B-flat to F; and the fourth drum (highest drum) from D to A. Timpani are popular in hip-hop music because the power of the low end is so effective (see example 6-7).

Example 6-7 Timpani range.

Percussion Instruments

A percussion instrument is defined as something that is struck or shaken; it can be made out of wood, metal, skin, or numerous other materials. Some percussion instruments have a traditional tone, but some do not.

Many sampled and analog percussion sounds are included in both software and hardware drum samplers; general MIDI patches with percussion are included with most synthesizers. Percussion is an integral part of drum programming and therefore simultaneously program percussion with the traditional drums.

Percussion plays a significant role in both the feel and the sonority of commercial arrangements. Percussion is an inherent member of the rhythm section. The parts should be scrutinized to make certain that they fit into the overall rhythmic puzzle. A part that is not quantized properly or that is out of character with the rest of the rhythmic groove will impair the feel.

Piano

The sound of the piano emanates when the player's hands depress the keys, which in turn triggers wooden hammers that strike the strings. Full-size pianos have 88 keys. The Bösendorfer piano (made in Austria] has 92 keys. The lowest note is F0. A number of pianos, including synthesized or sampled pianos, have fewer than 88 keys.

The piano is used as a solo instrument, as an accompanying instrument, to provide "tonal colors" such as playing in unison or in octaves with other instruments, or sparsely to highlight selected parts of the orchestration. It is the most versatile instrument.

Most pianists specialize in a style, such as classical, jazz, country, pop, rock, rhythm and blues, and so on. In all forms of music, the most important element of a performer's playing is being faithful to the style of a genre. For example, most rhythm-and-blues players are rooted in gospel music and have performed in churches; therefore, they have a traditional background and feel for rhythm and blues, which emanated from gospel music. Most country music performers were raised in the southern United States, where country music is the most popular music; the music is a part of their culture. The same concept applies to the traditions of jazz and other musical genres. The most accomplished musicians, in all musical styles, have an inherent affinity for the music they perform.

Range: The range of the piano is from A (8vb), written one octave below the bass clef, to C (15ma), written above the treble clef (see example 6-8).

Celesta (Celeste)

The celesta has a small keyboard with soft hammers that hit metal bars, creating a bell-like sound. The sound is pretty and soothing. The instrument is most effective when used to create "colors" and should not be overused. Melodic celesta passages, in combination with other instru-

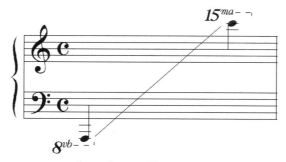

Example 6-8   Piano range.

ments, such as the flute or a woodwind section, create a sparkling sound. Arpeggiated passages and chords are also effectual when used sparsely.

Range: Parts are written in the bass and treble clefs and sound one octave above where they are written. The celesta is written from C in the bass clef to C two octaves above the treble clef (see example 6-9).

Example 6-9   Celesta range: staff indicates where the parts are written.

Percussive Instruments Played with Mallets

Vibraphone

For many years, the vibraphone (vibes) has been a popular instrument in jazz. The timbre has also been used extensively in film scores. The vibraphone is electric and has metal bars and a pedal that sustains the notes when depressed; a knob enables the player to adjust the speed of the vibrato. The notes are configured the same as a piano keyboard.

Normally, the vibraphone is played using two mallets, but parts are written for three and four mallets. Depending on the sound desired, the vibraphonist has an option of using hard or soft mallets. When using more than two mallets, the player requires time to change their configuration, and this must be taken into consideration when writing parts. If a tempo is too fast, the performer will not have enough time to arrange the mallets in the proper position. Vibes parts are often written as a combination with the piano (e.g., George Shearing).

Range: The vibraphone is a nontransposing instrument. Parts are written in the treble clef. It has a range from F, directly below middle C, to F, the fourth space above the treble clef. Vibraphones are constructed in different sizes and ranges (see example 6-10).

Example 6-10   Vibraphone range.

Xylophone

The xylophone is one of many instruments that have wooden bars. The bars are struck, most often with wooden hammer-like mallets. The xylophone is played in a manner similar to that of the vibraphone, except that the xylophone does not have a sustain pedal. The notes are configured the same as a piano keyboard. Used in moderation, the distinct wooden sound is effective when combined with orchestral instruments such as woodwinds. Xylophones are manufactured in different sizes, and consequently their ranges vary.

Range: Parts are written in the treble clef and sound one octave above where they are written. The lowest written note is F, below the treble clef, and the highest written note is C, above the treble clef (see example 6-11).

Example 6-11   Xylophone range: staff indicates where the parts are written.

Marimba

The marimba is similar to a xylophone and is struck with hard or soft hammer-like mallets. Similar to the xylophone, the marimba has wooden bars and no sustain pedal. The notes are configured the same as a piano keyboard. The marimba has a mellower sound than the xylophone.

Range: The marimba is a non-transposing instrument. Parts are written in the bass and treble clefs. The lowest note is C, on the second-to-the-bottom

♫ Balaphones (marimba-like instruments) are from the African countries, and their tunings and number of wooden bars vary from country to country; they are struck with mallets, which are made in a variety of sizes and materials. Their unique sound, used sparingly, is very effective.

space of the in the bass clef, and the highest note is C (8va), two octaves above the treble clef. Note: Marimbas are constructed in different sizes; therefore, their ranges vary. The bass marimba is very popular because it has a deep wooden sound that cannot be duplicated by any other instrument (see example 6-12).

Example 6-12   Marimba range.

Glockenspiel

The glockenspiel (bells) is a small instrument, consisting of two rows of graduated metal bars with no sustain pedal. It is played with two small wooden mallets, soft mallets, or brass mallets. It has a bell-like quality and is effective in combination with other instruments, such as the woodwinds.

Range: Parts are written in the treble clef and sound two octaves above where they are written. The lowest written note is G, below middle C, and the highest written note is C, above middle C (see example 6-13).

Example 6-13   Glockenspiel range: staff indicates where the parts are written.

Although the instrument can be played at a rapid pace, because the bells ring, the natural reverberation can create a cloudy sound. This must be taken into consideration when arranging a part. The instrument should be used tastefully, or the effect will not be appreciated.

Chimes

Chimes are long metal tubes that are hung vertically and configured like a piano keyboard. They are struck with wooden hammers and sound much like church bells. The sound should be used selectively.

Range: Parts are written in the treble clef and sound one octave above where they are written. The lowest written note is middle C, and the highest written note is F, on the top line (see example 6-14).

Example 6-14   Chimes range: staff indicates where the parts are written.

Latin Percussion

The most popular Latin percussive instruments are the conga drums, bongo drums, cowbells, go-go bells, and all types of shakers, guiro, timbales, claves, and maracas. Most Latin percussion originated in Africa. Afro-Cuban music developed from the rhythms of Africa and are the rhythms most often heard in popular music.

If an assignment specifies that the music should be composed in a specific Latin style, hire instrumentalists who are familiar with the music of that country (region). Every country and/or region has endemic instruments and musical traditions. Hiring a Cuban percussionist to play Mexican music would be analogous to hiring a rock-and-roll guitar player to perform a jazz solo. You cannot put a round peg in a square hole!

In commercial music, percussion players specialize in percussion styles and are usually not traditional drummers who also play drum kits and/or mallets. Orchestral percussion players are trained to play all orchestral percussion. We will concentrate on the most popular percussion.

Congas

Most conga players use two drums: a high-pitched drum and a low-pitched drum. Some use three or four drums, each with a different tuning. The drums are tuned by either tightening or loosening the drumheads. They are generally played with both hands.

Congas have been a staple in both Latin and popular music for many years. A well-played conga part fits perfectly with the rest of the rhythm section.

In Caribbean-Latin music, there is a variety of percussion, each playing in a traditional style. The percussion section must work as a unit. Conga players create a solid rhythmic foundation for the other

> ♫ The Conga set (a.k.a. congas) is comprised of the *quinto*, the highest-pitched drum; the *conga* or *segundo*, the middle-sized drum; and the *tumbadora*, the lowest-sounding drum.

percussionists. They have an excellent sense of time and technique.

Some conga players and percussionists specialize in playing rhythm and blues. It is a unique style of playing that has its roots in traditional Latin rhythms. (Latin rhythms emanate from African rhythms.)

Bongo Drums

Bongo drums are essentially high-pitched conga drums. Bongos are assembled as two drums that are held together with metal. Each drum can be tuned individually. Bongos played along with conga drums create an exceptional blend.

> ♫ The *hembra* (female) bongo is lower pitched than the *machu* (male) bongo, which is pitched higher. Many Latin bongo players also play the cowbell.

Bata Drums

Bata drums are similar to conga drums. *Oconcolo* is the small drum, *itotele* is the medium-sized drum, and the *iya* is the large drum. They are tunable, and many use buffalo hides for the drumhead. Batas are played with both hands.

Cowbells

Cowbells (taken from bells worn on cows' necks) are made of metal and played with a small stick. They are a fundamental part of the Caribbean-Latin rhythm section. It is traditional to play syncopated rhythms that help to form the rhythmic foundation of a groove.

Go-Go Bells

Go-go bells are, in essence, high-pitched cowbells and are played with a small stick. The parts are traditionally syncopated.

Shakers

Shakers are made in numerous sizes and shapes. They are usually made of gourds (a hard-skinned fruit) filled with a substance, such as beans or rice. Shakers are usually played by "shaking" a rhythm pattern that fits within a groove; they are also used to create a tonal color, as in film scores. A maraca is an example of a shaker.

Cabaza

A cabaza is a shaker-like instrument. It is a round piece of wood that is surrounded with bead-like metal strips and has a wooden handle. The cabaza is played by holding the instrument in one hand and rubbing the metal, in a rhythmic pattern, against the opposite hand. The effect is the same as that achieved with a shaker but sounds more metallic.

Tambourine

A tambourine is a single- or double-headed drum with small metal cymbal-like pieces surrounding the head. It is played by shaking and striking the head, usually with both hands. The tambourine is widely used in popular music as well as in Latin music.

Claves

The claves are two short thick pieces of wood that are hit together creating a rhythm pattern. Claves are used in Latin and popular music.

> ♩♪ Most Latin percussionists do not read music and are hired because of their unique rhythmic feel. If more than one player is being hired, it is wise to hire performers who have performed together; they will most likely play better as a unit than hiring random players.

The String Section

The string section, consisting of violins, violas, celli, and basses, is the backbone of a symphony orchestra. It is the most versatile section of the orchestra. The performers are capable of playing rapid passages, all dynamics from *pianissimo* (*pp* is the symbol to play very softly) to *fortissimo* (*ff* is the symbol to play extremely loud), and can create myriad effects by employing a multitude of bowing techniques. The beautiful blend of the instruments makes the string section unique. The strings accomplish many functions within an arrangement. Close harmonies, written in the middle to lower registers, produce warm-sounding "beds" (sustained chords); high unison violins can sail on top of the orchestra; and celli and violas, playing unison lines, glide through the baritone range, creating rich and full-sounding inner parts. Almost any emotion can be generated with a well-crafted string arrangement. Solo instruments, such as a solo violin or cello, can add contrast and beauty to the traditional sectional sonorities.

Strings blend well with other instruments. Some pleasing groupings are French horns with violas, bassoons with celli, tubas with basses, and flutes and oboes with violins. Adventuresome arrangers experiment with unusual combinations.

> ♩♪ Professional string players can perform almost any musical phrase that enters a composer's imagination. Write down all musical ideas and then edit them if needed. It is imperative that arrangers understand the fingering positions of string instruments. This allows them to take advantage of the versatility of the instruments.

String instruments are nontransposing instruments that sound where they are written, with the exception of the double bass, which sounds one octave below where notated. There is an extensive repertoire for violins and celli in all genres and a limited repertoire for violas and double basses. Double, triple, and quadruple stops (chords), which are notated with brackets around them, can be played on all the stringed instruments. Arrangers must be familiar with the time it takes performers to move from one position to another. Be certain that two notes are not on the same string, or the chord can obviously not be played. Double stops can be sustained, but triple and quadruple stops cannot be sustained since it is impossible for the bow to reach all the strings simultaneously; the stops are either plucked or bowed. If you have any doubts about what can be played, consult a string player.

Learn the various bowing techniques and technical limitations of the stringed instruments, or a composer/arranger's ability to write for strings will be greatly limited. It is impossible to achieve the variety of sounds that are available with a live string section on synthesizers or samplers because of the bowing techniques and "feel" that can be achieved only by live musicians. Most samplers offer a variety of bowings, but they are time consuming to program and will not sound as "real" as live performers. (If the strings are mixed at a low level, synthesized and sampled strings can sound remarkably realistic.)

Bowing techniques are an integral part of the sound of the string section. The main techniques follow.

Arco—To play with a bow; for example, after a pizzicato passage (plucked), the score is marked arco, meaning that the player resumes playing with a bow.

Pizzicato—To pluck the strings; the effect is extensively used and is a sound unique to strings.

Up-bow—the player moves the bow upward, as opposed to **down-bow**, where the player moves the bow down. Each technique creates a different sound.

A **slur** marking is a line (half moon) that connects a series of notes and indicates that the player should play those notes with one stroke of the bow. This creates a smooth-sounding passage. If there are no slurs indicated, the player alternates between up-bow and down-bow movements.

A **staccato** marking, which looks like a period symbol placed above or below the notes, indicates alternating up and down bows performed quickly.

Spiccato has the same symbol as staccato, but the bow bounces on the strings. The word *spiccato* should be indicated on the score to differentiate it from the *staccato* bowing technique.

Jeté—The bow "hits" the strings, which causes a bouncing effect. There is a down-bow marking and a slur marking, which indicate how many notes are hit.

Détaché (meaning detached) is marked with a line under each note. The bow must move quickly through the note and remain on the note for the duration of the note. Détaché is normally used with dynamics that are not too soft, and the note values and tempo must give the player enough time to perform the bowing. If the notes change too quickly, the bowing cannot be performed.

Louré has the same marking as détaché except that it contains slur markings that indicate that a series of notes should be played during one bowing direction, with a brief stop between attacks. Each time a new slur occurs, the direction of the bow changes.

Tremolo is created by the bow moving rapidly up and down through a certain note value without regard to tempo. It creates a dramatic result and is effective played at any dynamic marking. Tremolo is indicated by a series of lines under a note(s).

Sul ponticello—To play close to the bridge. This creates a very thin sound and works well while playing a tremolo.

Sul tasto—To play near or over the fingerboard. This creates a nondescript tone.

Col legno (meaning "with the wood") is achieved by hitting the strings with the wood of the bow. This creates a dramatic effect and is most effectively used in small staccato sections. The word *normal* is marked as an indication that the player should return to normal bowing.

Portamento is a sliding of the finger(s) from one note to another. (Portamento is often used in synthesizer programming.) This is marked with a line connecting the high note to the low note or the low note to the high note.

A **mute**, which is normally a piece of wood, is inserted on the bridge, creating a mellow, muffled sound. The part is marked **sordini** to indicate the use of mutes, and **senza sordini** indicates no mutes or to remove the mute.

Sur la touche—The bow is played higher up on the fingerboard than the bridge. This creates a pure and softer sound.

Vibrato is the signature sound of all string players. It is a rapid movement of the finger below the pitch but returns quickly to the correct pitch. Vibrato is a technique that is perfected by each player and one of the salient factors that determines a performer's unique sound. In early music, vibrato was frowned on but later became an accepted technique. If a composer does not want vibrato, it is marked in the score by writing *no vibrato* or *N.V.*

A **trill** is a rapid movement of the fingers from one note to another. It is marked in the score with the symbol *tr* and sometimes has the secondary note indicated in parentheses. If no note is indicated, the common practice is to trill between the written note and a note one-half or one full step higher.

Harmonics (the overtones of a note) can be played as individual tones on stringed instruments. This creates a delicate, glittering effect. Harmonics can be played in two ways on the violin: 1) **natural harmonics**, which are played on the open strings by lightly placing a finger a perfect fourth above the open string, resulting in a harmonic that sounds two octaves above the sound of the open string, and 2) **artificial harmonics**, which are played by placing a finger a perfect fourth above a stopped finger (a finger placed on a string to create a specific note). In this scenario, the harmonic sounds two octaves above the stopped note—not a fourth. For example, if the desired note is two octaves above the open G string, the finger is lightly placed on middle C. Harmonics are notated by placing a small, diamond-shaped symbol a fourth above the basic note.

We have discussed the most commonly used bowing techniques; there are additional bowings.

Violin

The violin is played by drawing a bow across the four strings, plucking the strings (pizzicato), or striking the strings (with the bow) in a percussive manner. Violinists place their fingers in various places (called positions) on the fingerboard. Practically, there are eight positions, but positions number as high as 15.

Range: The violin is a nontransposing instrument. Parts are written in the treble clef. It has four open strings, which are tuned in perfect fifths. The lowest open string is G, below middle C, followed by D, A, and E. The highest note is E, which sounds one octave higher than the third leger line above the treble clef (see examples 6-15 and 6-16).

Example 6-15   Violin open strings.

Example 6-16   Violin range.

The orchestral violin section is divided into two sections: first and second violins. The concertmaster of the orchestra has traditionally been the first violinist. (The concertmaster performs the solos written in the orchestral scores.)

Viola

The viola is played in exactly the same manner as a violin. The main difference is that because the viola is larger, it is more cumbersome for the violists to move rapidly through fingerings. This is a minor consideration since well-trained violists have excellent technique.

Range: The viola is a nontransposing instrument. Parts are written in the alto clef. If notes are written in a high register, the treble clef may be used. It has four open strings, which are tuned in perfect fifths. The lowest open string is C, one octave below middle C, followed by G, D, and A. The highest note is E, three leger lines above the treble clef (see examples 6-17 and 6-18).

Example 6-17   Viola open strings.

Example 6-18   Viola range.

Cello (Vioncello)

The cello is considered the bass of the orchestra. The cello is much larger than the viola and is played by sitting in a chair and holding the instrument between the player's legs. Because of the size of the cello, the fingering differs slightly from that of a viola. It is more difficult to navigate the fingerboard with the same agility and ease as a violin or viola.

Range: The cello is a nontransposing instrument. Music for the cello is written mostly in the bass clef. If notes are written in a high register, the tenor clef and treble clef may be used. The instrument is tuned in perfect fifths. The cello has four open strings, which are the same as those on the viola but one octave lower. The lowest string is C, two octaves below middle C, followed by G, D, and A. The highest note is A, one leger line above the treble clef (see examples 6-19 and 6-20).

Example 6-19   Cello open strings.

Example 6-20   Cello range.

Because of the cello's size, double stops and chords are more easily played on open strings.

Double Bass

The double basses, in a classic orchestral setting, usually play the same part as the celli but sound one octave lower than written. They are actually the sub-basses of the orchestra. The celli provide the clarity in the sound since they sound one octave higher. (In popular music, this same technique is commonly used when programming synthesized bass parts. For instance, a sub-bass might be doubled an octave higher with a different bass sound.)

The player holds the instrument while standing and/or sitting on a high stool. Because the instrument is so large and the bow is relatively small, the player cannot play legato passages or hold long notes with one bow stroke. The full, rich sound of pizzicato has made the upright bass the instrument of choice in traditional jazz ensembles.

Range: Parts are written in the bass clef and sound one octave lower than written. If notes are written in a high register, the tenor clef and treble clef may be used. It has four open strings, which are tuned in perfect fourths. The lowest open string is E, one line below the bass clef, followed by A, D, and G. The highest note is B-flat, located on the third line of the treble clef. Most concert double basses have a low C string (see examples 6-21 and 6-22).

Example 6-21   Double bass open strings.

Example 6-22   Double bass range: staff indicates where the parts are written.

The double bass, also referred to as an acoustic bass, is rarely used in pop music but is popular in jazz. Therefore, when a budget allows for only a small string section, the double bass is usually one of the first instruments to be eliminated. (Electric bass is usually the instrument of choice in commercial music.)

The string section consists of instruments that can play in very high registers (violins) to very low registers (double basses). This offers composers and arrangers a wide variety of tonal colors.

When writing an arrangement, the arranger might feel that the arrangement needs a "boost," which can be accomplished by building the string arrangement. For example, an arrangement could start with low strings and then add violas followed by violins. Creative string arranging is one of the most valuable skills of an arranger. (Because popular music tracks are usually recorded in sections, a band might arrange the rhythm track and hire an arranger to write a string arrangement.)

In a symphony orchestra, a large number of strings are needed to create a full, rich sound. This can be accomplished with fewer musicians in the studio by using a technique called overdubbing. Overdubbing means to record the same parts multiple times on additional tracks. (This is not always viable because of budget restrictions.)

If the number of musicians is limited, it is advisable for an arranger not to write the violin parts too high. Without a substantial number of violinists (at least eight playing in unison), the parts will sound very thin. By writing in lower registers and having all members of that section playing the same part, the section sounds richer. An experienced engineer can help generate a rich sound. Using the proper microphones and knowing how to position them is a major factor in the resulting sound.

Arrangers generally choose the instruments needed in the string section; the choices are based on the budget and the sound of a particular arrangement. For instance, only violins might be needed; four violas and two celli may accomplish the intended sound. Through experience, studio arrangers are able to select the proper string instruments that will sound best for a recording session.

Harp

The harp is an unusual instrument. It is plucked and has strings, pedals, and more than seven octaves. No other orchestral instrument can create the same sound. In an orchestral setting, the harp blends especially well with strings and woodwinds. It is also a beautiful solo instrument and a valued member of small combinations.

The harp is not considered a chromatic instrument. (The orchestrator must understand the technical limitations of the instrument in order to write chromatically.) A harp can play chords, single notes, arpeggios (broken chords), and glissandos (fingers sliding across the strings), which create a beautiful shimmering effect. A glissando (gliss), with the pitches alternating from high to low, low to high, or in random motion, is the signature sound of the harp. To be most effective in an orchestral setting, the harp should be used sparingly.

Range: The modern harp is nontransposing instrument. It has seven pedals, one for each scale degree. Each pedal represents a note in the diatonic scale. When the pedals are in their natural position, the harp is tuned in the key of C-flat. If the pedals are depressed to the second notch, the instrument is tuned in the key of C. If the pedals are depressed to the third position, the harp is tuned in the key of C-sharp. It takes time to adjust the pedals; therefore, a composer/arranger must take this into consideration when writing a harp part. Since the harp is complicated, if there are technical questions, consult with the harpist. Be aware of the most appropriate enharmonic spellings of the notes to make it easier for a harpist to change the pedals. Most harpists mark pedal changes on their parts. The harp is played with four fingers on each hand, and consequently the arranger should not write chords with more than four notes. Placing a small zero above a note(s) indicates harmonics. Harmonics sound one octave above the written note(s). The lowest open string is C-flat, one octave below the C-flat located on the second leger line below the bass clef; the highest note is G-sharp, one octave above the first space above the treble clef (see example 6-23).

Example 6-23　Harp range.

Synthesized Strings

There are many restrictions when programming synthesized or sampled strings. Because live string players use numerous bowing techniques and perform with a great deal of emotion, it is very difficult to duplicate the same sound on synthesizers or samplers. The following are several ways to make synthesizers or samples sound "real" on a recording.

Record the synthesizer parts and then add live players performing the same parts. The combination makes the synthesizers sound real and adds a human feel to an otherwise primarily electronic sound. The intonation, vibrato, and dynamics of the live strings bring animation to the synthesized parts. Sometimes the live strings sound full enough to eliminate the synthesized parts or to mix the synthesized parts at a low level. Another option is to play the lower parts on synthesizers and use live players to play the violin parts. The lower parts, being less obtrusive, will sometimes sound real within this context.

Mixing real and synthesized strings together can enhance the richness of the overall sound. This requires experimentation because the analog quality of some of the parts has to fit the tonality of the rest of the orchestration.

Since there are literally thousands of string samples, arrangers must be selective when trying to achieve a synergism with live strings. If the sonorities do not match, the combination will not work.

It is sometimes desirable to create an unusual sound. One way to achieve a creative sound is to choose interesting synthesized or sampled sounds mixed with live strings and add effects (signal processing).

When arranging synthesized parts, stay within the range of the live instruments. Some synthesizers allow programmers to play notes that are outside the range of the real sampled instrument. This automatically creates an unrealistic sound. Write within the tessitura (the best-sounding range) of the real instruments. This will cause the parts to sound more authentic.

Playing full chords, especially in the higher octaves, tends to sound thin and unrealistic on synthesizers. High, synthesized violins and violas sound best played in unison or octaves. If the violin and viola sections are small, the same theory applies to live string writing. A small section will not have the same effect as a symphony orchestra that has a full complement of violins and violas.

Do not make the synthesized strings too loud in the mix. Adding reverb and delay as well as keeping the parts relatively soft in the mix is an excellent disguise; the strings will sound more realistic.

Try not to write complicated parts. For example, when writing for a live string section, arrangers frequently write fast runs. This, generally, does not work well with synthesizers. One reason is that many synthesized sounds do not respond quickly enough, and therefore the sound is often behind the tempo. (If a part is carefully programmed and several live players are added to the synthesized parts, runs can sound realistic.)

Most professional string programs (sounds) offer sounds with a variety of bowing techniques (e.g., arco, staccato, and so on), dynamics (e.g., f and ppp), solo instruments, and full string sections. Even though these choices help to achieve realism, nothing can replace the "feel" of a live section.

String Combinations for the Studio

Since it is unusual to have a budget large enough to hire a full string section for a commercial, low-budget film, industrial film, and so on, arrangers must have options. The choice of instruments usually depends on the demands of the arrangement. Following are some suggestions.

Six first violins, five second violins, four violas, two celli, and one double bass (if needed) is a large string section for a commercial. The budget infrequently allows for a section this large.

Eight violins, two violas, and two celli will sound full in the studio as long as the violin parts are not written too high. Experimentation and experience help arrangers learn which studio combinations sound best for certain arranging styles.

Some arrangers might use only violins, violas, or celli. In the heyday of disco, almost all the records had live violin parts. Many arrangers only used six or eight live violins augmented by synthesizers.

There are several nontraditional uses of strings. The fiddle (violin) has been a mainstay of country, bluegrass, and Irish music for many years. The playing style is specialized. Many fiddle players cannot read music but improvise in the authentic musical style.

The solo violin has also been popular as a jazz solo instrument. The solo cello is used in rock-and-roll bands as well as in pop and folk groups.

Arrangers should be aware of the various styles and techniques used in multiple musical styles. Although many of the styles mentioned are based on improvisation, arrangers guide the performers.

The Brass Section

In popular music, brass plays many roles. Brass (and woodwinds) was used for accents and thematic unison melodic lines in old-school rhythm-and-blues tracks. Highlighting tracks with a surprise "blast" or long countermelodies is a trademark of rhythm and blues. Intricate brass and tasty ensemble parts have always been popular in traditional and commercial jazz arrangements.

Rhythm-and-blues horn sections are usually small and consist of brass and saxophone combinations. A typical section is two trumpets, one tenor saxophone, one trombone, and a baritone saxophone. To strengthen the sound in a recording studio, many producers double the horn parts.

The use of brass by master arranger Nelson Riddle in Frank Sinatra recordings is a fine example of how to incorporate brass in a commercial jazz style. The availability of mutes and plungers offers arrangers an array of tonal colors to choose from.

The most popular brass instruments in popular music are trumpets, trombones, French horns, and tubas. Throughout musical history, there have been many versions of these instruments (tuned to different keys). Most modern arrangers write for trumpets in B-flat, trombones in C, French horns in F, and tubas in C. There are instances when special instruments are used; for example, the piccolo trumpet (pitched in B-flat and sounding one octave above a B-flat trumpet) is popular in film scoring; sousaphones, baritone horns, and coronets are standard brass band and wind band instruments; and flügelhorns are used in all styles of music.

Because of the physical energy needed to play a brass instrument, arrangers must take the following into consideration:

1. Do not write the parts too high or too low for long periods of time. Players cannot sustain very high or very low parts for long periods of time without faltering. The embouchure (placement of lips) can become weak because of the muscular strain.
2. Trumpets are most effective when used in moderation. (Orchestration is the art of "painting" a musical picture; if the orchestrator uses too many of the same "colors," the orchestration will lack variety.)

Brass instruments have metal mouthpieces of various sizes. The player creates an embouchure (the placement of lips and tongue) and blows into the mouthpiece.

Trumpet in B-Flat

The trumpet is the highest of the brass instruments. It has three valves. By adjusting his embouchure, the player can change the natural harmonic overtones; by pressing various combinations of the three valves, half steps are achieved. Double and triple tonguing, slurring between notes, rapid trills, and special big-band playing techniques are all characteristic of the playing style.

In a large setting (e.g., big band or orchestra), there are usually three or four trumpets. Trumpets playing in octaves can be very powerful. Three- and four-part harmony produces a full and exciting sound.

Big bands always have a specialist called a lead trumpet player, who can play higher than the other players and sustain high parts for long periods of time. Normally, the second trumpet player has the role of the jazz soloist.

There are numerous concertos and chamber pieces written for trumpet. The sound of the trumpet can be altered through the use of three types of mutes:

- The **cup mute** is the softest sounding and blends well with other sections.
- The **straight mute** has a more cutting sound.

- The **harmon mute** has the thin, nasal sound.
- Trumpeters also use a **rubber plunger** or a plastic cup, which is held in one hand and opened and closed over the sound coming out of the bell. Sometimes the players use their hand to accomplish the same sound as a plunger.

The trumpet can be effective with the proper use of mutes. Playing a soft section using a cup mute and removing the mute and playing a fortissimo passage gives the illusion of two different instruments.

Muted trumpets with flutes, trumpets, and tenor saxophones playing in unison or in octaves, in addition to other orchestral combinations, make interesting sonorities.

Range: Parts are written in the treble clef and sound one step below where they are written. The lowest written note is F-sharp, below middle C, and the highest written note is D, above the treble clef. Professional trumpeters can play much higher (see example 6-24).

Example 6-24   Trumpet range: staff indicates where the parts are written.

Arrangers should not write high parts for a long period of time. High notes are very difficult to play, and the players may not consistently hit the notes with the correct intonation. Trumpets sound best in their middle range. They can sound powerful playing four-part harmony or playing in octaves (two trumpets high and two low) or in unison. Do not overwrite the trumpet parts; they are more effective when used as a distinct musical color. (The B-flat trumpet is the most popular trumpet used in commercial music. Trumpets are also constructed in other keys, e.g., trumpet in C.)

Tenor Slide Trombone in C

Adjusting a player's embouchure changes the natural overtones. The slide trombone does not have valves, and therefore the chromatics are achieved by adjusting the length of the slide. Since it is difficult to move the slide quickly, fast parts should not generally be written for the trombone, although many jazz trombonists have remarkable technical ability and can play almost as quickly as trumpeters.

Most big bands and orchestras have three or four trombonists. The bass trombone usually plays the lowest-pitched trombone part. A trombone section can sound smooth and full or loud and heroic, such as parts played in some marching band music. Trombones blend well with the lower strings, French horns, and tubas.

Whether arranged in harmony or unison lines, trombones have a distinct blend. The glissando is the most recognizable sound of the trombone because of the player's ability to slide from one note to another. Arrangers must study the instrument before writing a glissando since not all notes can slide to other notes. Low, percussive pedal tones are also a signature sound of the trombone. Some solo trombonists (e.g., Tommy Dorsey and J. J. Johnson) play with amazing dexterity, considering the limitations of the instrument.

The trombone is not popular as a solo instrument in the classical genre, although it is included in much brass chamber music.

Range: The tenor slide trombone is a nontransposing instrument. Parts are written in the bass clef. If notes are written in a high register, the tenor clef may be used. The lowest note is E, two octaves below middle C, and the highest note is B-flat, above middle C, which is notated in the tenor clef. Some trombonists can play higher. (Arrangers should not write too high without knowing the performer's ability to play the part.) They use the same style mutes as trumpets. The plunger is the most recognizable because as it enters and exits the bell, it creates an unusual "wah-wah" sound (see example 6-25).

Example 6-25   Tenor slide trombone range.

Valve trombones are rare. Some slide jazz trombonists also play valve trombones because it allows them to play faster. There is a distinct difference in sound between a valve and a slide trombone. Be certain of the desired sound before writing.

Bass Trombone in C

The bass trombone is a valuable addition to the low end of a band or orchestra. It provides a unique resonant and rich sound. No other instrument creates the same resonance when playing low notes. It is effective when playing in unison with tubas.

> ♩♪ During the Civil War, the marching bands used valve trombones with the bell facing over the trombonist's shoulder. The troops behind them could hear the sound more clearly. Other brass instruments were designed in the same manner.

Range: The bass trombone is a nontransposing instrument. Parts are written in the bass clef. If notes are written in a high register, the tenor clef may be used. The lowest note is B-flat, below the bass clef, and the highest note is B-flat, above middle C, which is notated in the tenor clef. Professional trombonists can play higher (see example 6-26).

Example 6-26   Bass trombone range.

French Horn in F

The modern French horn is pitched in the key of F. (Some symphony players prefer to use the horn in B-flat.) As with the other brass instruments just discussed, the French hornist changes the natural overtones of the instrument by changing her embouchure. French horns have three valves, which enable the player to achieve chromatic tones.

The majestic sound of French horns playing in unison or in fifths cuts through an orchestra with an important and sometimes soothing sound. The sound of the instrument is unique. The room seems to be filled with the magnificent sound. Most orchestras have three or four French hornists.

French horn players use cup mutes and straight mutes; unlike trumpeters, they cannot use a harmon mute. Players usually keep one hand over the bell in order to achieve a muffled, distant sound; they also play with an open bell. Do not write high parts for the French horn that last a long period of time. It is difficult to perform, and the sound of the horns will seem overused.

There are numerous solo French horn pieces written for orchestra and chamber music. Jazz French horn soloists are rare, but French horns are used in jazz orchestras. They blend with every section of the orchestra. Arguably, they are best used for legato passages, although staccato and sforzando passages are part of their signature sound. Arrangers must allow the players space to rest because the instrument is difficult to play and the performers' lips can easily become fatigued.

Range: French horn parts are written primarily in the treble clef and sound a perfect fifth below where it is written. If notes are written in a low register, the bass clef may be used. The lowest written note is F, below the bass clef, and the highest written note is D, the fourth line on the treble clef. Some hornists can play higher (see example 6-27).

Many arrangers do not write a key signature and notate the accidentals. This is the historical notation, although most contemporary arrangers use key signatures.

Example 6-27   French horn range: staff indicates where the parts are written.

Tuba in C

The tuba is the lowest-pitched brass instrument. (In symphony orchestras, some tubas are pitched in double B-flat or E-flat.)

The tuba and the bass trombone blend well playing in unison. The tuba adds a distinctive low sound to an orchestra or small group, such as in Dixieland or band music. It also blends well playing the lowest note of a trombone section. In this scenario, the bass trombone is usually written more like a tenor trombone part.

Tubas are pitched in various keys. Many have four or more valves, which help to achieve better intonation.

The tuba is not often used as a solo instrument. An exception is in the composition "Tubby the Tuba," a popular children's piece written by George Kleinsinger for symphony orchestra. Jazz tubists are rare.

Range: The modern C tuba is a nontransposing instrument. Parts are written in the bass clef. The lowest note is F, below the bass clef, and the highest note is G, above the bass clef. Professional tubists can play higher. Tubas are manufactured in different keys, such as tuba in B-flat (see example 6-28).

Example 6-28   Tuba range.

Brass Combinations for the Studio

Budget is a consideration when choosing a brass instrumental combination. With a modest budget, two trumpets, one tenor trombone, and a bass trombone will sound full if scored properly. If an assignment requires a small orchestra, try to include one or two French horns. No other instrument can produce the same sonority.

With budget restrictions, the tuba is usually the last instrument to be added. Most often, a tubist is hired because an arrangement specifically needs that sound, such as a Dixieland piece. (A tuba will not replace the sound of a double bass in a standard orchestral setting.)

The Woodwind Section

Woodwind is a deceptive term since many of modern instruments not constructed of wood are included in this category; for instance, flutes and saxophones are not made of wood. Woodwinds include the various flutes, clarinets, oboes, English horns, bassoons, and saxophones. As with the other instrumental sections of an orchestra, woodwinds provide distinct sounds by using various instrumental combinations. As a group, they blend well with almost all instrumental sections.

> ♩♩ Musicians who double or triple receive additional session payments.

Most commercial woodwind performers play two or three different woodwinds. This offers arrangers a wider selection of instruments to include because the colors of different sections can change. For instance, in letter A, a player might play clarinet, and in letter B, she may play a flute.

Flutes

All traditional flutes are held in a horizontal position and are played by blowing into a metal mouthpiece. The family of flutes consists of piccolo, flute, alto flute, and bass flute. (There are numerous wooden flutes.)

Piccolo in C

The piccolo is the highest and smallest flute and is used in both orchestras and bands. The most familiar sounds of this instrument are the technically challenging high countermelodies common to marches in addition to high trills. The piccolo also sounds good when played an octave above a unison passage. The instrument sounds one octave above the flute. The sound can be piercing, so it should be used sparingly. In most instances, one piccolo is sufficient, but for certain effects, three and four may be used, such as in marching bands.

Generally, flute players also play the piccolo. The fingering of a piccolo is the same as the fingering of a flute, but the very low and very high notes are more difficult to play.

Range: Piccolo parts are written in the treble clef and sound one octave above where it is written. The lowest written note is D, above middle C, and the highest written note is C (16va), above the treble clef. The most common piccolo is pitched in C, but there is also a D-flat piccolo (see example 6-29).

Flute in C

The most common flute is the C flute. The C flute is extensively used in jazz as well as in all forms of popular and classical music. Flute players

Example 6-29   Piccolo range: staff indicates where the parts are written.

have great dexterity and can perform almost anything. The repertoire consists of flute concertos in addition to extensive chamber music pieces. Flutes blend well with all woodwind and strings.

Range: The C flute is a nontransposing instrument. Parts are written in the treble clef. It sounds one octave below the piccolo. The lowest note is middle C, and the highest note is C (8va), written above the treble clef (see example 6-30).

Example 6-30   Flute in C range.

Alto Flute in G

The alto flute is a warm-sounding instrument and is popular in jazz. Three or four alto flutes playing in unison produce a soothing sound. Since they are soft, an arrangement has to be transparent so that the instrument can be heard. The alto flute takes more air to play than a C flute, so arrangers should not write parts that require as much physical dexterity as the C flute.

Range: Parts are written in the treble clef and sound a perfect fourth below where they are written. The lowest written note is middle C, and the highest written note is C, two octaves above the treble clef. Some flutists can play higher (see example 6-31).

Example 6-31   Alto flute range: staff indicates where the parts are written.

Bass Flute

The bass flute is an unusual instrument and can add a distinctive quality to an arrangement. It takes a lot of air to generate a sound, so the parts should not require short or fast sequences. Three or four bass flutes playing in unison produce an incredible sound. As with the alto flute, since the instrument does not project well, the arrangement must be sparse if it is to be heard.

Range: Parts are written in the treble clef and sound one octave below where they are written. The lowest written note is middle C, and the highest written note is C, located two octaves above the treble clef (see example 6-32).

Example 6-32   Bass flute range: staff indicates where the parts are written.

Wooden flutes are found in most cultures. Since each civilization has flutes that are unique and require individual playing techniques, study their musical culture before writing for the instrument.

Irish flutes, Renaissance flutes, bamboo flutes, and Native American flutes are among the many types of wooden flutes. The following are descriptions of some ethnic flutes.

Irish Flute

The Irish flute contains six holes, with the lowest note being a D above middle C; the flute will sound a D major scale as the holes are opened, with the top note being a C-sharp. This enables the flutist to easily play in the keys of D major and G major, which will accommodate many traditional Irish melodies. Adding metal keys that are attached to the wood can expand the range of the flute. The flutes are made in a variety of keys.

Baroque Flutes

Baroque flutes obtain an authentic sound of the period. By cross-fingering, a flutist who specializes in the baroque style can play a full chromatic scale. Some baroque flutes have two separate joint sections, which enable the players to tune to the baroque pitch of A-415 or the standard A-440 pitch used today.

Renaissance Flutes

Renaissance flutes should be used to replicate sixteenth-century Renaissance music. The Renaissance flute is a transverse flute and was probably used from the late fifteenth century to the second half of the seventeenth.

Boxwood was the most common material used to make Renaissance flutes, but some were made of various fruitwoods. Most tenor flutes were made in one piece, and most of the bass flutes were made in two parts. They were built in three sizes:

- The bass flute is tuned in G minor, and the range is two octaves from G to G.
- The tenor flute is tuned in D minor; the range is two and a half octaves from D to A.
- Descant, or highest flute, is tuned in A minor; sometimes the tenor plays this part.

Native American Flutes

Native American flutes are made in many shapes and sizes. They can be made of cedar, redwood, or walnut. The flutes have either five or six holes and are tuned to traditional minor scales. Study the tribes and theory of Native American flute playing if trying to emulate a specific tribe.

Wooden Ocarinas

Wooden ocarinas are chromatically tuned flutes made out of a variety of woods. They have an unusual oval shape.

Recorder

A recorder is held vertically and has a two-octave range. The recorder is made in many sizes. It is difficult to vary dynamics with this instrument.

Shakuhachi Flutes of Japan

Shakuhachi flutes are traditionally made of bamboo (some modern flutes are made of maple), are held vertically, and are built in many sizes. The bamboo is taken from the very bottom of a bamboo tree. The traditional tuning is in the key of D.

There are four finger holes on the front and a thumbhole on the back. The mouthpiece is open on the top of the open pipe. The flutist can play in a very expressive manner by using various blowing techniques and half-hole fingering.

The original Zen music for Shakuhachi is called Honkyoku and is played with bamboo flutes tuned only to the bamboo; since there is no traditional tuning and the tuning varies between instruments, Honkyoku music is only played solo.

Chinese Dizi Bamboo Flute (*D'tzu* or *Ahu Di*)

The dizi is similar to a traditional modern flute (held horizontally) but is made of bamboo. It has one blowhole, one membrane hole, six finger holes, and two pairs of holes at the end. Some dizis are made with 7 or 12 keys, but those are not traditional instruments. The dizi dates back to the Yuan dynasty (A.D.1279–1368).

The two types of dizi flutes are the bon di and the qun di. In the north, the flute was used in the Bon Zi Opera, located in northern China; the singing was accompanied by the bon di. The flute is pitched higher than the qun di. The Quan Opera, located in southern China, was accompanied by the qun di. Dizi players generally use three fingers. The average range is two octaves plus several additional notes.

Chinese Xiao Bamboo Flute

The xiao is played vertically and provided the basic design for the Japanese Shakuhachi bamboo flute.

Peruvian Pan Flute (*Zampona*)

The pan flute is made of bamboo shoots in various sizes and keys. It is one of the oldest instruments in the world. Its sound, which is beautiful and soothing yet can be highly dramatic, has been very popular in film music. The instrument sounds enjoyable playing either slow or fast music. The European pan flute player Zamfir is the most popular modern-day proponent of the instrument.

African Flutes

Flutes are part of most African cultures. Most are made of bamboo, but other materials are used, including wood, gourds, clay, horns, and various other materials. Some are built to be played like a traditional flute (transverse), while others are held vertically. Some are round or oval. Most African flutes have two to six holes.

Didgeridoo

The didgeridoo originated in northern Australia and is recognized as "the sound of Australia." It is a long flute-like instrument made from tree trunks and limbs that are cleaned out to make the tube hollow; most are made from bamboo. It has a low sound and is often played with complex rhythm patterns. It is a popular sound in film music.

The player vibrates his lips and gently blows into the instrument while simultaneously projecting sounds of various animals with his vocal chords. Some animals are very difficult to project, and replication of their sounds requires an expert. They are built in a variety of sizes.

Clarinets

Most clarinets have plastic mouthpieces; some are made of glass, crystal, wood, and hard rubbers. They have a single reed attached. The instrument is held vertically. There are a variety of clarinets currently being used:

- Clarinets are pitched in B-flat, A, and E-flat.
- The alto clarinet is pitched in E-flat.
- The bass clarinet is pitched in B-flat.

Clarinet in B-Flat

The B-flat clarinet is the standard clarinet used in popular music. (Clarinets are built in many keys.) The clarinet is one of the most popular instruments in both jazz (e.g., Benny Goodman) and orchestral music. Clarinetists have facile techniques, and the instrument has a wide range. A clarinet section has a beautiful mellow sound and can create a "cushion" to an arrangement. Solo clarinet has a pure, round tone and is used extensively for solos in both classical music and jazz. In a Dixieland band, a clarinet can sound raucous playing a rhythmic song and soothing when playing a ballad. Clarinets blend beautifully with the other woodwinds and strings. An extensive repertoire is written for clarinet.

Range: Parts are written in the treble clef and sound one step lower than where they are written. The lowest written note is E, below the treble clef, and the highest written note is A, one octave above the treble clef. Some clarinetists can play higher (see example 6-33).

Example 6-33 B-flat clarinet range: staff indicates where the parts are written.

Clarinet in A

Range: Parts are written in the treble clef and sound a minor third lower than where they are written. The lowest written note is E, below middle C, and the highest written note is A, above the treble clef (see example 6-34).

Example 6-34   A clarinet range: staff indicates where the parts are written.

Clarinet in E-Flat

Note: The E-flat clarinet is small and has a more piercing timbre than the B-flat clarinet.

Range: Parts are written in the treble clef and sound a minor third higher than where they are written. The lowest written note is E, below middle C, and the highest written note is A, two octaves above the treble clef. It is possible to play higher (see example 6-35).

Example 6-35   E-flat clarinet range: staff indicates where the parts are written.

Alto Clarinet in E-Flat

The alto clarinet is pitched in E-flat. The alto clarinet is written in the treble clef and sounds a major sixth lower. The lowest written note is E, below middle C, and the highest written note is E, above the treble clef (see example 6-36).

Bass Clarinet in B-Flat

The bass clarinet in B-flat has a deep, resonant low end. It sounds one octave lower than the B-flat clarinet. When used in combination with other clarinets, it usually plays the lowest note—analogous of the role the bari-

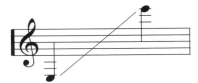

Example 6-36   Alto clarinet in E-flat range: staff indicates where the parts are written.

tone saxophone plays in the saxophone section. It is also used to play low auxiliary parts in many orchestral arrangements and blends well with other low instruments, such as celli and trombones.

Range: Parts are written in the treble clef and sound a major ninth lower than the written part. The lowest written note is E, below the treble clef, and the highest written note is G, one octave above the treble clef. Professional clarinetists can play higher (see example 6-37).

Example 6-37   Bass clarinet in B-flat range: staff indicates where the parts are written.

Oboe

The oboe uses a double reed, made of cane, instead of a plastic mouthpiece that holds a single reed. The oboe blends well with other woodwinds and especially sounds good playing in unison, harmony, or octaves with flutes. Oboists have great technical dexterity and can perform complicated passages with ease.

The oboe is a beautiful solo instrument that can depict either sadness or playfulness. Because it can make a "nasal" sound, the instrument is also used to create a feeling of humor, as does the bassoon. Many concertos and chamber selections have been written for the oboe.

Range: The oboe is a nontransposing instrument. Parts are written in the treble clef. The lowest note is B-flat, below middle C, and the highest note is F, above the treble clef (see example 6-38).

English Horn in F

The English horn is a tenor oboe and uses a double reed, made of cane. It has a beautiful, deep, rich sound that is showcased when playing solos.

Range: Parts are written in the treble clef and sound a perfect fifth above where they are written. The lowest written note is B, below middle

Example 6-38   Oboe range.

C, and the highest written note is F, one octave above the treble clef (see example 6-39).

Example 6-39   English horn in F range: staff indicates where the parts are written.

Bassoon

The bassoon is the lowest of the commonly used double-reed instruments. It has a beautiful, almost muted quality. A bassoon, along with a bass clarinet, typically plays the low part in a woodwind section.

When played in its low register, it can take on the role of a comedian. When playing a melody in a middle or high register, it can sound beautiful. The bassoon blends well with almost any orchestral instrument.

There are a limited number of concertos and chamber pieces written for the bassoon when compared to the repertoire written for flutes and clarinets.

Range: The bassoon is a nontransposing instrument. Parts are written in the bass clef. If notes are written in a high register, the tenor clef may be used. The lowest note is B-flat, below the bass clef, and the highest note is E-flat, on the top space of the treble clef. The E-flat is notated using the tenor clef (see example 6-40).

Example 6-40   Bassoon range.

Contrabassoon

Range: Parts are written in bass clef and sound one octave below where they are written. The lowest written note is B-flat, below the bass clef, and the highest written note is F, above middle C.

Note: In a commercial orchestra setting, the instrument is rarely used with the exception of film scores (see example 6-41).

Example 6-41   Contrabassoon range: staff indicates where the parts are written.

Woodwind Combinations for the Studio

Many woodwind combinations work well. The following are some suggestions:

- Flutes and clarinets playing in octaves
- Clarinet, oboe, and C flute playing in unison
- C flute and oboe in unison or playing in harmony
- Flute, oboe, clarinet, and bassoon or bass clarinet playing in harmony
- Oboe and clarinet playing in octaves
- Clarinet with bass clarinet or bassoon playing one octave below
- Two flutes playing in harmony
- Two oboes playing in harmony
- Two bassoons and two clarinets playing in harmony
- Flute playing the highest octave, oboe playing one octave below, and clarinet one octave below the oboe

Almost any combination sounds good. Many of these groupings blend well with other sections of the orchestra:

- Flutes with violins
- Bassoons with celli
- Bassoons and bass clarinet with bass trombone and tuba
- Clarinets with almost any instrument
- Muted trumpets and flutes

Saxophones

Although saxophones are not made of wood, they are considered wood-winds. But they are also listed in their own category. They have plastic mouthpieces with a single reed attached.

The saxophones used in contemporary music are soprano, alto, tenor, baritone, bass, and contrabass. (The bass and contrabass saxophones are rarely used except for specific purposes.)

Example 6-42   Saxophones: staff indicates where the parts are written for all saxophones.

Saxophones are not considered a standard orchestral instrument. In modern concert music, composers (e.g., Richard Strauss and Bizet) have included saxophones in their scores. Chamber works and concertos have been written for them. They have always been an intrinsic part of commercial orchestras, bands, and jazz groups as well as concert and marching bands. French composers have used saxophones extensively to create the dominant sound in French band music.

The standard saxophone section consists of two altos, two tenors, and a baritone. In unusual circumstances, the baritone player doubles with a bass saxophone. The soprano saxophone has become a popular instrument, especially in jazz (e.g., John Coltrane) and smooth jazz (e.g., Kenny G).

The saxophone section has a beautiful blend. When the music is written in close harmony, the section can sound like one instrument; few other sections sound as cohesive. Another unique section sound results from writing octaves and unisons. Parts can be written to be played at lightning speed because professional saxophone players have extraordinary technique. This is partially attributed to the fact that saxophones are the easiest of the woodwinds to produce a sound. Saxophones blend with almost any section. They are especially rich sounding when played in the middle to low octaves along with the strings. The baritone is often written in combination with the bass trombone and tuba. Most commercial saxophone players also play clarinet and flute; some also play double reeds, such as the oboe, English horn, and bassoon.

Range: All saxophones have the same written range and are fingered in the same manner. Saxophones are built in various keys. They all have the same written range: B-flat or B, below middle C, to E or F, above the treble clef (see example 6-42).

Soprano Saxophone

The soprano saxophone is the highest-pitched of the instruments, and it is shaped more like a clarinet than the other saxophones. (Some sopranos look like small alto saxophones.) It is mostly used as a solo instrument, especially in jazz. Having a beautiful mellow sound, it is also very effective in playing solo parts in film scores because the sound does not interfere with the dialogue the way, for example, a trumpet could. Soprano saxophones sound one step lower than where written.

Alto Saxophone

The alto saxophone usually plays the lead part in a saxophone section. (Sometimes the lead is played by the soprano saxophone.) There are typically two altos in a section. The second alto normally plays the part directly below the lead alto; sometimes a tenor plays the second part, and the second alto plays the third part. The alto players are usually accomplished jazz soloists and play solos in big-band arrangements. Alto saxophones are frequently used in small jazz combos. They sound a major sixth below the written note.

Tenor Saxophone

The B-flat tenor saxophone is pitched in the key of B-flat. Two tenors are normally used in a full section. They normally play the third and fourth parts in a typical section. The tenor is, arguably, the most popular saxophone used in jazz. Tenors blend exceptionally well with trombones. In fact, two tenors and two trombones can sound like a trombone section. The B-flat tenor saxophone sounds a major ninth below where written.

Baritone Saxophone

The E-flat baritone saxophone usually plays the lowest note in the saxophone section. It is also an effective solo instrument, primarily in jazz, vintage rock-and-roll, and rhythm-and-blues music. It produces a unique rich, deep, raspy sound that cannot be duplicated by any other instrument. The E-flat baritone saxophone sounds an octave and a major sixth below where written.

> ♩♩ The baritone is rarely used for jazz solos, but there have been some extraordinary jazz musicians who have made the instrument popular, such as Jerry Mulligan, Pepper Adams, and Ronnie Cuber.

Bass Saxophone

The B-flat bass saxophone is the least used of the modern saxophones. It has an unusually deep sound and should be reserved for special use. The

B-flat bass saxophone sounds two octaves and a full step below where written.

Saxophone Combinations for the Studio

If there is a limited budget, an alto and two tenors or two altos and a tenor will blend well. Generally, a baritone will be the last saxophone to be added unless that sound is generic to the style of arrangement, such as fifties rock and roll. Saxophones are pliable instruments and work with almost any orchestral or band combination.

General Combinations for the Studio

Some budgets only allow for a small horn section. The following are some examples of instrument sections that will blend:

- Two trumpets, a tenor sax, and a baritone sax
- One trumpet and one tenor sax, playing in octaves or in unison
- Two trumpets and two trombones
- One trumpet, one alto sax, and one tenor sax
- Three trumpets, a tenor sax, and one tenor trombone

If a part is well written, various combinations will sound good.

Voices

Voices are used to sing lead vocals and background vocals and as part of the orchestration (without words). The following are the general ranges of the various vocal groupings.

Soprano 1

Range: Parts are written in the treble clef and sound where they are written. The lowest note is B-flat, below middle C, and the highest note is C, above the treble clef. Some singers can sing higher or lower (see example 6-43).

Soprano 2

Range: Parts are written in the treble clef and sound where they are written. The lowest note is A, below middle C, and the highest note is G, above the treble clef. Some singers can sing higher or lower (see example 6-44).

Example 6-43   Soprano 1 range.

Example 6-44   Soprano 2 range.

Alto 1

Range: Parts are written in the treble clef and sound where they are written. The lowest note is G, below middle C, and the highest note is F, on the top line. Some singers can sing higher or lower (see example 6-45).

Example 6-45   Alto 1 range.

Alto 2

Range: Parts are written in the treble clef and sound where they are written. The lowest note is F, below middle C, and the highest note is E-flat, on the top space. Some singers can sing higher or lower (see example 6-46).

Example 6-46   Alto 2 range.

Tenor 1

Range: Parts are written in the treble clef and sound one octave lower than where they are written. The lowest written note is middle C, and the highest written note is C, above the treble clef. Some singers can sing higher or lower (see example 6-47).

Example 6-47   Tenor 1 range.

Tenor 2

Range: Parts are written in the treble clef and sound one octave lower than where they are written. The lowest written note is A, below middle C, and the highest written note is A, above the treble clef. Some singers can sing higher or lower (see example 6-48).

Example 6-48   Tenor 2 range.

Bass 1 (Baritone)

Range: Parts are written in the bass clef and sound where they are written. The lowest written note is F, below the bass clef, and the highest written note is F, above the bass clef. Some singers can sing higher or lower (see example 6-49).

Example 6-49   Bass 1 range.

Bass 2

Range: Parts are written in the bass clef and sound where they are written. The lowest written note is C, below the bass clef, and the highest written note is E-flat, above the bass clef. Some singers can sing higher or lower (see example 6-50).

Conclusion

Arranging and orchestration provide the colors for the composer/arranger. Arrangers must be careful not to "overarrange." When a part is

Example 6-50 Bass 2 range.

too busy or dense, the arrangement tends to sound muddled and has a lack of clarity. When composing jingles, arrangements should surround and enhance the melody and the lyric, not overpower it.

A composer should try to internalize the sound of an arrangement while composing, followed by either writing the arrangement or hiring an arranger. Study arranging, orchestration, and a multitude of styles. The more styles an arranger can tackle, the more assignments he or she is able to undertake. Without well-crafted arrangements and orchestrations, music would be boring.

Assignments

1. Compose music for a 15-second commercial (invent a product) and write three rhythm section arrangements, each with a different style.
2. Using the rhythm section arrangement as a foundation, add strings, brass, and woodwinds.

7

Jingle Writing

The recorded history of advertising music began when music printing became economical. During the nineteenth century, the street cry was transmuted into the jingle on trade cards and in newspaper and magazine advertisements. Some companies advertised on sheet music and in

> ♫ Although the term *jingle* is distasteful to some composers, songs for commercials are referred as jingles throughout the book.

music collections; others published their own music. In early twentieth-century England, Beecham's Pills issued a series of portfolios that included popular songs, folksongs, numbers from operettas and other light classical selections, and excerpts from Handel and Mendelssohn oratorios, all interspersed with advertising copy and music specifically intended to promote Beecham's product. Although lacking obvious jingles, the portfolios included dances such as the "Guinea-a-Box Polka" (alluding to the price of Beecham's Pills), the "St. Helen's Waltz" (that being where they were manufactured), the "Beecham's Chimes Galop" and "Beecham's March to Health" (www.grovemusic.com).

Musical Commercial Saves
Wheaties from Extinction

Wheaties made advertising history as the first product to feature a singing commercial on network radio. Its first airing took place on Christmas Eve 1926. Four male singers known as "The Wheaties Quartet" sang the soon-to-be-famous "Have You Tried Wheaties" jingle. The commercial was a barometer on how popular Wheaties was with the people. Sales increased in areas where the people heard the commercial. Unfortunately, the musical commercial was heard in only a very limited area of the United States. In those regions where the musical commercial wasn't heard, sales floundered badly.

With the product's sagging popularity, General Mills, the makers of Wheaties, came within a whisker of discontinuing the production and selling of Wheaties. At a company staff meeting, an advertising executive for Wheaties suggested a business model that would save the cereal. He stated that since the sales were good in those regions where the Wheaties musical commercial was heard, why not air the commercial in as many regions of the country as possible? To summarize, the musical commercials were aired, sales improved, and Wheaties quickly became one of the most popular breakfast cereals.

Jingles are miniature songs. In the 1940s, Pepsi-Cola broadcast the first national jingle, "Pepsi-Cola Hits the Spot." Some jingles have become popular songs; for example, "I'd Like to Teach the World to Sing" was originally a jingle for Coke. Many popular songs have been used as jingles; "Like a Rock" became an anthem for Chevrolet.

> ♫ In 1841 the first advertising agency opened in the United States. The name of the company was Volney B. Palmer, and they were located in Philadelphia (www .old-time.com/commercials/ wheaties.html).

Most popular songs are formatted to include a musical buildup to a memorable chorus (or hook). Since the average popular song is 3 minutes, the composer has time to build a compositional structure. Jingle writing does not afford composers the same luxury; a jingle must immediately grab the attention of the audience. Most successful jingles are catchy and memorable.

Soft-drink companies have traditionally used jingles as the crux of their advertising, such as Coke and Pepsi. General Electric's slogan (and singing logo) "GE, We Bring Good Things to Life" has been the heart of their advertising for decades. The elements that make a song catchy are the following:

- More conjunct (stepwise) motion than disjunctive (skips) motion in the melodic structure.
- Memorable after the first hearing.
- The average person can easily sing along.

Lyrics can create an image for a company. Advertising agencies devote a painstaking amount of time developing effective lyrics for jingles. The message must be clear and precise. It is not unusual for an agency to spend months refining lyrics and creating alternative lyrics for campaigns or "pool-outs," which are multiple commercials designed around a central idea.

Since most advertising campaigns mirror popular culture, many creatives use examples of contemporary songs to demonstrate the style of music most appropriate for their commercial(s). The agency and client are concerned about appealing to the demographic and/or psychographic psyche of their consumers and/or potential consumers. They are therefore discriminating about the style of music chosen. Not being "musically" offensive to their target audience is of great concern. Focus group testing becomes an important factor in helping to choose the final commercial and the final music. Focus-group participants are asked to comment on the various components of a potential commercial; for example, if the music is not well received, the agency will most likely revise or change the music.

The Ford Motor Company conducted research to determine the genre of music, if any, their pickup truck customers preferred. They found that they generally favored country music. This type of information, in conjunction with additional relevant knowledge, helps agencies develop profiles of their consumers. Research is essential to advertising agencies when designing campaign strategies.

Several music houses are normally hired to submit jingle demos for most national or regional commercials. After extensive focus group testing, the final music is selected. The commercial(s) is usually tested in a region and, if successful, is aired regionally and/or nationally. (This is the usual modus operandi for the selection of jingles.)

Licensing Popular Songs

Licensing popular songs for commercials has been an accepted practice for many years. Familiarity helps the audience immediately associate the product with a song. Sometimes, agency copywriters write alternative lyrics to popular melodies; other clients use songs in their original form but edit the musical format so that announcers and/or actors can read the copy over a familiar musical bed. For example, the introduction (no vocals) to the Bee Gees song "Stayin' Alive" might repeatedly loop under the copy. Some agencies license original recordings and fade the music at the end of the commercial without any editing.

High-profile artists such as Sting, Beyoncé, and Elton John have performed on commercials. When music celebrities were first used on commercials, many believed they were jeopardizing their credibility. As time passed, the exposure was so rewarding that the stigma was lifted. Artists' sales have soared after appearing in well-produced, high-profile commercials.

Celebrities know the format and visual "look" of a commercial before agreeing to participate. Artists will walk off the set or will not allow their music to be licensed if they feel their integrity is being compromised. Managers and agents are concerned with protecting their clients' images and therefore include safeguards within agency contracts.

Popular artists receive considerable fees for their participation; compensation can be in the millions of dollars. Substantial fees are also paid to license popular music, such as the music of The Beatles.

In 2002, a European group called Dirty Vegas scored considerable success with the song "Days Go By," which was heard on a campaign for the Mitsubishi Eclipse automobile. The agency spent $30 million in media buying, consequently providing great exposure for the song. The song jetted to the top of the dance charts in *Billboard* magazine and progressed to mainstream radio, selling over 1 million units.

This affirms the power of advertising. Most likely, without the commercial, the song would never have received the amount of airplay it received on commercial radio because it did not fit the style of music played on pop radio in the United States at that time. When listeners request to hear a song, as in this case, radio stations play it to accommodate their listeners. (Radio stations are interested in gaining audience share. The larger their audience, the more they can charge for advertising.)

Listeners call radio stations to request songs or to ask the titles of songs recently played. Most radio stations do not announce the titles of the songs because they want listeners to call in and ask for the information; this helps them determine which songs are popular with their listeners.

"How were the phones?" is the industry expression that means that the station wants to determine how many phone calls were received immediately after a record was played. Sometimes, if there are minimal phone calls, programmers will delete a record from their playlist; when there are numerous calls ("heavy phones"), they will consider adding a song to their regular playlist, which results in increased airplay. This depends on a song's continuous popularity, which is measured by sales. If sales do not result from continuous airplay yet the listeners keep requesting a song, the song is considered a *turntable hit*. A turntable hit does not produce monetary benefit to a record label but does bring considerable subliminal audience recognition to a commercial and generate performance royalties.

Between obtaining a synchronization license from a music publisher and obtaining the rights to use the original sound recording, clients are willing to pay fees to obtain the synchronization rights to a popular song. The terms of rights agreements vary. To illustrate, the use of a song might be limited to a category, such as soft drinks. The same song could simultaneously be used in a car commercial because it is in a noncompetitive product category. The licensing fee to exclusively license a song (instrumental) is substantially higher.

The rights might stipulate a one-year term with a specified number of uses during that term. The agreement usually contains built-in options with additional fee schedules.

Rights agreements are complex and therefore should be negotiated by an expert. Most large agencies have in-house attorneys who negotiate deals with music publishers, record companies, and individual rights holders. Private clearance companies clear (receive permission) and research song licenses. (They are compensated with a percentage of the synchronization fee.) Agreements are not standard and are therefore always negotiated.

Jingles

Many successful songwriters do not write well-crafted jingles. Writing miniature songs is a special craft that requires the ability to compress the song form. A skillful jingle writer can write a 30-second hook, meaning that both the verse and the chorus is memorable. The average duration of a television jingle is 30 seconds; most jingles are edited to 15-second versions. Some 30-second versions are called "lifts," meaning that they are edited ("lifted") from a longer version. ("Lifting" does not necessarily indicate that the track was cut and pasted. Most often, the composition and arrangement have to be rewritten to fit the time.) The average radio commercial is 60 seconds, meaning that the jingle has to also work in a shorter format, such as 30 seconds. Analogous to an underscore, a composer might write a jingle that works in a 60-second format but not work when it is edited to 30 seconds. Composers must be aware of this potential dilemma during the writing process. Agencies will expect the majority of jingles to be adaptable.

Most campaigns require that the music not only adapt to different timings but also adapt to various arranging styles. Most national prestigious advertising campaigns are played for at least a year, and the agency will most likely film a variety of commercials based around a central idea, called a "pool-out."

This suggests a need for musical variety. A jingle will most likely go through many incarnations before airing. Prior to selecting a final jingle, agencies frequently request demos arranged in three or four styles. Clients will most likely spend large sums purchasing airtime and will not risk selecting a jingle that is not adaptable.

Most successful jingles have a very strong "hook" line that becomes a musical logo for the product. (The lyric of the logo is generally used in an accompanying print campaign.) Sometimes, the melody of the jingle is played instrumentally (called a "bed"), and only the hook line is sung as a tagline or sung intermittently throughout the commercial; announcer's copy or dialogue is usually inserted between the singing. (The spaces are referred to as "donuts.") For example, the announcer says, "The _____ is the safest car on the road," and the singers sing, "Buckle up for safety." Then the announcer says, "The car has been voted the safest car on the road for the past three years," followed by the singers singing, "Buckle up for safety." This format continues throughout the commercial.

Lyrics Written by Copywriters

Agency copywriters generally write the lyrics for jingles. Frequently, this creates a problem for composers because most agency copywriters are not lyricists. Writers are usually given a "laundry list" of topics to be included in a lyric. Many copywriters literally just write a ''list'' with a minimum of lyrical cohesiveness. They try to incorporate too many ideas, not realizing that the lyric must fit a tempo and predetermined length.

The best approach for composers is to discuss the lyrical problems with a copywriter prior to writing the melody. Writers generally revise their lyrics after hearing a logical and musical explanation of why the lyrics need editing. Problems occur when clients insist that all the submitted copy points are included in one lyric. Sometimes, to fit the time restrictions, the tempo becomes so fast that it is impossible for the audience to understand the words. Plead with the creatives to make further revisions; sometimes adjectives or nouns can be removed without affecting the content of the lyric.

During a recording session, the clarity of the lyrics is paramount. If the lyrics are not understood, a rerecord is inevitable (at the expense of the music company). Hire singers who specialize in singing jingles. They understand the importance of diction, and they work quickly.

Lyrics Written by Music House Lyricists

When music companies are asked to write lyrics, it is usually by a small agency in a local market. It is rare for a large agency to request lyrics from an outside source. (The agency copywriters normally write lyrics.)

If the assignment includes writing lyrics, hire a lyricist with advertising experience. There are freelance writers who write lyrics for commercials. They understand advertising music and know how to analyze an assignment. Stay in close contact with the agency creatives while the lyrics are being written. The lyrics are the ''key to success.'' If a client does not approve the lyrics, the agency will hire another music house. Lyrics are always approved by the agency prior to recording a demo.

Because the main ingredient in most lyrics or advertising campaigns is a ''hook line,'' a lyricist must become familiar with the advertising strategy of the product and write a line that will satisfy both the agency and the client. Since the lyric is a crucial part of the strategy, it is best when the agency writer provides the hook line and a lyricist writes the lyric incorporating the hook line. Most agency writers agree to let the music company's lyricist rewrite or write the lyric and make it ''musical.'' It is rare that egos interrupt the creation of high-quality advertising.

Demos

The process of developing jingles and submitting them to agencies and their clients is the same as submitting underscore demos. As a general rule, try to submit three pieces of music:

1. Write what the creatives ask for.
2. Write what *you* want to write (assuming you have a dissimilar conception).
3. Write additional music that is in an unexpected musical direction. (Do not be afraid to take chances.)

Agencies traditionally offer low budgets to produce demos. Because of affordable recording technology, demos are no longer demos in the traditional sense; most demos sound similar to finals. If a jingle is chosen to go on the air, the jingle is usually revised so that it will fit a film or be adjusted to accommodate new dialogue or announcer's copy. In addition, musicians and/or singers may be added to enhance the track.

Approaching a Jingle

Writing a jingle is not unlike writing an underscore. The creatives generally give the jingle writer a storyboard. The storyboard contains a scene-by-scene pictorial of the commercial with the lyrics written under each cell. The storyboard is laid out exactly the same as a storyboard used for underscoring; it contains camera directions, detailed drawings of each frame of picture, lyrics, and dialogue. The following is a list of ideas that might help a composer write a jingle.

Clarity. As previously mentioned, the main objective is that the lyrics must clearly deliver a client's message. This also applies to the production of the recording and the musical performances. An acceptable recording is difficult to achieve if the composition is not well written. A composer should be aware that certain words "sing better" when the proper number of syllables and the appropriate rhythmic values are assigned to each word. For example, if a word has more than one syllable, assign a note to each syllable. If the word is *concentrate*, it is better to have three eighth notes than three sixteenth notes or only two notes; when sung, the word will be easier to understand.

Notate rhythmic values. Assign rhythmic values to each word before writing the actual pitches. This will aid in making the lyric sound conversational. It will also help in emphasizing the proper words. The composer should mark Xs on the score paper with rhythmic values (eighth notes, sixteenth notes, and so on) and indicate whether the note should rise or fall. Write the lyric under each rhythmic value and then write the melody using each rhythmic value as a guide. This will help make the delivery of the jingle more conversational.

The product name is the most important word in the lyric. A client's goal is to sell one's products. The note or notes assigned to the product name must emphasize the name of the product so that the audience remembers the product.

Most jingles have a melodic logo that is repeated several times throughout the jingle; this is called a "hook." If the audience cannot remember the hook, the jingle will probably not impact the audience. A composer must be certain that the musical focal point of a jingle is the product name. If a lyric writer does not repeat the name of the product often enough to help create an image, suggest that the name be added more often. Sometimes the best solution is to revise the jingle and seek approval from the creatives. Several problems can occur when writing jingles:

- The commercial may be too long if a portion of the original lyric is not deleted.
- It may not be acceptable to delete certain sections of the lyric. The client might insist that particular ideas remain in the lyric. Experimentation aids in reaching acceptable solutions.

Melodic simplicity. A memorable jingle is usually simple and "catchy." Since commercials are short, try to make the entire jingle a hook. The goal should be that the audience remembers the entire jingle. (Sometimes this is not possible because of the structure of the lyric.)

The song should not have a wide range, unless there is musical justification. Keep the notes within singing range of the average person so they can sing along. Most of the time, the use of conjunctive motion makes a melody more memorable.

There are exceptions to this general rule. The creatives might ask for a jazz jingle or operatic aria. This indicates that they are expecting a well-written piece of music, and the music does not necessarily have to be memorable in the traditional sense. When an agency is expecting to hear a catchy jingle, they will usually tell the composer. If the assignment is to write a traditional jingle, make it catchy; otherwise, just *make it good.*

Donuts. Most jingles have "donuts" (music without lyrics), primarily in the middle of the jingle. This space, or donut, is typically used for the actors or announcer to deliver a message. During the donut, play the vocal melody instrumentally so that the audience hears the main theme music during the dialogue. The strategy is to aid the audience in remembering the melody and lyric, which in turn helps them recall the product name.

Harmony. Most jingles are harmonically simple. This does not mean that the song has to sound trite or redundant. Many of the most popular songs have simple chord structures. If the melody is interesting and memorable, the song will most likely make an impression with the audience.

Arrangement and orchestration. Since the style of music will be predetermined, the arrangement and orchestration should sound authentic. Hire an arranger who is familiar with the style. If the genre is rock and roll, use a rock-and-roll rhythm section and not a full orchestra playing nontraditional parts. The arrangement should be interesting and creative. Since most advertising jingles mirror contemporary songs, listen to and analyze the structure and arrangements of songs closest to the style of music the creatives want.

Jingle writers are traditionally not arrangers. They generally specialize in jingle writing, which is highly competitive and lucrative. Jingle writers work closely with arrangers, just as film composers often work closely with orchestrators.

Check the key with the singer(s) before writing an arrangement. The wrong key can create serious problems at a recording session. If the key is out of the vocalists' ranges or they have to strain their vocal chords, the jingle will fail.

The key also affects the harmonic structure of an arrangement. For example, if the key is changed after the arrangement has been completed, the woodwind or string orchestration might require inversions because the harmonies might be too high or too low for the instruments in the original orchestration.

To avoid this problem, before writing an arrangement, make certain that the agency has approved the choice of the lead singer; audition the lead singer (either in person or on the telephone), and choose the most comfortable key. If the track requires improvisation, do not make the key too high or too low because the singer will have limited room to improvise.

All singers have a break in their voices. It usually occurs between their chest or middle vocal range and their head voice (their high range). If the key is not correct, the melody could lie where the voice breaks. This problem must be avoided. Most singers with technical training will not have a noticeable break in their voices. Ask the singers if the key affects this potential problem.

If the jingle requires a solo singer, submit several demo tapes. The creatives will generally select the voice they feel is appropriate for the commercial. Most creatives are particular about the choice of singer(s); this becomes personal preference. Three qualified singers might be submitted for the job, but only one may appeal to the creatives and to the client.

In rare instances, an agency will request that more than one lead singer record the final music track. This usually occurs for several reasons:

- The creatives want to choose the finalist after hearing several complete vocals.
- They might want to broadcast the commercial with two or more lead singers; this creates variety.
- The creatives might want a female lead and also a male lead. (If this occurs, the arrangement will almost certainly have to be copied in two different keys. Be aware of the potential orchestral inversion problems previously discussed.)
- The creatives might want to experiment by recording a duet—two

females, two males, or one of each. Reminder: Make certain that the keys are correct for each version.

Male or female lead singer. Ask the creatives if they prefer a male or a female lead singer or possibly a duet with alternating lines and harmonies. A vocal arrangement (e.g., close harmonies, open harmonies, solo voices, and so on) can determine the success of a jingle. Often the lyric dictates the form.

If the objective is that the singer(s) sounds "full," double the vocal(s); if the objective is to create intimacy, do not double the vocal(s) and ask the singer(s) to stand close to the microphone. (Standing too close to the microphone can cause distortion or digital error.) Most experienced studio singers have developed proficient microphone techniques and a sense of how to achieve the objectives of music producers. The singers generally make suggestions on how to achieve the musical goals.

Background singers. The decision to hire background singers is both creative and financial. Most jingles require backgrounds to expand the parts and create variety within the vocal arrangement. Jingles are generally structured with the verse sung by a solo voice and the background singers entering during the chorus, usually emphasizing the name of the product. When hiring background singers, there are several crucial factors to consider:

- They must have perfect intonation.
- Their voices should be similar in character so that they blend.
- They must have the ability to sing in the style of music being recorded.
- Phrasing is of utmost importance. (They have to sing as an ensemble, not as soloists.)
- With a large group of singers, always double the melody before doubling other parts. This will balance the blend.
- Make certain that they sing at relatively the same volume or the backgrounds will not sound balanced on the recording.
- If arranging for a large chorus, try to assign an equal number of singers to each part to create the proper balance within the chorus. Assigning more singers to the lead part will make the melody louder, which is sometimes desirable.

The number of singers has to be cleared by the agency and client before the recording session. The cost in both session fees and residual payments is calculated on the basis of the media buy. If the music track is a jingle, this is not normally a problem. If the singers are used primarily as a section of the band and they are not featured, this might cause a predicament. Some clients have policies concerning the use of singers. One of the leading advertisers does not allow voices on underscorings. In their opinion, the cost of residuals makes it prohibitive.

Overdubbing. Most background vocals are doubled or tripled during recording sessions. Lead singers are often doubled or tripled. Overdubbing creates a full sound, which is more effective in certain musical styles than others.

Overdubbing becomes a creative choice that is determined by the composer, arranger, and/or music producer. Additional fees are paid for overdubbing. The agency must approve the expense, in writing, prior to the session.

In states that do not require musicians and singers to belong to unions, the performers are generally paid one fee, which is called a *buyout*. The agency has the right to use of the jingle in perpetuity.

> ♫ I once hired three singers for an underscoring. The producer failed to inform me that it was the policy of the advertiser not to use singers on an underscoring. After the track was completed, I had to remix the track and eliminate the singers. The missing vocal parts were transcribed for synthesizers.

Hiring musicians. The choice of musicians is vital to the success of commercials. As previously mentioned, authenticity is the key to success. Always try to capture the authentic musical style of a jingle. For instance, if a jazz guitarist is hired to play on a rock-and-roll jingle, the part will most likely not sound authentic. It would be advantageous to hire a contractor to engage the most qualified musicians—particularly if the style of music or the instrumentation is unusual.

The following are the most common compositional mistakes and should be avoided in jingle writing (refer also to chapter 5).

When writing for television, start the music approximately seven frames into the film and finish the music half a second before the film ends (30 video frames per second in the United States). It takes time for a video to "roll in" and attain the proper speed; at the end, time is needed to transition out of the film smoothly. If the music continues to the very end, the transition to the next event would be too abrupt.

Not all music starts at the beginning of a commercial and stops at the end. For instance, the music might begin 10 seconds into the commercial and end at 25 seconds.

Do not compose a jingle that is too long to accommodate a shorter version of

> ♫ Because of new digital technology, it might not be necessary to follow this standard. The music can begin on the first frame of picture and end on the last frame of picture if a station uses digital technology; there is no need for a "roll-in" or stopping the music half a second before the film ends. Not all stations, both in and/or out of the United States, use the most current technology.

the same commercial. The most frequent assignment is to write a 30-second jingle that can be shortened to 15 seconds. Depending on the musical needs of the film, one suggestion is to write short thematic fragments that are easily adaptable and lend themselves to modulation, helping to keep the composition interesting. Another suggestion is to write a theme that is no longer than 12 seconds, leaving space for an introduction and ending in the 15-second version and room for expansion in the longer version. (This proposal is based on the assumption that the tempos of the various versions are the same.)

Before writing, experiment with a variety of tempos; each commercial included in a campaign might require a diversity of arrangements and tempos. This helps determine the flexibility of the theme. Not all jingles adapt well.

It is often difficult to write an extended jingle that works in its original format as well as in all variations. In this situation, try to compose the jingle so that the first or second part of the jingle can be used as independent themes. This is a common problem when compressing the music from a 30-second version to fit a 10-second version. The theme might work well in 30- and 15-second versions, but there is not enough time to fit the entire piece in 9 seconds. A solution might be to select a section of the original theme. The audience will still identify with the original theme because they will recognize the phrase that has been "lifted."

Most agencies accept this practice because they realize that the original composition has to be edited to solve the timing issues. Since most of the airplay will probably be the 30-second and 15-second versions, they are willing to make this compromise.

Some jingles, although well constructed, do not adequately adapt to various musical styles and tempos. Although a theme might fit other styles and tempos, the composition sounds best in its original form. If thematic variations are needed, experiment before the original composition is presented to the agency.

> ♩♩ Film composer Danny Elfman writes short, identifiable themes so that a four- or five-note excerpt heard within a cue will immediately create an identity for the audience (e.g., *Spider-Man 2*).

Once a jingle has been approved, the integrity of the composition must remain. A problem can result if the composition is not adaptable to different arrangements. It will be noticeable that the theme is missing or incomplete. If the theme has to be compressed for additional versions, inform the creatives before writing.

After approving the theme and discussing the various versions, the agency might add another version. If the theme will not fit in its entirety, present the best solution and explain the problem to the creatives. There is usually an acceptable solution.

The composition might contain odd time signatures, which could

make the rhythm or melody feel unnatural. This normally occurs if the composer wants to start a new musical statement over a specific part of the film. For example, if a scene changes from pictures of mountains to the inside of a department store, the composer will most likely want the singers to start a new section over the scene change rather than continue the previous melodic line. The measure prior to the scene change might require an odd time signature so that the overall timing is correct. (Solutions to these problems are discussed in chapter 5.)

Listen closely to the frequency range of the dialogue or announcer. A common error is to write in the same frequency range as the actors or announcer. This applies to all instrumental sections of a jingle. If this occurs, the composition will often sound busy and cluttered. One solution is to choose a key and tessitura that will not conflict with the voices. Think of the dialogue as part of the orchestration. This also has to be addressed when writing a repetitive theme. Sometimes, sparse writing is an effective solution—*there are no rules*. Whatever works—use.

Production Tips

Always separate the elements of the recorded track. The separate elements are referred to as *stems*. In addition to a full mix, mix each of the following stems separately:

- Instrumental-only track
- Lead vocal–only track
- Background vocals–only track

It is sometimes advisable to further divide the stems: solo instruments, bass and drum, and so on. Try to anticipate potential mix problems and act accordingly.

Agencies often request remixes. Working with stems enables music companies to work quickly and not lose the ambience of the original mix because the signal processing is recorded on the stems. For instance, if the agency wants the lead singer to re-sing the lead vocal, overdub the lead singer over the premixed instrumental track. The most common reasons for a remix are the following.

Lyric clarity. If the lyrics are not easily understood, a re-sing will always be required. Diction is of paramount concern when recording vocals for a commercial.

Creative reasons. The lyrics are changed for creative reasons. The client will generally request a copy and possibly lyric changes up until the copies of the commercial(s) are shipped to the stations.

Legal changes. The lyrics might have to be changed for legal reasons. Agency attorneys check the legality of lyrics and copy. To protect the public, the Federal Trade Commission has devised specific rules known as "truth in advertising." It is illegal to make false statements or promises in advertisements.

The Federal Trade Commission

The FTC states the following:

- Advertising must be truthful and nondeceptive.
- Advertisers must have evidence to back up their claims.
- Advertisements cannot be unfair.

Additional laws apply to ads for specialized products such as consumer leases, credit, 900 telephone numbers, and products sold through mail order or telephone sales. And every state has consumer protection laws that govern ads running in that state.

Pointers

Hire recording engineers who specialize in recording commercials. They work quickly and save the music company expenses in both their hourly fees and their studio time. Mixing commercials is a specialty, and record engineers have not necessarily mastered the techniques of mixing commercials:

- Vocals have to be absolutely clear and equalized specifically for broadcasting.
- The tracks are, most often, compressed so that they are present at low listening levels.
- Always mix on small speakers and at a low listening level. The objective is to try to replicate the sound of an average home television and/or radio.
- If time permits, play the mix on a car sound system and on an average home system. The mix must be clear and present when heard on multiple sound systems—if not, *remix*.

Recording engineers have the luxury of time—not so with commercials. There are almost always deadlines because of time buys on stations and new media; the commercial(s) have to be sent to the stations by a specified date. Keep in mind that *music is generally the last creative element added to a commercial before the final mix.*

Hire professional, flexible, and cooperative singers. Because clarity and expression are important, it is common for the agency creatives and/ or the music producer to record multiple vocal takes. They might request minor changes or request that the parts be rearranged. For instance, a creative might say, "I can't hear the 't' on the word it," or, "The background vocals are masking certain lyrics." Jingle singers anticipate comments of this nature and are diplomatic when communicating with music producers and agency creatives. Hire background singers whose voices blend. Lead singers are not necessarily skilled background singers and vice versa. If needed, ask the singers for recommendations.

Hire musicians who are experienced in recording jingles. They are generally accustomed to the pressure of working quickly and accurately. Some studio players who play only on records are not as fast. The longer it takes to record, the more the session costs. The overage is generally deducted from the music company's budget.

Find out the technical format required by the agency to be used for the final "playback" of music onto the film/tape. DAT (digital audiotape) used to be the preferred format but has been replaced by burning data, such as AIFF or wave files, on a CD or DVD. Many files are sent via the Internet.

The following is my interview with Dr. Patricia Fleitas, director of choral studies at Florida Atlantic University in Boca Raton, Florida:

MZ: How does a nonsinger learn to coach a singer?

Patricia: From a stylistic standpoint and a musical standpoint, [it is advantageous] if the singer has technical knowledge. If the person knows what they are doing with their voice, then the musician who is a nonsinger can still coach in the musical aspect of the production. For example, a jazz specialist doesn't have to be a vocalist to teach and coach a jazz-style production, the same way that in classical music the vocal coach, most of the time, is a nonsinger.

MZ: How do you approach singers who are not technically trained?

Patricia: There is a lot of natural talent. [The singer should be] accurate for the style, sing in tune, and the production of the voice [should be] nonoffensive. A lot of the times when singers have intonation problems, the issue is technical. You have to understand the instrument to negotiate the music . . . to accommodate the score.

MZ: How do you help a singer improve their intonation?

Patricia: The first thing to look for is what they are doing physically. Look at breath support . . . on how they are inhaling the breath and how they are supporting the voice. The next thing is how the mechanics [of voice] are working. A depressed larynx can be one reason for intonation problems, misplacement of a vowel, an overmodification of a vowel sound, a lack of articulation. Breath is at the center of all of this.

MZ: Can you help a singer who cannot hear that their intonation is not accurate?

Patricia: That is a problem with musicianship. I think we are limited in how much we can help. If [the singer] is young, we can expose them to listening, and that will help. I heard that you can increase the musical IQ of a child up until grade 4, and the best way to do so is through a cappella singing.

MZ: Can singers be taught to blend?

Patricia: Absolutely. The way to blend sounds is to line up the vowel placements, the vowel shapes, and the articulation of the consonants. In any kind of ensemble the performers have to listen to each other. I think of the voice in terms of colors, and I feel that the amount of colors in each individual voice is a very big palette . . . by the time we put each individual's pallet of colors in an ensemble, we have a canvas of colorful sound that is infinite.

MZ: How do you work around the break point in a singer's voice—going from a chest voice to a head voice?

Patricia: That is done in the training studio, not in the coaching. You even out the registration, meaning you even out the voice from the top down without any breaks. I classify a voice not necessarily by the range but by where the voice sounds the prettiest.

MZ: Do you feel that all popular singers should have technical training?

Patricia: I do, because what I think technical training provides is health . . . too many singers go for style [before they have technique].

MZ: Many popular singers feel it would be a detriment to study voice because it would change or maybe ruin their style. Do you agree?

Patricia: No, but I can understand why they feel that way. When you hear someone like Pavarotti or Plácido Domingo singing something in the popular genre, it sounds very operatic. [She added that style does not have to change by learning to sing correctly and learning not to damage the voice.]

Vocal Ranges

The five main categories for singers are soprano, alto, tenor, baritone, and bass. Most commercial female singers have ranges between soprano and alto, and most male singers have ranges between the tenor and baritone ranges.

If the tessitura (the predominant pitch range) of a piece is too high or low, ask the singer(s) if he or she can sing comfortably within the written range. Most singers have difficulty singing in the top of their range for long periods of time. The best vocal range is where the vocalist feels most comfortable. (It is often wise to experiment with several keys.)

Conclusion

Singing and writing jingles is lucrative. The fees are higher than underscores, as are the residual payments. Jingle singing and writing is a highly competitive and profitable business. Successful jingle writers usually devote their careers to only writing jingles. It is an unusual skill and takes a long time to master.

The following is my interview with Marshall Grantham, creative director and composer for Russo/Grantham Productions, a commercial music house in New York City:

MZ: What is the difference between composing for radio and composing for television [commercials]?

Marshall: Jingles for television and radio are similar because the song is the same. Radio is much more about creating the right mood to sit under the voice. I find radio easier because you can be more musical; there are less hit points to worry about. It's more a matter of hitting the target of the mood that they're shooting for.

MZ: How often are you asked to write the lyric for a jingle?

Marshall: Twenty percent of the time we are asked to write the lyrics, and 30 percent of the time we are asked to smooth out the lyrics. A good copywriter overwrites and asks you to edit it and run it by me. [Marshall said it is wise to ask the copywriters which "lyrics are in stone." What are the salient points? For example, how often should the product be mentioned in the lyric? Ask specific questions.]

MZ: Do you have a procedure for writing a jingle?

Marshall: I'm a writer in my head. I already have the melody, the chorus, the verse before I even sit down at the keyboard.

MZ: When writing an underscore, where are potential problems with picture changes occurring on odd beats?

Marshall: I try not to give too many strange measures. [He tries to keep the meter the same and work around the hits that occur on odd beats. For example, he will sometimes have each new melodic section begin on the second beat rather than change the meter so that it occurs on the first beat.]

MZ: Before you record a demo, do you play the composition for the creative people?

Marshall: No. We go along the lines that they are not going to picture the stuff very well. We'd rather explore three or four ideas and produce them. More often than not, when we play them something in its infancy, they can't picture it.

MZ: What percentages of your recording sessions have live musicians?

Marshall: Not many—maybe 10 percent. Almost everything is programmed—we will still use live brass almost all the time—for finals, we try to bring in six or eight string players. [He said they combine the live strings with the synthesized strings to produce a more realistic sound.]

MZ: How many acoustic orchestras do you record in a year?

Marshall: None. I just did a spot where we had 14 live players—several years ago we had 40—it hardly happens anymore. [Referring to budgets, Marshall said they usually tell the agency if they want X number of live musicians or singers, the budget will be X, and if they want live players mixed with synthesizers, the budget will be Y.]

MZ: What is your advice to young jingle writers?

Marshall: You are going to need good production values and a good setup [referring to a synthesizer setup]. I don't think it's a world anymore where you are going to give a rough idea of a jingle—there are no demos anymore [meaning the demos have to sound like final productions]. You are going to need to be a good engineer, producer, and songwriter yourself—you might need to work without pay, at first—you are going to need every bit of the demo money, if you are paid, and you will want to pump it all into the demos.

MZ: What percentage of the time does the agency's demo budget cover your production costs?

Marshall: We technically lose money on every one (demos) just because we use our facilities [meaning studios]—I would say we lose money on every demo. We go for the win to make up for the loss. [Meaning there is almost always a competition to get the final job.]

Marshall: [In response to a question about underscoring.] Underscoring is having a knowledge of flow of picture, editing, and how to marry that sound to that picture. [He suggests that young composers tape commercials from television and score them for practice. Some composers offer to score demos without payment.] You never know, they might get lucky. . . . I think that anyone getting into commercial music who can't produce and program is definitely not going to make it. It's a programming world at this point . . . maybe one in a hundred [composers who apply to his company] can compose, program, engineer, and produce. . . . I think the most important thing is to be well rounded in things you are going to need to make a living. Study the crafts of composing and arranging. I find a lot of composers are weak in arranging.

The following is my interview with two-time Grammy Award–winning singer Cissy Houston (the former leader of the Sweet Inspirations—one of the most successful background singing groups in recorded music history—who sang backgrounds on more than 500 hit records):

MZ: What is the difference between singing on a commercial and singing on a record?

Cissy: With commercials you have to be quick because time is money . . . they want people who are quick and give them the kind of expression that they need.

MZ: Does the fact that the lyric has to be exceptionally clear when singing a commercial affect your singing style?

Cissy: I don't know that it affects your singing style because I'm fussy about my diction anyway. It just makes you kind of nervous sometimes when you have to do that kind of thing in 30 seconds or 60 seconds—you've got to get that message across the way they want you to do it. Sometimes they go over something over and over again, and sometimes they come right back to the first one, which is the best one.

MZ: On average, how many takes do you record when singing on a commercial?

Cissy: Maybe eight to 10. [Cissy said that sometimes the producer combines the best lines from each take to compile the final vocal.]

MZ: Since you have been so successful as a background singer, what is it you look for when hiring background singers to sing with you?

Cissy: I look for somebody who is quick and who is paying attention and who is on time . . . you have to have a good blend . . . people who are serious about their work . . . some people come in and want to play games—that really annoys me.

MZ: Some lead singers are not good background singers and vice versa. Since you have worn both hats, can you tell me the differences?

Cissy: It's really hard to be a great background singer. When it comes to backgrounds, you have to blend with other people and listen to other people singing—most people don't—they listen to themselves or just don't have that blend.

MZ: How does a young singer break into studio work?

Cissy: I would suggest that they learn to read [music] . . . you still have to have a good sound and soul in your voice. [She said that reading helps a singer to record faster. Since commercials always have specific budgets, all professional musicians and singers have to work quickly, or they will not be hired.]

MZ: How important is it to be versatile both as a lead singer and as a background singer when doing commercials?

Cissy: I guess that is why I was so successful, because I think it is very important to be versatile. You have to be able to give different sounds . . . you might need to do a white sound or an operatic sound or whatever it takes—you might need to do a blues—you know what I mean?

MZ: When you are hiring background singers, do you generally give each singer their part, or do you just sing the lead and have them come up with their own parts?

Cissy: I always come up with the backgrounds, unless they [the arranger] have certain backgrounds that they want. With the Sweet Inspirations, we would just break into harmony—we really knew what we were doing. [She said that singers with that ability are hard to find.]

MZ: How does a singer trying to break in get a demo reel together?

Cissy: Sing songs and show people what type of voice they have . . . do a versatile tape where they can do different things. I would suggest that would be the only way that I see that you can do it. Commercials are very hard to break into and it's a tight-knit situation . . . they're very, very guarded.

MZ: Do you think that most young singers should have a vocal coach so they learn to sing properly?

Cissy: I really do . . . [some] they scream and that's not singing . . . I work on feelings, and that's what I like to give.

MZ: Is there any advice you would like to offer young singers?

Cissy: Just go to school and learn—that's the easy way—but don't lose your feeling.

Assignments

1. Write a 30-second lyric for a ficticious product. Write a memorable melody that includes a "hook line" and/or chorus. Select the correct key both for the lead singer and the background singers.
2. Arrange the 30-second jingle (from #1) in two or more musical styles and tempos. Also write 15-second versions.

8

Composing Music for Radio Commercials

Radio Commercials versus Television Commercials

Radio commercials generally have copy and music throughout the commercials. The music often has to create virtual images for the listeners.

Some television commercials do not have dialogue or a voice-over. When a music underscore is added, the pictures will most likely require hits, which create impact. The pictures and the music are woven into the fabric of the emotional content of the commercial. If the same basic commercial is adapted for radio, the underscore might not require the same number of hits. Television and radio commercials can have essentially the same concept but require different music. Do not assume that the same music will create similar impact for both mediums. Composing for radio commercials is analogous to composing for television commercials, except for some composers it is more challenging and for others less restrictive.

Watching films helps composers create musical images. With radio commercials, listening to actors and/or announcers requires composers to use their imaginations to produce musical imagery. Composers are afforded more freedom in radio because the musical hits are not generally as precise as television hits. In some instances, this affords composers the opportunity to write a more cohesive piece of music because of the lack of restrictions (e.g., composing to picture).

If the final dialogue or announcer's copy has not been prerecorded, ask the

> ♫ Writers must be accurate with the timings of their readings. For instance, if the commercial is 60 seconds, it is common for writers to write copy that cannot be read in less than 62 seconds. This creates problems for composers. The writer has to shorten the dialogue before the composer can write.

copywriter to record a pilot track. Listening to the dialogue or announcer's copy makes the composing process easier. At times, it is difficult to understand the intention of a writer by only reading the script; hearing the dialogue clarifies the true meaning of the copy.

If the agency does not provide a pilot track, ask the writer questions. Make certain that the writer's intentions are absolutely clear. Several people reading the same script may interpret it in dissimilar ways.

Sometimes agencies want the radio music completed before recording the dialogue. The producer may play the music for the actors and/or announcer while they are recording. The music helps to establish the proper mood.

Frequently, a radio commercial contains the same basic music as a television version. The difference is usually in the duration. The average radio commercial is 60 seconds, and the average television commercial is 30 seconds; therefore, the composition must be expanded from the radio version.

In some instances, the television music does not adapt for the radio version because the pictures enhance the effectiveness of the music. Writing new music can be difficult because the composer has to reconceptualize a commercial that has basically the same message as the television version. The best advice is *not* to listen to the television music and approach the radio version as a new commercial.

Approach

If the commercials are recorded only for radio, initiate the same procedure and analysis used for television commercials—ask the same questions. The objective is to discover the most appropriate musical style and obtain the approval of the creatives. Discuss everything in detail before composing and arranging.

Procedure

Understand the script. The music will not work if the composer lacks a thorough understanding of the script and the emotional impact required of the music. Ask the creatives to play an example of a musical style that would be appropriate. If they do not have an example, assemble some samples that seem suitable. Play them for the creatives and decide on an acceptable musical style and direction.

Time each section. Break the script down by timing each section. Determine where the music should change and mark the script with detailed notes.

Lay out the score exactly the same as a television commercial. Decide on a tempo(s) and write down on the score paper or in a computer music-sequencing program where musical changes should occur (e.g., new thematic material, hits, tempo changes, and so on). Try to visualize pictures. ''Draw'' the pictures musically.

Determine the hits by the connotation of the words. The music might be more important to the final success of radio commercials than it is to television commercials because of one less element—pictures. Write music that will create visual images in the listener's mind.

Determine the tempo(s) and meter(s) of each measure before writing. Without this preparation, it is difficult to lay out the score inasmuch as the dialogue will not match the measure numbers. When reading the script to a metronome click, composers can determine if there will be any odd meters within the piece. The score could possibly have a 4/4, 3/4, and a 2/4 measure consecutively and continue with an array of beats per measure. The goal is to write a piece of music that does not sound disruptive.

Radio Budgets

Radio music budgets are generally less than television budgets, which affects number of musicians and vocalists that can be hired. Problems can result. Most radio commercials are expanded versions of television commercials, but the radio budgets might not allow the music house to hire the same number of singers and musicians used in the television spots. Discuss this with the creatives before submitting a budget. The agency may request the same production budget for the radio music so that the music will sound the same. If the budget is not approved, explain to the creatives that the track will not sound the same and what the differences will be. Do not "surprise" them at the session. When collaborating with nonmusicians, it is important to be transparent when explaining music. They might claim they understand your intentions, but at the recording session the first question that is frequently asked is, "Why doesn't it sound the same as the television music?"

> ♩♩ Arrangers can combine synthesizers with live musicians to help make the track sound similar to the television version. Although this technique will certainly help, nothing replaces the sound of live performers. Synthesizers cannot replicate the individuality and feel of live musicians.

Analysis

The following is a radio commercial written by a copywriter and submitted to a composer as a worksheet.

Council on Family Health's "Read the Label" Campaign
60-Second "Corner"

SFX: Mystery detective music

Announcer (echo as in an alleyway): Psst . . . listen over here. Gotta tell you something . . . when it comes to taking medicine, what you don't know CAN hurt you. Be a know-it-all. Read the medicine label. Hey, it's your body. So, you'd better make it your business to find out everything about everything that goes inside it. The when to—the why to—the don't do—and especially—the never do. Because, sometimes a medicine that works for one person isn't going to work for another. Or, sometimes, certain foods, beverages, or other medicines you take might interfere with how safely and effectively the medicine you take works. Or, you might even have forgotten the right dosage or what hour you're supposed to take it. Or . . . you get the point. So, when it comes to getting better safely and effectively, with no unpleasant surprises inside your body—be a know-it-all and read the label. This message brought to you by the Council on Family Health and the FDA.

To help the writing process, the composer must dissect the commercial into timings and indicate the overall feel of the music. The goal for the following commercial was to make the music light and almost "cartoon-like." Try to internalize a basic musical mood when reading the dialogue.

Use the following commercial as a practice exercise, prerecording the dialogue and using the suggested timings as a guide.

SFX: Mystery Detective Music

Announcer (echo as in an alleyway): (Approximate timings per section)
Psst . . . listen over here. Gotta tell you something . . . [4 seconds]
When it comes to taking medicine, what you don't know CAN hurt you. [5 seconds]
Be a know-it-all. Read the medicine label. [2.5 seconds]
Hey, it's your body. So, you'd better make it your business to find out everything about everything that goes inside it. [6 seconds]
The when to—the why to—[2 seconds]
The don't do—[1.5 seconds]
And especially—the never do. [2.5 seconds]
Because sometimes a medicine that works for one person isn't going to work for another. [5 seconds]
Or, sometimes, certain foods, beverages, or other medicines you take might interfere with how safely and effectively the medicine you take works. [9 seconds]
Or, you might even have forgotten the right dosage or what hour you're supposed to take it. [6 seconds]
Or . . . you get the point. [2 seconds]
So, when it comes to getting better safely and effectively, with no unpleasant surprises inside your body—[6 seconds]
Be a know-it-all and read the label. [3 seconds]
This message brought to you by the Council on Family Health and the FDA [5 seconds]
Total of 59.5 seconds

Radio Jingles

Radio jingles are usually 1 minute in length and generally mirror the television versions of the same campaign (assuming there is a television version). Radio campaigns normally require several arrangements of the basic jingle. As mentioned in chapter 7, make certain that the jingle is adaptable.

Music houses, mostly located in the smaller markets, record generic radio and television jingles in almost every musical style. They license the same jingle to different markets for a specified period of time. The music house includes the name of the product in each new lyric. Of course, you might hear the same jingle in multiple markets, but it is not usually a concern to local advertisers. Their customers will most likely never hear the other versions.

The same process is used to license local news themes and station IDs to various markets. Most station IDs (and many generic commercials) are recorded in Dallas because Texas is a right-to-work state, and it is not mandatory for musicians and singers to be union members. The performers do not necessarily receive the equivalent of union scale, pension and health benefits, or residual payments.

Conclusion

Writing music for radio has to be approached as a distinctive craft. Compose the music so that the audience can visualize the commercial. Play the music without hearing the dialogue and determine if the meaning of the commercial is still conveyed.

If the music is written to "go against the picture" (e.g., writing happy music when sad music seems more appropriate), the dialogue must be heard to understand the meaning of the music. This compositional method is used more often in television than in radio.

Assignment

Analyze the following commercial and compose several different pieces. Record the script on a recorder or in a sequencing program and use it as a reference when composing. The reading should not exceed 30 seconds.

Council on Family Health's "Read the Label" Campaign

"Come to Me"

Hey, it's your body. So, you'd better make it your business to find out about everything that goes inside it.

When people want to know about the medicine they're taking, they come to me for the answers.

Who am I?

I tell you when you should take it, if you should take it, how often you should take it, what you should take it with, what you shouldn't take with it.

Who am I?

The label.

Be a know-it-all.

Read the label.

This message brought to you by the Council on Family Health and the FDA.

9

Corporate Videos and Infomercials

Long-Form Commercials

More often than not, the music in corporate videos sounds like library music (stock music) and, therefore, is ordinarily less effective than original music. Scored music greatly enhances the overall impact of the videos. The same concept applies to motion pictures, television programs, or television and radio commercials.

As a producer/director, I cannot allow cost to motivate whether I use original music or not. For me, it is better, and oftentimes more cost effective, to use a talented composer of synthesized music than wasting time and money searching for and securing the rights to stock music.

For me, persuading a group of bankers, insurance brokers, or doctors, through the use of corporate video, is no different than a feature film director's need to stimulate an audience in the local Cineplex. My job is to motivate the viewer to accept and use the product I've been asked by my client to sell; no different, in concept, than a feature film director [who] is asked by his or her producers to "sell" the story that gives credence to that feature film. Original music helps do that.

—Dennis Powers, president, Dennis Powers Productions

Corporate Videos

Corporate video is an inclusive term for many genres of videos made for businesses. Included are training videos, product videos, and informational videos. Some businesses, such as pharmaceutical companies, introduce new products by producing informational corporate videos that are released to the press as well as to their employees. Some are detailed and technical. For example, the press will want to know the medical terminology used to describe a new drug. A newspaper columnist or a television reporter has to gather enough information to inform the public.

Some salespeople travel with laptop computers and a CD-ROM of a corporate video and use it as a sales tool for prospective clients. Corporate videos are played in department stores to give an in-depth perspective of a product to potential consumers. It is common to see an exercise video looping (repeating) on a television screen while a nearby salesperson is giving a live demonstration and taking orders. Almost every genre of business uses corporate videos to promote and inform its employees and customers, including cruise ship companies, travel agencies, and industrial show production companies.

Directors

Some film production companies specialize in producing corporate videos. Composers generally interact with either producers or directors. The videos vary in duration. (I have composed music for 60-minute corporate videos and 10-minute corporate videos.)

Unlike commercials, composers are usually hired after the film or video has been shot. Scoring corporate videos is similar to scoring television programs, except that something is being "sold." Dramatic and informational segments may be incorporated within the production. There is no standardized format. Executives from marketing departments of corporate clients meet with producers and directors and express corporate goals and messages. The writers must incorporate their directives in the scripts. The scripts are revised until the clients give final approval and "greenlights" the production. (Many corporate directors and producers are also writers.)

Spotting Session

The video is shown to the composer, after which the director and/or producer "spot" the film with the composer. A spotting session is a discussion of the overall concept of the music, which scenes should be scored, and which events ought to be "hit." The decisions made at spotting sessions are crucial to the success of a film because an inappropriate style of music can send the wrong message to the viewers and hinder the effectiveness of the film.

The composer creates a cue sheet, which is a map of each cue. The action and the timing of each event is notated either in a sequencing program or written. Music editors supply cue sheets for film composers who are working on films with substantial budgets.

Composers are usually asked to send a demonstration reel (of their music) that contains examples of music that is similar in style to the music required for the video. The production company normally plays the most suitable reels for their clients and subsequently receives approval to hire a composer. Clients always approve the music because music can shape the overall effect of the video. Composers must write music that will appeal to a client's target audience. If a video is targeted for a specific demographic, the music must appeal to that audience. It is the same musical approach used when scoring commercials.

Musical Approach

Since most corporate videos are long form, composers have to conceive of a score that is more comparable to a television or film score than to a commercial. Composers may write a theme and variations or approach each cue as an individual piece, using a compositional device to "sew" the score together so that it sounds unified. The musical approach is always discussed with the producer and/or director. Agree on which events must be hit and whether the hit(s) should be subtle or direct.

Some videos are produced in segments, with each segment introduced by a separation banner, such as "THE OFFICE," "THE FACTORY," and so on. The composer might suggest that each segment title be on the screen for the identical number of seconds, and an identifiable musical logo can be played each time a title card appears. This helps to create unity within the score.

There are instances where music is not appropriate. I scored a video promoting a pharmaceutical product that could benefit paraplegics. In certain segments, the director did not want to include music because the scenes were more dramatic without music.

Some corporate videos have elaborate openings that require music that is closer to the style of music for commercials than cinematic music. Some contain animated corporate logos that instantly create an image for a company. Sometimes, a reprise of the opening video segment is used in the closing segment and should be scored with a similar arrangement.

Budget

Because most corporate videos have low budgets, the majority of the scores are synthesized. For example, if a company is producing an elaborate video for a corporate meeting, the budget might be sizable enough to hire a small orchestra. Producers generally offer composers an all-inclusive ("all-in") budget, which is normally nonnegotiable. (The composers must deliver a complete score for the agreed-on budget; the music company absorbs overage.) The music budget is frequently the first budget item to be reduced if cost overruns occur. To cut expenditures, directors and producers use stock music instead of original scores. Most significant videos have original scores because directors want the music to match the picture and not sound like a nondescript bed of music.

The following is my interview with Dennis Powers, director and writer of corporate videos:

MZ: What is a corporate video?

Dennis: There are many kinds of corporate videos . . . generally speaking, a corporate video outlines or describes what it is about a corporation that makes it unique . . . makes it special . . . makes it different. It describes the corporation and gives the viewer a feeling for what the corporation does . . . who are the people who run the corporation, and what the talent pool is like that makes the corporation run. These are definitions that are sort of general, but that's mostly the kind of work that I do. There are other corporate videos that are more specific and targeted to different audiences, depending on what the corporation does. Pfizer, for instance, will do videos for certain divisions that explain or describe a certain product. Sometimes those corporate videos go out to people who sell the products or go out to doctors, for instance, and then there are other corporate videos that are strategic and slightly more cerebral that kind of give more of a sense of what a corporation is about. It doesn't have to be specific information, but it can be more like a mood or a feeling or an essence of what a corporation stands for.

MZ: How does working on a corporate video differ from working on a commercial?

Dennis: A corporate video, just by the nature of being longer, has more information. It's like taking a commercial and stretching it out, but, I treat it pretty much the same way as I would treat a commercial. I think that the shooting and editing [of the film] and [scoring] the music are all inherently important . . . the way I treat corporate videos, because of my background in commercials, would be to look at a subject, to delineate what that subject is, and then to fine-line certain aspects of it . . . almost like treating it as individual commercials. So, I think you have the luxury in a corporate video of telling more stories, of getting into personalities within the corporation, or developing characters in a way, like you would in a movie.

MZ: How often are corporate videos made for in-house use?

Dennis: Probably about 50 percent of what I do remains in-house—[the purpose is] to motivate employees—to give specific information that the upper management wants them to understand more thoroughly. About 50 percent [of my videos] goes to the outside [for other purposes]. [Dennis produced several videos of the Boys Club of Harlem playing basketball in China and in Cuba.]

MZ: Do you consider the videos you produced for the Boys Club corporate videos?

Dennis: They're principally used for fund-raising. The Boys Club pieces, both the Beijing, the China piece, and the Cuba piece, are essentially to inform the public that the Boys Club wants to reach out . . . so that's the workhorse . . . they take these videos around to various schools that they are trying to get Boys Club kids into . . . prep schools, particularly on the East coast, to show the kinds of things that the Boys Club is doing . . . but it's motivational and fund-raising more than anything else . . . in this context, it's more documentary in nature, and through storytelling in documentary fashion, you can get people involved, and they kind of get the feeling of what you are doing, and it becomes motivational, and the motivation, of course, becomes one of financial gift giving.

Music for corporate videos is a hybrid between scoring commercials and scoring documentaries. It provides composers with an opportunity to be creative without the restrictions of a shorter format.

Infomercials

Infomercials are long-form commercials that usually run either 30 or 60 minutes, which is the length of an average television program. (Infomercials are also played on the radio but less frequently than on television.) They are advertisements. *Infomercials are designed to prompt immediate consumer response.* Customers are encouraged to call a toll-free number or access an Internet site, which enables them to order the product.

Another form of infomercial is called direct-response television (a.k.a. DRTV). Most DRTV infomercials have a duration of 1 or 2 minutes but are sometimes longer or shorter. As with long-form infomercials, the goal is to receive an immediate direct response from the audience—*sales.*

Although infomercials are designed to result in immediate phone or Internet sales, surveys have shown a direct correlation between the showing of infomercials and increased sales in retail stores.

Airtime

Since most infomercials are broadcast at unusual hours—mostly after midnight—this presents an opportunity to purchase airtime at inexpensive rates. Media companies purchase bulk time and resell it to infomercial companies. Both cable and broadcasting time is available, but the majority of the bulk time is on cable channels.

A survey showed that 15 percent of all televisions are on at 1:00 A.M. and that more than 66 percent of cable television viewers surf the channels. This presents an opportunity for the viewers to watch an infomercial. Sometimes it is difficult to tell when a program is an infomercial until the hard sell occurs. Many celebrities have successfully promoted products in infomercials and are compensated by receiving a percentage of sales. A successful infomercial can generate substantial sales, although most are not successful. They are usually tested in a region and played for one or two weekends. If considerable sales are not achieved, the infomercial is typically canceled.

The following list contains some of the most successful infomercials:

- Jane Fonda: Fitness Trends for the Nineties (treadmill)
- Psychic Friends Network (1-900 line)
- Bruce Jenner: PowerWalk Plus (treadmill)
- Connie Sellecca and John Tesh: Growing in Love and Hidden Keys
- Jake Steinfeld: Body by Jake (hip and thigh exercise machine)
- Barbara De Angelis: Making Love Work
- Health Rider (fitness machine)
- Popeil Pasta Maker
- Anthony Robbins: Personal Power #4 (self-improvement)

The following is my interview with Mark Mayhew, of Mayhew/Breen Productions, one of the most successful infomercial producers.

MZ: What is an infomercial?

Mark: An infomercial is a 28-minute and 30-second broadcast piece that is used to sell a product or to convey information about a product.

MZ: Other than the length, how does an infomercial differ from a commercial?

Mark: A commercial is designed to enhance the image of a product and create an awareness that can be acted on later on, whether it's in a store or in some other way. An infomercial demands a direct response—thus the name ''direct response.'' [The audience] calls for information about a product at that moment or actually buys something.

MZ: What is the role of music in an infomercial?

Mark: [It] is not unlike its role in a commercial, but in an infomercial we use music to enhance the need to buy. We have one of the most difficult jobs, and that is to get people up off their comfortable seat and get to a phone and take down a number. We use music to enhance that need. We use it to help us drive the sale.

MZ: Is creating an infomercial different from creating a commercial?

Mark: It's not fundamentally different, in that you're working on a product for which you're creating an image. In traditional advertising, that image does not have to be acted upon in that minute. In our business, we're still creating an image for the product, but we hope to get direct response. The function of music is identical, in that it has to enhance the message in what we're trying to do.

MZ: Is scoring an infomercial closer to scoring a television program than scoring a commercial?

Mark: It is much closer to doing a television show. I think that the whole process of the infomercial is much closer to a television program than it is to image advertising. In order to keep someone involved for half an hour, you have to tell them a story that is interesting, you have to repeat the story in different ways, you have to convey your information.

MZ: Do most of the composers who compose music for commercials also compose music for infomercials?

Mark: I would say, probably, yes. I don't really know people who [just compose for infomercials].

MZ: Are you hired by advertising companies?

Mark: We are almost never hired by [an] advertising agency. We are mostly hired by marketing companies—occasionally, we will work with an advertising agency that has been asked to do an infomercial and doesn't want to touch it. On occasion, we are hired by a wealthy entrepreneur who wants to do something on his own.

MZ: What warrants keeping an infomercial on the air?

Mark: It takes sales that are able to comfortably cover the cost of media plus the cost of the production of the item. For instance, if you spend your thousand dollars to buy your half hour, and you make a thousand dollars, most likely you're going to go out of business very quickly because you're not covering any of the additional cost. You may have covered the cost of media time, but you haven't covered the cost of the infomercial, the manufacturing for the infomercial, and all of the prototype work.

MZ: What percentage of infomercials makes money?

Mark: Maybe one out of 25.

MZ: Are most of the products tested before spending the money to produce and promote an infomercial?

Mark: Not necessarily—it's a high-risk, high-return business.

MZ: What infomercials have you produced?

Mark: In fitness we have done Body by Jake, Cable Flex with Jackie Chan, Ab-Flex, Fast Track with Cathy Rigby—we've done shows for Quaker State Motor Oil, Bayliner Boats, and Bose Speakers, with Herbie Hancock.

Music for Infomercials

Infomercials present an interesting challenge to composers. It is similar to composing music for television programs, including the commercials.

Infomercials generally include a congenial host(s) who makes the audience feel comfortable. Most viewers are not cognizant of the fact that they are watching a long-form commercial until the call-to-action (CTA) sequence. The CTA is the actual commercial—hard sell—that occurs recurrently within the infomercial format. The viewer is expected to call in an order or order via the Internet. Production companies routinely spend a substantial portion of their budgets producing the CTA sequences. Their objective is to demonstrate the reason a product is superior to competitive products (if competition exists) or to explain why their product is unique. If the CTAs are not well constructed, the product, generally, will not sell. The CTAs always include a toll-free telephone number, the features of the product, the price, credit card information or check information, the address, and sometimes a Web address. Most of them boast a guaranteed return policy (within a certain time frame).

Prior to showing the CTAs, the viewer listens to numerous testimonials from satisfied customers. The testimonials are usually scattered throughout the program and can be very effective in motivating an audience to purchase the product.

Approaching the Score

During spotting sessions, the music is discussed in detail. Most infomercials have noninvasive scores because the director does not want the audience to experience any diversions from the program content. The director and/or producer generally wants the music to create "a musical atmosphere." The director typically tells the composer where the music should be assertive. This generally occurs during the CTA sequences. Since CTAs are commercials within informercials, these sections are sometimes scored using the same compositional techniques used to score commercials. Infomercials vary in style, and composers should not assume that all infomercials are approached (from a musical vantage point) the same. The pertinent questions that composers ask the creatives when scoring commercials should also be asked of infomercial directors.

Bumpers

Bumpers are short pieces of music that separate sections within videos (or television programs). Infomercial bumper music is usually repeated each time a segment changes (e.g., testimonials followed by demonstration or a CTA segment). Sometimes the duration of bumpers varies, but the basic music remains similar. Bumpers are used in television programs before going to commercial breaks and also to reenter programs. A well-designed, memorable bumper can create a signature sound. [Listen to track #11 on the enclosed CD.]

Testimonials

Testimonials by satisfied customers are significant segments. Some directors want the same basic music for each testimonial. Sometimes the arrangements and durations vary, but the basic theme music remains the same. The music used to accompany testimonials should create product identity.

Opening Theme

Compose an identifiable theme for the opening. Some directors want composers to develop scores by incorporating variations of the theme music. Rearranging the theme as well as using motifs taken from the theme's melody are common practice. This technique is often used in film scoring. If a composer decides to incorporate this approach, get approval from the director prior to composing the music.

Conclusion

Composers must try to compose a cohesive score rather than individual cues with no musical relationship. Approach an infomercial or corporate video as if writing a film score rather than a commercial. The purpose is to sell or inform—not necessarily to entertain, although the film/video must keep the audience's attention. (Some music companies specialize in composing music for infomercials, and other companies specialize in composing music for corporate videos.)

Assignments

1. Watch several infomercials on television. Compare the manner in which the program is formatted with the placement and use of music.
2. Record testimonials and CTAs from an infomercial, mute the music, and compose original music for those segments. (Suggestion: write down the dialogue and record it, using your voice, into a computer music-sequencing program.)
3. Prior to composing, watch and analyze several corporate videos. Compare the general formats and note their similarities and differences.

10

Theatrical Trailer Music

Motion Picture Trailer Music

Los Angeles–based composer Kevin Christopher Teasley provided portions of the information contained in this chapter. He has composed music and created sound design for the theatrical trailers *I Am Legend, Beowulf, Rambo 4: John Rambo, The Happening, Jumper, The Spiderwick Chronicles, Fantastic Four 2: Rise of the Silver Surfer, Live Free or Die Hard, Rush Hour 3, Night at the Museum, The Accidental Husband, Lions for Lambs, The Perfect Holiday,* and *Dreamgirls,* among many others.

Composing music for theatrical trailers is a unique and complex subgenre of motion picture scoring and scoring commercials. Many composers who compose music for commercials also compose music for trailers (also known as feature film advertising).

Trailers are viewed in theaters or on television, the Internet, and DVDs or via additional new media formats (e.g., cross-promotional, home entertainment, in store, closed-circuit television, "making ofs," pay per view/on demand, hotel/airplane, cruise ship, and now mobile entertainment). The purpose of trailers is to attract an audience. Theatrical motion pictures or television programs (miniseries, series television, Internet series, and so on) must be advertised and marketed. The editor's job is to create an appealing and compelling compilation of the most exciting, humorous, dramatic, and/or poignant scenes of a film that will not reveal salient information about the film's content yet will attract an audience. *A trailer is a commercial! The film is a product! The studio is the client! The audience is the consumer!*

Companies that specialize in this genre edit theatrical trailers. The motion picture company usually provides the editing company with a digitized copy of the picture. The studios' marketing directors provide guidance to the editors. A clearer "chain of command" is the marketing director/creative executives of the film studio providing guidance/notes to the producer at the trailer editorial company. Sometimes the information is forwarded directly to "superstar trailer editors." The producer then deciphers the information, has "scripts" written, and adds his or her creative input to develop trailer/television spots. Studio executives are often vague and will request, for example, "a young male spot," and the producer/editor will edit and write a "creative" spot.

As with commercials, trailers are almost always tested with audiences in focus groups. If a film is tested, depending on the reaction of the audience, trailers may be reedited, and the music might change.

Generally, the motion picture company has final approval of the trailer. Often, a trailer is approved by a "committee" at the film studio, such as an A-list director (Steven Spielberg), an A-list actor (Tom Cruise), and an A-list producer (Jerry Bruckheimer). The following are basic definitions of various genres of trailers.

Theatrical trailers. Theatrical trailers are shown in motion picture theaters. The average trailer is 2 to 2.5 minutes in length. The footage (pictures) is taken either from a completed film or from sections of a film that might still be in production. In some instances, scenes not incorporated in the film are included in trailers. The average trailer is released three to six months prior to a film's release.

Although most theatrical trailers are designed to appeal to a general audience, the studios may release a variety of trailers that are geared to appeal to targeted demographics. For example, if a film is made to attract a young male audience, the promotional trailer might be edited to appeal to the same demographic, and/or the music might change to accommodate the tastes of a specific demographic.

Television trailer. Theatrical trailers, created for television, are usually edited specifically for television. It is a completely different genre than editing a general audience trailer that is shown in theaters; therefore, not only may the selection of the scenes differ, but the music generally may vary according to the targeted demographic. The trailers are usually 30 seconds, although companion trailers can be 15 or 10 seconds. In rare instances, the trailer might run for one minute. "Blockbuster" or "tent pole" movies can have up to 30 or more different television spots.

The studio might authorize a media-buying company to purchase advertising time for select high-budgeted films. After a period of time, the trailers are sometimes "refreshed" to keep the audience's attention. For example, if a film is being considered for an Oscar nomination, the "refreshed" trailer might include critics' reviews.

Trailers for television events, such as the Olympics, are usually created by television networks or by advertising agencies. Music used for television events is either licensed or written by composers who generally score commercials or specialize in scoring various styles of television music (e.g., music for sports events, news programs, and so on). The composers are accustomed to working in short formats.

If the television division of a film company (e.g., Warner Bros. Television) is preparing to syndicate a television series, the studio prepares promos (trailers) as part of their sales presentation. The syndicated stations might use the trailers, or the stations prepare new promos.

"Teasers" (a.k.a. short trailers). Short trailers are often referred to as "teasers" and are substantially shorter in length than theatrical trailers. Most are 60 to 90 seconds. They are usually shown six to eight months prior to a film's release and are often created while the film is still in production. Some teasers are released a year before a film's release. For instance, if a *Harry Potter* film is being released during the holiday season, the studio might also promote the next *Harry Potter* film that will be released during the following holiday season.

Trailers designed for the international market. Trailers are usually designed to appeal to a general audience. Since one trailer will usually not appeal to all countries, most studios design trailers that target a specific culture. This, naturally, affects the choice of music. For instance, in a trailer designed for the U.S. market, hip-hop music might be appropriate; in a country located in Southeast Asia, hip-hop might not be popular; therefore, the music would be replaced by a musical genre that would appeal to the culture of Southeast Asia. This theory also applies to the scenes selected for a trailer. In one country, it might be acceptable to show more violence than would be acceptable in another territory.

Trailers designed for the home video market. The opening segment of most DVDs contains feature film trailers, which are generally used in the theaters. Sometimes, the trailers are altered. For example, if the film featured on a DVD appeals to an ethnic market (e.g., a film made in India for the Indian market), the trailer might be reedited and the music changed so that the trailer appeals to the targeted demographic. Commercial spots (usually 15 to 30 seconds), which advertise release dates of future DVDs, are also included on DVDs. This has become an important marketing tool. Additional spots for Blu-Ray and HD DVDs are also being advertised.

Trailers designed for the Internet. Some trailers are designed specifically for the Internet, while select websites play full-length, general audience theatrical trailers. Teasers are also played on the Internet.

Library Music

As mentioned, because trailers are designed to appeal to multiple demographic, psychographic, and ethnic audiences, the same music is not necessarily appropriate for all trailers. Consequently, the music varies. Generally, if a popular song is licensed for a lucrative synchronization fee, the song will be heard in most

♩♪ A number of studios primarily license library music for trailers, while other studios hire composers to write original music that is included with the library music.

of the trailers. (Companies pay larger synchronization fees for music used in multiple genres.) It depends on how crucial the song is to a film. For major motion pictures, as many as 30 variations of a trailer might be edited. Each trailer is designed to appeal to a specific market. For instance, for television, a trailer might be 10, 15, or 30 seconds. The various lengths are normally shorter versions of a 30-second trailer. Trailers might be geared to appeal to the Hispanic market, African American market, the international market, the MTV or YouTube markets, and so on. Each version may have different scenes and different music.

Approximately half the music used in trailers is licensed from record companies, music libraries, composers, and/or recording artists; 25 percent of the music may be from the film (source, score, or sound track) if the music in the film is strongly associated with the film (e.g., the theme from *Star Wars* or *Superman*), and 25 percent of the music is custom scored. The film studio owns the original music composed for the trailer in perpetuity. This is referred to as a "buyout."

Music libraries are comprised of music that is owned by the libraries and licensed to various licensees, usually on a nonexclusive basis. Most music libraries contain cues (musical pieces of various lengths) that, it is hoped, appeal to producers and editors of trailers. Library music is divided into categories. The following are some of the musical subgenres.

- Dramatic
- Action
- Romantic
- Horror
- Jazz (traditional or smooth)
- Orchestral
- Rock
- Pop
- New Age
- Country
- Chill-out
- Combos (playing various forms of music)
- Rhythm and blues
- Hip-hop

Large music libraries control thousands of cues (compositions) for potential licensees to peruse. Musical cues that might be selected by trailer producers or editors must be mixed in 5.1 surround sound as well as in stereo, although many theaters are currently converting to 7.1 surround sound. If cues were mixed in stereo, the music companies would be required to remix the composition in surround sound. Since the music-for-trailers business can be lucrative for composers, music publishers, and music libraries, it is prudent to mix most cues in various technical formats. It will save time and expense at a later date.

Most composers who write for library companies retain their royalties (writer's share), and the music library retains the rights to the publisher's share. Composers are generally not paid to write cues for music libraries. This practice is referred to as "writing on spec (speculation)." One might ask, "Why do composers devote time to writing on spec?" The answer is that library cues might be licensed numerous times, generating considerable fees from synchronization licenses and performance royalties from use on broadcast television, cable television, Internet advertising, and so forth. (No composers' royalties are derived from theatrical performances of trailers.) Successful library composers can generate substantial compensation if they are prolific and their music is regularly licensed.

Original Trailer Music

Composers who compose theatrical scores might be asked to write new music for portions of the trailers for films they scored. It is rare that music from the films is used in the trailers, unless the music is identifiable with the picture (e.g., *Star Wars* or *Superman*). The genre(s) of music used in some of the trailers may differ from the tone of the music scored for the film. For example, Clint Eastwood's film *Flags of Our Fathers* has a traditional orchestral score, yet the television trailer has a contemporary score; the theatrical trailer incorporates the theme from the original score, which is written in a traditional style.

Independent composers are hired to write original music and/or soundalike cues. Soundalikes are compositions that sound like something else (or "in the spirit of"), such as the theme to *The Lord of the Rings*. This is usually due to the expense of licensing high-profiled music. Composers must be careful not to plagiarize. A standard assignment may be to compose an action cue that will remind the creators of a cue or theme used in XYZ film. Since professional composers purchase high-quality instrumental samples, working with a relatively low budget allows them to produce orchestral compositions that sound remarkably "live." Mixing samples with several live musicians makes it difficult for an audience to realize that a live orchestra is not performing the music. In addition, much of the music is mixed at a lower level than the dialogue and sound effects, making it even more difficult for an audience to recognize that the music is synthesized.

It is uncommon for one composer, using a live orchestra, to score an entire trailer. Music executives generally do not want to incur the expense of paying for musicians, engineers, studios, and other expenses when they can accomplish most of their musical goals by licensing music at relatively low licensing fees. Although rare, the trailer for the CGI animated film *Monster House* was custom scored with a live orchestra.

SMPTE (Society of Motion Picture and Television Engineers) time code is burned in, so film companies can lay back the music to the correct video address. Composers, as in commercials, must have the ability to capture the emotion of the scene(s) and work quickly. The goal is to satisfy the creative staff at both the trailer company and the motion picture or television studio. There is a direct parallel between composing music for trailer companies and composing music for advertising agencies. The composers experience the same time restrictions, and their work is normally judged by a group of people rather than by an individual, such as a film director, which is industry standard in feature films. (Studio executives usually get involved with the creative aspects of the music after the director. Unless a director is an A-list director, the studio has to approve the hiring of a composer.)

Technical Considerations

Although theatrical trailers will be played in theaters and heard in either 5.1 or 7.1 surround sound, listen on small speakers when composing. Listening on large speakers can easily distort a composer's ability to evaluate a composition and the impact of the music. Most music sounds more dynamic when played at a loud level on a sizable speaker system. As in writing music for commercials, the better the music sounds at a low level on home speakers, the more impact the music will have when heard in theaters.

Most trailer companies have mini-theaters with surround-sound systems. The films and the music are tested in their theaters before being reviewed by the film companies.

The final music is usually saved as an OMF (Open Media Framework) file as well as Pro Tools Sessions, the industry standard. The OMF file is given to the mixers at the studio and/or the final "mix stage" or "dub stage." The mix/dub stage is used solely to mix theatrical trailers in a large mix room that resembles an actual theater. The final mixing session consists of blending the dialogue, music,

> ♩♪ *Book trailers* serve the same purpose as movie trailers. They entice viewers to buy the books. Writers such as best-selling author Michael Connelly are using book trailers as a marketing tool. His trailers have original music, use seasoned actors, and contain high production values. Some of his trailers run as long as 11 minutes. Other trailers, from various authors, run 30 seconds and 60 seconds, the length of the average television and radio commercial. View several book trailers by going to michaelconnelly.com (author Michael Connelly) and donbrunsbooks.com (author Don Bruns).

and sound effects. If, for instance, the studio engineers decide to load the music into a Pro Tools file, the OMF file must be converted to a Pro Tools format. There are several software conversion programs.

In the future, digital distribution of motion pictures to theaters will become the standard. The film studios will have the ability to alter trailers and instantly distribute them to theaters. There are approximately 3,100 U.S. screens equipped with 2k digital equipment. Major rollouts are planned to begin in 2008. National Cine Media [controls Regal, Cinemark, and AMC] has a three-year rollout planned to start in 2008. Access ITX has about 3,400 screens now operating [those include Carmike and Rave]. Technicolor is doing a beta test in about 200 screens. Dolby and Kodak are late starters. Sony electronics equipped the Muvico Rosemont theater, which opened to the public on September 14, 2007, with Sony 4k digital projectors in all 18 screens. This is the first theater in the United States with this equipment. Sony is planning a rollout of all Muvico theaters starting in November 2007 running through 2008. Sony recently announced a deal to supply AMC with 54 Digital 4k projectors in four theaters under construction.

1. Majors have most of their product available digitally, and independents are starting to make some films available in digital. The problem indies face is on limited-run films and the expansion to secondary markets. Using the same digital prints they have to pay virtual print fees in each new market.
2. All studios get [to show] two trailers with their films.
3. Trailers are placed based on the audience. They are rarely changed during run of film, but this will be easier in the digital world.

—Hank Lightstone, senior vice president, Muvico Theaters

AFM Agreement

The following information is adapted from the Television and Radio Commercial Announcements Agreement of the American Federation of Musicians (AFM). (Read the agreement for the latest revisions, which can be found on the Internet. The following information is being reproduced with the permission of the AFM.)

Nonbroadcast use. For use of commercials in any and all nonbroadcast media (e.g., theaters, trade shows open to the public, closed-circuit television, in-store point of sale, phone hold, in-stadium, give-aways), excluding the Internet, videocassettes, and other devices for the home video market, all musicians shall be paid an amount equal to the conversion fee provided for in Article XIV(5), for each 52-week period of nonbroadcast use. For an up-front payment of 150% of the conversion fee, the employer may obtain two consecutive 52-week periods of nonbroadcast use.

Assignments

1. Download a motion picture trailer from the Internet. Remove the sound and rerecord the announcer copy and dialogue. (Sync the dialogue as closely as possible.) Add sound effects and compose and record a score.

2. Download a television trailer from the Internet. Remove the sound and rerecord the announcer copy and dialogue. (Sync the dialogue as closely as possible.) Add sound effects and compose and record a score.

11

Video Game Music

> Computer Space is the first video game developed for the arcades. One player pilots a rocket ship and fights two flying saucers; when two gamers played, they competed against each other. . . . Nutting Associates released the game in 1971, followed in 1972 with Pong, also developed for the arcades. . . . U.S. sales of game software for January–May [2007] hit 85.9 million units, up 13.5% from the prior year, with a retail value of $2.74 billion—a 21% gain, according to Anita Frazier, toys and video games analyst for NPD Group, which tracks sales at retail.
>
> —*Billboard* magazine July 28, 2007

The video game business accumulates sales topping $30 billion per year. Development costs for complex games can reach $15 million; marketing and advertising are also pricey.

A game has to achieve the same level of interest from a game player as a viewer receives from watching a compelling motion picture. Most likely, a game probably has to be even more gripping because of the number of hours spent playing a game. If a gamer is not emotionally involved in a game's plot, the game will have a minimal chance of achieving commercial success. Gamers should be able to understand how to play with an extremely short learning curve; a one-on-one tutorial is ideal. If a game is too complex, many gamers will not be interested.

Since game development is costly, game publishers have devised additional revenue streams. In addition to traditional retail sales, game music is sold primarily on the Internet (e.g., iTunes) and as ringtones. The music is also being licensed for commercials, CDs, feature films, television programs, and other businesses that provide licensing opportunities. For example, music from the game "Myst III: Exile Main Theme" was used in the theatrical trailer for the motion picture *Peter Pan*. The music publisher (usually owned by the game publisher) and

> ♫ The average age of a video game player is 30, and 60 percent of heads of households in the United States play games, according to the Entertainment Software Association (May 2006).

the composer can receive substantial royalties from these sources of revenue. These rights are referred to as *ancillary rights*. (Ancillary rights occur when music composed for games is used in other mediums. Composers' compensation for these rights is negotiable.)

Another revenue stream is derived from product placement within a game, which has been a source of revenue for the motion picture and television industries for many years. For instance, a game character might be drinking Pepsi-Cola, or a character is watching a Sony television set. Product placement in games is expected to generate hundreds of millions of dollars by 2010, according to Yankee Research, a research and consulting service.

♩♩ Video game music is also heard on the concert stage. Major symphony orchestras perform the music, which is synchronized with clips from popular video games; laser beams shoot across the audience. The presentation is called *Video Games Live*, with attendance of over 100,000 worldwide as of August 2007. Video game composer Tommy Tallarico is the host and one of the founders of *Video Games Live*.

Game Platforms

The three companies that manufacture competitive consoles are Microsoft's Xbox 360, Nintendo's Wii (pronounced "we"), and Sony's PlayStation 3. These platforms offer game players the option of playing against opponents via the Internet. Gamers can also download the most recent program updates, which include new music as well as new versions of games. New games are also planned for the PC format. The platform competition is healthy for the industry and keeps consumers interested in the medium.

The game industry is one of the primary sources of revenue in the entertainment industry. Game companies not only create games but also base game ideas on motion picture franchises, which are licensed. Electronic Arts created games

♩♩ "Hosted by Victor Lucas, Julie Stoffer and Tommy Tallarico, Electric Playground is a Telly Award–winning show that goes on location and behind the scenes of the video game industry to provide interviews with game developers, previews of upcoming games, industry news, technology features and celebrity gamer segments, as well as a look at the latest gadgets, toys and comics that gamers are interested in" (www.g4tv.com/electricplayground/index.html).

based on *The Lord of the Rings*, *James Bond*, and *Harry Potter*. Game publishers are also developing games created using the personas of music superstars. Rapper 50 Cent is featured in the game "50 Cent: Bulletproff," which "sold 1 million units in less than 2 months" (*Billboard*, May 13, 2006). Game companies search for new ideas that will keep gamers interested in the medium.

Music has developed into one of the most essential elements of video games. Full orchestral scores that accompany games are now common. The most sought after film composers are scoring games. In addition to underscoring, licensing songs recorded by popular artists is routine.

♩♪ Rapper 50 Cent sampled a song written by me and Aram Schefrin for the game "50 Cent: Bulletproff." The track is called "I'm a Rider." 50 Cent wrote and performed the rap.

Home entertainment systems are available at reasonable prices; consequently, most avid game players own sophisticated audio and visual reproduction systems, adding to the excitement of the gaming experience. Purchasing games has created a negative impact on the sale of music and motion pictures. The game, music, and motion picture industries are all vying for consumers' leisure expenditures. These subjects are discussed in the remainder of this chapter.

Portions of the following material are from an interview with Steve Schnur, worldwide executive of music and audio for Electronic Arts for *Billboard* magazine, November 10, 2007:

[Referring to popular music being licensed for use in video games] This is the beginning of music and film and TV becoming interactive vs. linear forms of entertainment. Interactive media is the only way media is going to be delivered in the future.

Writing music for video games differs from writing music for films. Video games are interactive entertainment and game players, therefore, must feel as though they are a part of the experience. If the music, sound effects, and dialogue do not contain the same artistic value as the audio on major motion picture soundtracks, the games would not be competitive in the video game market. Most game players own high-definition televisions and surround sound speaker systems; the visual and audio component of games has to equal the experience of viewing feature films on home state-of-the-art entertainment systems.

Film composers compose music after viewing completed films. The films have been edited. Usually temp (temporary) musical tracks (music taken from other sources, e.g. CDs, commercials and other films) have been added. This helps to communicate a director's musical vision to a composer.

In addition to hearing the dialogue, many of the films contain either the final sound effects or temporary sound effects. Hearing or envisioning the sound effects is essential to composers because it affects the style of music they write for particular scenes. If the sound effects are going to be prominent in the final audio mix, which is comprised of dialogue, music, and/or sound effects, composers must write music that will be audible, but not compete with the other elements. For example, it might be difficult to hear a lightly orchestrated musical cue if countless explosions happen simultaneously and the actors' voices are agitated and loud.

Film composers study a film in order to understand the underlying motivations and subtleties of the characters. Composers are able to communicate and interact with directors who help them determine the proper musical solutions to various complex dramatic and/or comical situations. Musical solutions are subjective and can pose conflicts between composers and directors. When composers and directors decide on a musical direction, the process becomes less problematic.

Game composers do not write while viewing the final video. They, most often, receive a description of the game, which may be a storyboard containing cartoon-like pictures of the characters, detailed descriptions of the characters, and the various situations the characters will encounter throughout the game. [Therefore, Steve Schnur seeks out composers who have well-defined communicative skills; talent, including the ability to write memorable musical themes and thematic variations; and musical vision.] Composers often suggest interesting musical solutions that differ from the original views of the creative team. Jobs are frequently awarded to them. Many composers are competent but do not contribute a unique musical perspective. Creators generally want them to expand on their basic musical visions.

> ♪♪ Consumers download music from games. "Steve Schnur . . . claims that 24% of those who played the latest Madden NFL game either bought or otherwise downloaded a song they discovered on the game's soundtrack, which included music from the musical groups, Fall Out Boy, Foo Fighters, and Godsmack, among others. For the car racing game, Need for Speed, that figure rose to 34%" (*Billboard*, May 20, 2006).

Composers must work with both music directors and the game producers. [Not all video game companies have musical directors.] If a creative team cannot communicate in an imaginative manner with composers, the musical solutions expected of composers will generally not meet the vision of the creative team. In the video game industry, composers are considered an intrinsic part of the creative team. Music makes as significant a contribution to the game as does the animation and the computer graphics.

Another difference between film composition and game music composition is that film music is written in a linear fashion. Viewers watch films from beginning to end. Game com-

> ♪♪ "MTV Games/Harmonix's Rock Band, with Electronic Arts distribution and marketing, is the first game to let users earn the ability to download full albums from such acts as the Who via Xbox Live or PlayStation Network" (*Billboard*, July 28, 2007).

posing is not written in a linear format. Game players have the power to control the behavior of the characters; they control the outcome of the game. For instance, if a character is directed to go to the left, they might encounter a hostile situation; if they go to the right, they might encounter a friendly situation, and so forth. The musical cues [specific compositions] must be written so that the transition from one musical mood to another does not sound disruptive. In many ways, this makes game writing more complex than film writing. Games vary from fifty minutes of music to more than one hundred and twenty minutes of music, with an average of sixty minutes. It depends on the complexity of a game.

The Composition Process

As in any form of musical composition that accompanies visual images, composers must first decide on the genre of music that will most appropriately complement a game. Game scores may require traditional romantic or heroic filmesque scores, rock and roll, jazz, a combination of styles, and so on. It is helpful for game music composers to be versatile. Versatile composers receive more assignments than composers who specialize in one or two musical genres. Composers should display their musical strengths on their demo reels and on their websites. (Most game composers have a website that is used to market their work. It is easier for a potential employer to hear their work and read their credits and other essential information.)

This reiterates the importance of musical training; learning the techniques of writing to visual images is relatively simple compared to learning composition and orchestration.

Executive producers and creative teams from the game publishers usually have clear visions of musical styles most appropriate for their projects. Often, they play musical examples to communicate the style of music they envision. The purpose of the examples is to present an overview of their musical expectations. The creatives want composers to write in their own styles and not copy the exact approach taken by the composers of the examples. They are asking composers not to plagiarize but merely to understand the musical direction that, in their opinion, will be most suitable for a project.

♩♩ Steve Schnur stated that in his search for composers, he is most interested in a competent composer who may not understand the technique of writing to film or games but who writes melodic themes and well-constructed melodic content. He can hire someone to help a composer with the technical requirements (musical "hits," transitions in the proper keys, and so on).

- Many game composers begin the process by composing several themes. It is hoped that the creative team selects one to be used as the title theme or the main theme.
- The opening theme music may also be used as the closing theme, or a new theme might be composed for the closing theme.
- In addition to a closing theme, there may be short compositions, called "stings" (very short sounds or short pieces of music), that indicate if game players have won or lost the game or if the players are pushing "buttons" or performing additional tasks that require short sound effects or short musical sounds. If the choice is to write a musical sting, one approach is to write thematic material that has previously been used in the game. It helps to create a unified score.

Musical Thread

All musical scoring should have a "thread" that "sews" the score together. The thread can be the various themes, musical moods, tonality, orchestration, instrumentation, or other elements that formulate a homogeneous score.

Some composers develop the main theme into numerous variations from the viewpoint of both composition and orchestration design. One cue might be mixed in many incarnations. For example, the main theme could be a full orchestral arrangement, one breakdown could be mixed without brass, another breakdown will contain strings only, and so on. In addition to developing cues (musical selections) during the mixing process, a composer might record numerous arrangements of the same basic music. For instance, the original tempo might be at 120 beats per minute and sound heroic, while an additional arrangement of the same theme might be at 80 beats per minute and sound

> ♪♪ Study motion picture scores because many game scores contain sound tracks written in the style of traditional film scores. Also study the orchestration techniques used by eminent film orchestrators. Film-scoring workshops are offered by the performance-rights societies BMI and ASCAP as well as by film composers and orchestrators. It can be advantageous to attend.

sad. This technique is used in film composition. The composer's job is to capture the emotion(s) of a particular situation, which is determined by a game player's manipulation of the options offered within the game.

Not all game music is developed from one central theme. A composer might compose a theme and variations for each major character. A number of themes may be composed for use throughout the game, but the themes are not necessarily associated with characters. The themes might be based on emotions or moods.

Demos (Mock-Ups)

All cues are eventually performed on samplers and synthesizers as a musical demonstration. After the score has been approved, the parts will be performed either completely or partially by live musicians or remain synthesized. Since all cues must be heard prior to the final recording, there is a logistical problem that must be solved. *Most game music is complex, and the sampled instruments should sound real.* Composers make a substantial investment purchasing not only studio equipment but also sound libraries. Some composers own multiple samplers, such as Giga Studio or virtual samplers, to ease the time it takes to search for proper sounds. Because strings players use multiple bowing techniques, one sampler might be loaded with staccato violins, arco violins, pizzicato celli, and various dynamic ranges, such as *p* (piano), *f* (forte), and so on. Another sampler might contain brass with various dynamic mark-

♩♩ Available orchestral samples are of such high quality that it is sometimes difficult to determine that a real orchestra did not record a cue. The unique feel provided by live musicians and conductors' interpretations of the music is missing when samples are used. For instance, although myriad string bowing samples are available, it is cumbersome to smoothly emulate the various techniques used by live string players. The same is true of other sampled sections of the orchestra, such as full string sections, woodwinds, French horns, and so on.

ings and a variety of effects, such as muted trumpets (with a choice of various mutes, such as harmon mute, cup mute, and so on), French horns playing portamento, sliding trombones, and other effects. The third sampler may be loaded with woodwinds and percussion. There are many variations of each instrument, making it is time consuming to continually view libraries in order to find preferred sounds. In addition to the use of samples, synthesizers are usually combined with real orchestral samples.

Time Constraints

Many film composers are required to write and record scores in eight weeks and sometimes less. Because of the complexities of creating games, the final music might not be recorded for a year. As a game develops, so does the score. Composers are asked to compose new music for new situations that occur as a game develops. They may work for several months and then wait a month until receiving new instructions to write additional music. It is a very long and arduous creative process.

As with commercials, composers must not be enticed to plagiarize music written by other composers or music the composer has written for other projects. In an effort to avoid legal problems, many game publishers hire musicologists to analyze the music written for their games. The scores must be original.

Sound Effects

Composers work closely with sound designers and/or sound design teams. Most composers do not hear the sound effects before they compose. Since game composers are not viewing or hearing the audio for the final game, they must internalize the imagined sound effects and the manner in which the sounds will affect their compositional process. This parallels the process used in film scoring with the exception that film composers, most often, will hear most of the sound effects or temp sound effects while they are composing. This offers the advantage of hearing the music while simultaneously hearing dialogue and effects. Composers are able to determine if the sound effects and dialogue mask the music.

Most sound effects are created specifically for games with substantial budgets. Games with sizable production budgets generally do not employ sound effects libraries. Creating original effects is costly and requires the same creative skills and talent used by Foley artists (creators of sound effects) in the film industry. If a game presents the illusion that it takes place during World War II, the sound designers might fire and record weapons from that historic period. Their goal is to create authentic effects.

Reactions to sound effects from creative teams are subjective. Sound designers might create multiple effects for a requested sound before a creative team agrees that one or more of the sounds work in the game. If the effects are rejected, the sound designers create new effects until the creatives are satisfied.

> ♩♪ I interviewed a sound designer who was working on a sports video game. A team of six sound engineers simultaneously recorded a crowd of 50,000 sports fans at a stadium. Since the audio is mixed in 5.1 surround sound, the crowd effects sound as if the game player is in a real stadium. The game had a sizable budget for the creation of the sound design. Complex and expensive sound effects recording sessions are usually reserved for feature films; this is an unusual example for a video game.

Since games are mixed in 5.1 surround sound, a game with poorly designed effects could fail in the competitive marketplace. As the industry grows, so do the expectations of game players. Consumers are exposed to superior sound and realistic, clear pictures with fluid motion. Developers producing mediocre work usually cannot compete against companies producing state-of-the-art games.

When game developers have limited budgets, composers may be asked to create the sound effects. It behooves composers to learn this craft. Most composers who write music for commercials and industrial videos are familiar with designing sound effects. There are innumerable sound effects libraries available for purchase, and most composers own several libraries. Many of the libraries do not have copyright restrictions, allowing composers to use the effects (without a licensing fee) without infringing on the rights of the copyright owners.

Certain effects are created by combining and editing synthesized and sampled sounds, such as space ships and additional "Star Wars" types of effects. Various audio effects (plug-ins) are used to morph basic sounds into unique effects. Delays, filters, pitch bending, compression, echo, reverberation, and pitch shifting are some of the devices used to manipulate sounds.

If certain realistic sound effects have to be created by recording the actual source (e.g., an airplane taking off or a car starting), composers must have the proper microphones and additional technical equipment to achieve the best results. Most important is capturing the sounds so that they sound authentic. This is a difficult and time-consuming process and should not be the responsibility of composers unless there are severe budgetary constraints. Some composers command additional creative fees if they create the sound effects.

> ♩♪ It can take composers equal time to design effects as it does to compose and record the music.

Voice-Overs

In low-budget projects, composers might be asked to cast and record the voices of the game characters. This can be a precarious situation. Pleasing the creative team is as vulnerable a task as having their music accepted and approved.

If casting the voices becomes a composer's responsibility, make certain that the creative team attends the auditions and the final recording sessions. Voice performances are crucial to the success of games.

Most major video game developers do not expect composers to cast and record the voices. This is generally the responsibility of the executive producer, producer, and the creative team. The creatives usually have a definite vision of how the characters should sound and behave.

> ♩♪ It would be a reasonable assumption that a high voice playing Darth Vader in the *Star Wars* films would not have been as effective as the low-resonant voice of the actor James Earl Jones.

Hiring and recording the actors requires the composers (and game developer) to abide by the SAG (Screen Actors Guild) or AFTRA (American Federation of Television and Radio Artists) agreements. These unions are responsible for negotiating scale payments and also protecting the rights of performers, including singers, actors, and dancers. Some voice-overs are recorded in right-to-work states where union membership is not required; therefore, the fees are negotiable.

> ♩♩ Nonunion actors and nonunion musicians can perform one job with union actors and union musicians before they are required to join the appropriate union in states where union membership is mandatory.

Live Orchestral Music

When video games first became popular, most of the music was synthesized, and the music was not an important component of the games. Much of the music was substandard compared to music written in almost any other medium. As all components of video games became more complex and imaginative, so did the quality of the music. Today, large orchestras record almost 100 percent of the music composed for games designed by Electronic Arts. The size of the orchestras varies from 70 to 90 musicians. Other game developers also use large orchestras.

When budget constraints exist, companies record with nonunion musicians who reside outside the United States or in right-to-work states in the United States. (Employers do not pay pension and health benefits to musicians in right-to-work states.)

The initial recording is not necessarily less costly, but there are no "back-end" payments due. This means that game publishers own the rights to use the music in perpetuity without having to pay residuals or reuse fees.

Portions of the following section are based on an interview with composer Jack Wall. He has composed music for the following games: "Mass Effect," "Jade Empire," "Myst IV: Revelation," "Rise of the Kasai," "Splinter Cell: Pandora Tomorrow," "Myst III: Exile," and many more.

> ♩ Almost all major film scores are orchestrated by orchestrators rather than by the composers primarily because of time constraints. Games with substantial budgets allow composers to hire orchestrators, but composers with limited budgets arrange and orchestrate their scores.

The music written for a game is not fully approved until all of the elements of the game have been approved. The composer is then given "the green light" to record the final score. Because of time restrictions, some composers hire orchestrators. Unlike film music, game music is usually not altered during the studio recording sessions; budgets do not allow for rewriting. The mock-ups (synthesized music cues) are approved before the final recording. Film composers usually rewrite and/or reorchestrate certain cues. "Film budgets are usually higher than those allotted for game music recording although this is changing remarkably from year to year and before long, they may equal or surpass film music budgets."—Jack Wall

Composition

Since game music requires certain sections of games to work as a unit, the key of the music in those sections is important. One solution is to write the various sectional cues in the same or related key, such as C minor followed by E-flat major. Game players can steer the stories in many directions. If the key varies, the music might sound jarring. As with film composition, the music is supposed to create an emotional mood and not necessarily be "heard." Therefore, the composers create musical techniques that allow smooth musical transitions. "However, overall, game music tends to be more 'foreground,' driving the actions, where film music needs to lie underneath dialog much of the time and thus be 'background'" (Jack Wall).

Another musical technique is to record a loop (repeated section) and add and/or change the music or sound design that is performed over the identical loop, also known as a "bed." This affords composers options without changing the mood. This technique can subliminally keep game players from becoming bored. The music could become monotonous because it is repetitive. Creating stems (orchestral sections rather than the entire orchestra) enables the musical phrases to be stretched so that it extends the time it takes for the melodic content, or sound design content, to be heard over the loop. This process also keeps the music interesting. For example, stems might consist of a percussion track, a melody track, a countermelody track, ambient effects, and so

♩♪ One of the main differences between film music and game music is that it might take a player 30 or 40 hours to play a game; therefore, the music has to remain interesting for a longer period of time than the time it takes to watch a film, which is designed in a linear mode. The viewer watches the film from beginning to end. Games are not linear. The player determines the direction of the game.

on. This format must be designed so that the stems work simultaneously. For instance, if the percussion track is playing, the melody can be added, followed by the countermelody, and so on. Musical chaos occurs if the sections are not written correctly.

- As mentioned earlier in the chapter, some composers begin the compositional process by writing multiple themes.
- Some composers write individual themes for the main characters. When a character appears, there might be various arrangements of that character's theme. If a character is in a frightening situation, the "frightening" arrangement of the theme is selected; if the character has a love scene, the "love" arrangement is played. (This is a common technique in motion picture scoring.)
- Some composers write pieces and assign an emotion to each piece. For instance, a title of a series of pieces could be "Heroic," "Sad," "Love," "Fear," and so on. In essence, the composer creates a music library for the game. Each category might have 10 compositions that will fit a specific mood.

Portions of the following section are based on an interview with composer Christopher Lennertz. He has composed music for the following games: "Medal of Honor: Rising Sun," "Pacific Assault," "European Assault Gun," "James Bond: From Russia with Love," "Warhawk," and "The Simpsons."

The average composition is written in a linear design but not music for video games. Because the game player has a choice of what path the game takes, the music must be written so that the A musical section can work not only with the B section but also with the C, D, or E sections of the music. If the game player goes left, the A section might go to the D musical section; if the game player goes right, the B section might go to the E musical section. This is a complex compositional challenge and is unique to writing music for games. As mentioned earlier, the key plays an important role in this compositional technique. The composer usually remains in one key when these potential situations can occur in a specific section of a game. Essentially, the music must be composed so that each section sounds like a completed piece of music; it should not sound as if it has a direct relationship to other sections of the composition.

Composers' Instructions

Since, in most instances, game music composers do not see the game before composing the music, they are given written directions that include a description of the scenes, the timings, the musical mood, the intensity of music, and the possible scenes that the game player might enter. The instructions for a scene might be described as Mood: Fear; Music Intensity: Level 2–3 (level settings 1–5, 5 being the highest); and Music Length: 20 seconds. There might be arrows pointing to descriptions of different scenes that the game player may enter. Therefore, the music must smoothly shift from one musical section to another, as mentioned in the previous paragraph.

General Information

Not all game publishers have budgets to hire full orchestras to accompany their games. Consequently, game composers have to compose, arrange, and orchestrate complete scores using samplers and synthesizers. They must also become competent engineers. Games with minimal budgets do not generally afford composers the ability to hire engineers. It is wise to hire minimum numbers of musicians to accompany the sampled and synthesized parts so that the score sounds more "humanized." As mentioned earlier in the book, adding several live musicians to sampled or synthesized sections as well as using live musicians as soloists can often make an entire orchestral section or solo sound real. Composers must select the most appropriate use of the live players. For example, if a budget allows for only five live musicians, you might not hire a live vibraphone player if the part sounds acceptable when played with a sample. If the vibraphone part were a jazz solo, then it would be wise to hire a jazz vibraphonist. Only the composer can make these decisions. Unfortunately, in most areas of music composition and recording in the commercial music business, the composer is often confronting budgetary issues and crucial artistic decisions that are related to the budget. In the past several years, the high quality of orchestral samples (as well as synthesized effects) has enabled composers and programmers to produce sampled and synthesized recordings that sound remarkably real. The music is usually mixed lower in level than the sound effects and the dialogue, helping to mask some of the unrealistic sounds.

As mentioned, composers might be responsible for designing and recording the sound effects and also recording the dialogue. Additional compensation is rarely given for these additional duties. In some instances, the composers are asked to mix all the audio, which includes the music, sound effects, and dialogue. Unfortunately, inexperienced composers often have to perform extra duties.

Small companies, with low budgets, might offer composers licensing deals rather than composition and production fees. The composer retains all rights to their music as compensation for not receiving fees. The composer licenses the exclusive rights—to the game publisher—to use the music for a limited (negotiated) period of time. When the term expires, the composer owns the music. He or she may license the music for use in commercials, films, CDs, and so on but most likely not for other games. Owning the music copyright can be valuable if the game is successful.

The Business of Video Game Composition

Confidentiality (Nondisclosure) Agreements

Composers are required to sign confidentiality agreements, also known as nondisclosure agreements, before game publishers disclose information about a game and/or hire composers to write the music. Standard confidentiality agreements state that composers not reveal the following:

- The name of the project
- Information regarding the characters
- Information concerning the graphics
- Advertising and marketing strategies
- Technical information
- Game platform information

In essence, composers are not authorized to reveal any information about a project to unauthorized parties. Many agreements prohibit composers from disclosing that they are composing music for a specific game or game publisher. The agreements are valid even if a composer does not accept an assignment or the assignment is not offered to the composer.

Game Composers' Contractual Agreements

Most agreements have standard clauses. Composers who have substantial "track records" (success) can often negotiate higher fees and percentages of the ancillary rights than composers who have not attained the same level of success.

The following list of headings is included in all composers' agreements. Agreements are not standard. Therefore, they are customized following the completion of negotiations between game publishers' attorneys and composers' attorneys. (The following headings are an outline of the information stated in an average agreement. Attorneys may negotiate more multifaceted deals.)

Composers' fees. Fees paid to composers are normally based on a predetermined number of minutes of original music required for the game. If the number of minutes of music exceeds the agreed-on amount, there is usually a formula that determines additional compensation. Composers are usually paid on a per-minute basis. Consequently, if a composer writes 10 extra minutes and the fee is $1,000 per minute (with a guaranteed minimum fee), the composer would receive an additional $10,000.

Recording budget. The cost of the final recording is generally handled in one of two ways:

- As an all-in buyout. The composers are paid one fee and are expected to pay the recording and mixing costs.

- The company pays the recording costs, and the composers' fees are paid directly to the composers.

The recording budget is stated within the agreement. If the recording budget changes, there must be an addendum made to the original agreement. For several reasons, companies usually make allowances for the recording budget to change. The following are some of the reasons:

- The budget for the creation of the game might exceed the projected budget; therefore, the company reduces the recording budget.
- The company might not require as much music as they originally anticipated.
- The company may decide to license songs; consequently, they require less original scoring.

Completion period. Composers are expected to complete the assignment within a specified time period that is stated in the agreement. For example, if a composer is hired for nine months, the game publisher might state that 30 minutes of music must be composed and recorded (with sampled and synthesized mock-ups) within the first four months. If a composer does not meet this obligation or the creative work is not acceptable, the employer has the right to fire the composer. If the composer is fired, the employer is obligated to pay for the work completed or pay the total fee stated in the contract. (This clause can be complex, and the terms are negotiable.)

If a game publisher is late with their development, composers are generally compensated for the extended time period. If composers are late completing the music, they may be penalized. For instance, for each day a composer is late, a portion of the final fee is deducted.

Payment schedule. Most complex games require the services of composers for a considerable time period; it may take a composer one year to complete the music for a game. (This does not mean that composers are writing continuously for a year. There may be periods of time when they work on other projects. For this to occur, the game company must grant permission to the composer. This is usually stated in the agreement. Composers are obligated to abide by the contractual agreement.)

The payment schedule is negotiable. Some composers receive one-third of their fee when the agreement is signed; a second payment in the middle of the contracted time period and the final payment on completion of the music and acceptance of the score by the employer. Some composers receive an advance before composing, and the employer pays the remainder of the fee on completion of the score and acceptance of the music. Payment schedules are negotiable.

Work-made-for-hire agreements. Most game companies ask composers to sign work-made-for-hire agreements. (Work-made-for-hire agreements are a part of the U.S. copyright law.) The agreements state that the company (game publisher) owns all rights to the original music composed, paid for, and used in a game. Composers do not usually receive "back-end rights," meaning that they do not receive royalties based on sales or ancillary usage. (Certain composers may receive a royalty.) The rights to cues (individual compositions within a project) not used in a game usually revert back to the composer after the final music has been completed and accepted by the game publisher.

Ancillary rights. Some composers receive royalties when their game music is used in other mediums, such as in motion pictures, television, CDs, commercials, and additional formats. Composers' royalty rates are negotiable.

Some composers receive bonuses if unit sales of games exceed a predetermined number. Established composers may receive a royalty after expenses have been recouped, but this is a rarity.

Composers' credits. Clearly state the manner in which composers' credits are listed on game jackets and in the advertising and marketing campaigns for the games. Credit is important to composers because other game publishers (and music buyers) are made aware of their work. Publicity brings new opportunities.

Most agreements also state that the company has the right to publish the name and likeness of composers. This can be advantageous to both composers and game publishers. For instance, if John Williams wrote the score, his name could certainly influence potential customers to purchase the game. Games containing songs by well-known recording artists can help sell games. For lesser-known composers, having their names publicized can expose them to future employers.

Litigation. If contractual problems or disagreements occur, the agreement states the means by which disputes may be handled. Some agreements state that disputes are litigated in a court of law. Other agreements state that an arbitration panel will settle a dispute. The panel's judgment is usually irrevocable.

Legal proceedings generally take place in the state where the employer is located. Most often, disputes are settled out of court.

Expenses. If composers incur approved expenses, the employer agrees to pay. For instance, many scores are recorded in cities and countries other than the city where a composer lives. This requires flight, hotel, and food expenses. The company might ask the composer to orchestrate the score for a 60-piece orchestra and then request that it be scored for an 80-piece orchestra. If the agreement states that the composer is required to pay the cost of the music recording sessions (an all-in budget deal), the budget overage is paid by the employer.

Cross-collateral implications. Some A-list composers may receive royalties on a per-unit-sold basis, which begins after the game publisher has recouped its investment. Since there are multiple video game platforms, the attorneys representing composers must try not to allow the company to cross collateralize the game expenses for the various game formats (e.g., PlayStation, Xbox, and Nintendo) against composers' royalties). The negotiations may become confrontational, and the outcome can depend on the relationship the company has with the composer. For instance, do they want to work with the composer on future projects?

Testing

Games are beta tested before they are released to the public. Game developers want to be certain that potential game buyers accept the entertainment value of a game, the musical score, the graphics, the voices, the sound design, and how quickly a player can learn to play the game. If these elements do not test well, some of the elements will be redesigned and retested until the test results convince a publisher that their games are ready to be released into a highly competitive marketplace. Game publishers are committed to investing advertising and marketing dollars. Therefore, they want to anticipate a financially sound outcome, and testing helps them prognosticate their chances of success.

Conclusion

This discussion has focused on most of the terms included in generic video game agreements for composers. All agreements with game publishers are complex; consequently, composers should consult with attorneys who specialize in entertainment law and who also have expertise in negotiating video game agreements for composers.

Examples of Video Game Business Agreements
Musical Composition License

Licensing songs and instrumentals for use in video games can be extremely complex. A song might have six writers; each writer has a publishing company. All companies must agree on the terms of the license. In most instances, favored-nations deals are offered to each writer and publisher (each writer and publisher receives the same deal). This is not always acceptable to all involved parties and might require further negotiations. One writer might claim that he wrote 25 percent of the song, another might claim that she wrote 50 percent of the music, and so on.

An additional problem might occur if samples are used within the recordings. This involves clearing not only the writers' and publishers' shares but also the shares of each record company that owns the master sound recording rights to the samples. The entire process can become a legal nightmare. When determining the value of samples, the number of minutes a sample is heard and the popularity of the sample usually determine its value.

Game publishers will either offer a fee for a "buyout," which requires no further payments unless the composition(s) is used in a format other than the game format (e.g., the song is used on a CD or in a motion picture).

Standard Agreement

The following is a synopsis of a standard agreement (not a legal document) between composers and game companies for the use of a song(s) (instrumental[s]) within a video game and also for "third-party" usage of the song(s) (e.g., theatrical trailers, CDs, commercials, and so on).

The first paragraph states the name of the parties entering into the agreement, the date and term (length) of the agreement, and the name(s) of the composition(s). Whereas (company name) desires to use the Composition(s) in the interactive software game entitled (name of game [the "Product"]) and to make copies of the Compositions and Product ("Copies") for distribution to the public, the parties mutually agree as follows:

License. The Company pays a fee for the usage and in return receives the following in the licensed territory (territories) on a nonexclusive or exclusive basis:

- The Company has the right to use the Composition and Arrangement in various formats. For instance, they may use the vocals with various background arrangements, use only the instrumental portion of the track, use portions of the song, and so on. They basically have the right to use the music in any format as long as the integrity of the Composition(s) is not compromised. For instance, the music cannot be used in a pornographic context.
- The Company has the right to use the Composition(s) as introductions to portions of the game, ending pieces ("outros"), "cinematics" (a movie within a game), and game trailers (promotions).
- The Company has the right to promote the game at trade shows, additional promotional venues, magazine promotions, platform demonstrations, Internet promotions, and additional forms of promotions.
- The Composition(s) (within the game) can be used in various game platforms (e.g., Xbox, PlayStation, and Nintendo).
- The Company has the right to manufacture, market, distribute, and sell the game to the public.
- The Company also has the right to sublicense the rights for the purposes of manufacturing, distributing, and marketing the game.

Term. The term shall be for (number of years) from the initial date of release of the game. The Company will have the option to extend the license either on the same terms specified in the agreement or with additional stipulations.

Territory. The rights are usually worldwide, unless there are unusual circumstances. For instance, if an established song (instrumental) has a variety of publishers throughout the world, the Company must obtain licenses from each publisher. This is not usually a problem.

Fee. In some agreements, composers and publishers are paid a one-time fee for all rights in perpetuity. In other agreements, composers and publishers may receive royalties after the Company has recouped their advance against royalties. All agreements are negotiable.

Warranties. Licensor warrants and represents:

- The composers and publishers have to state that they can legally enter into the Agreement.
- The Licensee must state that they are not infringing on the rights of any third parties.
- The Licensee must state that the composition(s) does not include unauthorized use of samples from other compositions without obtaining the rights.
- They must state that they own the copyright and publishing rights.
- If there are multiple writers and multiple publishers, the division of ownership must be stated. For example, John (writer) owns 10 percent of the writer's royalties, Jim (writer) owns 90 percent of the writer's royalties, XXX Music Publishing owns 10 percent of the music publishing royalties (territory must be stated), YYY owns 90 percent of the publishing royalties (territory must be stated), and so on.

Indemnification. The Licensor indemnifies and holds harmless the Licensee against any Licensor's breach of the License.

Assignment. The parties may assign this agreement to third parties. For instance, if the Company is sold, the new Company will inherit the agreement.

♪♪ The previous sample agreement is not a legal document. The terms stated are an outline of the general terms that would be legally stated by an entertainment attorney.

Legal fees and limitation on damages. In the event that either party claims that an agreement has been breached, this clause will define how the legal issues will be resolved (e.g., arbitration or through the court system).

Miscellaneous. This clause names the state in which the agreement will be litigated in the event of a claim.

Writer/Publisher Agreement

The following is an example of an agreement between composers and publishers when sampled tracks are used as background tracks containing new melodies and/or hip-hop lyrics that are performed over the sampled track. This example of a sample breakdown agreement is used for some video games.

The original title of the sampled song is changed to a new title, thereby creating a new song. The percentages of ownership are stated within a new agreement.

> New Composition: [name of new song title]
> Timing:
> Artist: [name of artist]
> Songwriter #1: 50 percent
> Songwriter #2: 25 percent
> Songwriter #3: 25 percent
> Name of publisher #1 (ASCAP): 50 percent
> Name of publisher #2 (BMI): 50 percent
> The new song is sampled from: [name of original song]

In witness whereof the parties have entered into this Agreement the day and year (add day and year).

> [name of game publisher]
> [signatures of all writers and publishers]

The Agreement is registered as a new composition with the publishers as well as with the performing-rights organizations (e.g., ASCAP, BMI, and SESAC in the United States and with the equivalent foreign publishers and performing-rights organizations).

AFM (American Federation of Musicians of the United States and Canada)

Because conditions may vary with individual companies and video game projects, the composer and/or contractor should consult with the AFM before comprising a budget or proceeding with a video game recording session in the United States. (These agreements may be used throughout the United States and Canada and are generally considered a one-off, or a single, engagement agreement.) The AFM currently offers the following video game agreements:

- AFM Experimental Video Game Agreement—Option 1
- AFM Experimental Video Game Agreement—Option 2
- AFM Combined-Use Video Game Agreement

These agreements provide information on the following topics:

- Premium overtime
- Breaks
- Minutes of music
- Use of music
- Sound track albums
- Leader
- Contractor
- Pension
- Health and welfare
- Music preparation
- Payments
- Promotional use
- Credits
- Cartage
- Cancellation
- Grievance and arbitration
- Union security

For the most current terms and financial information, contact the American Federation of Musicians' Electronic Media Services Division, West Coast Office, 3550 Wilshire Blvd., Suite 1900, Los Angeles, CA 90010. Phone: (213) 251-4510, ext. 202. Website: www.afm.org.

Founded in 1896, the AFM is the largest organization in the world dedicated to representing the interests of professional musicians. With more than 90,000 members, the AFM represents all types of professional musicians, including those who record music for sound recordings, film scores, and radio, television, and commercial announcements, and those who perform music of every genre in every sort of venue from small jazz clubs to symphony orchestra halls to major stadiums. Whether negotiating fair agreements, protecting ownership of recorded music, securing benefits such as health care and pension, or lobbying legislators, the AFM is committed to raising industry standards and placing the professional musician in the foreground of the cultural landscape.

Assignments

1. Play a video game. Choose several sections and score them. Select a different musical direction than the music heard on the game.
2. If possible, mix your music in 5.1 surround sound. If not, record a stereo mix. Play your music back while viewing the game. (It is important to ascertain if your music is appropriate for the project.)

12

Internet Commercials, Website Music, and Made-for-the-Internet Video Programs

Many commercials that can be viewed on the Web are the same commercials made for television; the majority of Internet commercials are 30 seconds. As advertising on the Internet grows, more video ads will be designed for the Internet. Because the effectiveness of video advertising for the Web is yet unproven, video companies have to produce the videos at a much lesser cost than budgets spent for television commercials. Music houses must also agree to compose Web music at a reduced rate. Ads specifically designed for the Web will most likely be shorter than the average television commercial; they will probably average 5 to 10 seconds. Advertising incorporated in television programs viewed on the Web averages 30 seconds. As more agencies specialize in Web-only advertising, the quality of the productions will increase.

Original Web music is also written to enhance the effectiveness of websites. The music is designed as traditional underscoring. Music adds to the viewer's experience and, it is hoped, makes the Web message more effective.

Arguably, the most effective use of Web advertising to date has been *The Hire* film series, created for BMW. The company hired several of the Hollywood's foremost directors to create eight mini-films (long-form commercials) designed to promote the high performance of BMW cars. Over 100 million viewers saw the films. The series won numerous awards and was the forerunner of creating films designed for the Web. (The films are no longer available for viewing on the Web.)

> ♫ The average age of a video game player is 30, and 60 percent of heads of households in the United States play games, according to the Entertainment Software Association (May 2006).

The newest form of entertainment is "television-style" series created for the Internet. These shows are not necessarily full-length programs. For instance, some programs are 8 minutes or shorter. The producers experiment with various lengths; they have to develop a format that will keep the attention of the audience so that the audience watches the new episodes.

Some of the programs show commercials prior to the program. The viewer cannot bypass the commercials, thereby assuring the advertisers that their commercials will be watched. Since the production costs of the programs are much less than the production costs of television programs, the advertising rates are less, and the advertiser can reach their target audience. The advertiser has the opportunity to learn more about their target audience since the websites are interactive. The viewers might respond to questions or click on links that provide the advertisers with a more accurate profile of their demographic. This information helps advertisers design advertising that appeals to their target audience. The following are some of the made-for-the-Internet programs:

Prom Queen is a made-for-the-Internet teen soap opera, produced by the former chief executive officer of the Walt Disney Company, Michael Eisner. The series has 80 short-form episodes. The film *Hairspray* was a major sponsor. The episodes are scored with original music. The viewers can interact via video blogs, comments, profiles, and so on. The first season of the program was shown between April 1 and June 20, 2007, and received 15 million views. Because of this success, a spin-off, *Prom Queen: Summer Heat*, debuted on August 27, 2007.

Afterworld, an animated show created by Electric Farm Entertainment that runs 2 to 3 minutes per episode, has 130 episodes and cost $3 million to produce. Companies are investing large sums to produce high-quality programming. This program also has original underscoring.

Funny or Die, cofounded by Will Farrell, is a comedy video-based website. Many popular comedians and new comedians contribute to this site. Some of the videos have been viewed by millions of viewers. They are all short form.

Quarterlife, an Internet series, was created by the highly successful team of Marshall Herskovitz and Edward Zwick. Some of their projects include *Blood Diamond*, *Legends of the Fall*, and *My So-Called Life*. Creators with their achievements elevate the credibility of Internet entertainment.

Advertisers are supporting this new format because the programs are reaching the younger generation who can afford to purchase their products. This format offers new opportunities for composers to write both commercials and underscoring for Web-based programming.

The television networks are showing entire episodes of their successful programs on the web, the day after they are broadcast in prime time. There was concern by the networks that this practice would decrease the number of viewers, but the opposite occurred: the number of viewers increased. Viewers miss episodes or do not record them. This affords them the opportunity to see the programs.

Broadcast television generates approximately $60 billion in advertising revenue, and the video Web market generates approximately $10 billion. This proves that advertisers are being drawn to the Web.

Research shows that the average person spends about 34 percent of their free time watching television and that folks with broadband (cable or DSL) spend 32 percent of their time online.

To keep the audience's interest while the television program *Battlestar Galactica* was on hiatus, the producers produced ministories on the Web, providing fans with small bits of information about the new season. This helped to keep the audience interested until the program returned to television. Fans can follow up with online chat rooms in which their core audience can interact with each other.

Prediction: Television and the Internet will become one format (e.g., Apple television).

13

The Business of Commercials

Although the primary focus of this book is the creative process of composing music for commercials, an overview of the *business of commercials* is necessary.

In the United States, New York, Los Angeles, Chicago, and Nashville are the hubs for national advertising. In these locales, most musicians and singers are union members, entitling them to receive union-scale session payments and residual payments. Residual payments are additional payments to musicians and singers based on the length of time a commercial is broadcast and the number of regions in which it is broadcast. These payments also apply to performances on the Internet, satellite radio, and cell phones as well as motion picture theaters, cable television, and additional new platforms referred to as "new media." The various unions (AFM, SAG, AFTRA, and SESAC, discussed later in this chapter) have dissimilar payment scales that are periodically renegotiated with representatives of the advertising industry.

Composers do *not* receive residuals. For many years, composers have unsuccessfully lobbied for this benefit. To compensate for the loss of this potential income, some music companies charge sizable creative fees.

Composers who write for music houses are almost always included on the musicians' and singers' contracts. This allows them to collect session fees and receive residual payments.

Marketing a Music Company

Demonstration Reels

Music houses or independent composers submit audio reels and video reels that serve as a demonstration of their work. It is advisable that each reel does not exceed 7 to 10 minutes in duration.

When agency producers solicit reels, they are usually specific about the style of music they are searching for. Try to customize a reel for each individual request. It is difficult to be chosen for a job without demonstrating a piece of music that sounds similar to the style of music that the agency is requesting. Three or four examples are usually sufficient. If an agency is not familiar with a composer's work, also send a composite reel that incorporates various musical styles.

It is advisable to keep a music library that is filed by category, such as jazz, jingles, rock and roll, rhythm and blues, and so on. File subgenres, such as male rock-and-roll vocals, light female vocals, and so on. Design an easily accessible filing system, which will simplify the process of accessing samples. Some music companies have numerous reels that are divided into categories. For instance, they may have children's reels, World Music reels, jingle reels, and various other genres. Keep the reels updated. When new musical genres become popular, assemble new reels (e.g., Reggaeton).

Singers submit demo reels to music companies and advertising agencies, which collect reels of outstanding singers and file them by category. For example, some singers specialize in rock and roll, others in country music, and so on. When working on jingles, the creatives will ask the music house to submit demo reels of lead singers. It is advisable to submit several reels and ask the agency creatives to choose the lead singer. If they do not like a singer's performance at the recording session, they will request a new singer, and the music company will generally incur the additional expense unless the agency selected the singer.

It is beneficial for music companies and independent composers to create an image. For example, some composers specialize in jingles and others in underscoring and sound design. Always market the most exemplary work. Do not accept an assignment that is not suitable for your talents. A poorly executed job will cause an unpleasant situation with the agency (and the client) and result in an irreconcilable relationship with the agency. No composer is an expert in all musical genres.

Create business cards, stationery, and a website that depicts your company's image. Websites enable potential clients to play both video and audio samples. The websites should include a history of the music company and bios of each composer and jingle writer. A well-designed website creates a company's image.

Representatives

Most jingle houses and some individual composers have representatives, referred to as *reps*. Their job is to approach advertising agencies in a sales capacity. They meet with agency creatives and develop relationships that hopefully lead to employment.

A typical meeting includes playing the music company's most recent video and audio sample reels. Their objective is to determine when an agency will need the services of a music company and the style of music they will be in search of. Agencies usually arrange their shooting schedules several months in advance and sometimes will reveal the information.

A creative rep asks the music house to assemble a distinctive music reel that contains music that will, it is hoped, appeal to the agency for an impending job. If the agency producer likes the reel, he or she may use some of the music on a temp (temporary) track when editing the commercial. Since most music is not available to be licensed, if the producer feels a particular piece would suit the commercial, he or she may ask the music house to write an original composition in the same style. The job might be awarded to the music house.

Reps often negotiate fees and calculate budgets. Their job description varies between companies. It is advisable that reps attend recording sessions to "hand-hold" the agency creatives and to be the intermediary between the agency and the music company. Sessions can become unruly when there are too many chefs in the kitchen. One person from the music company should be the liaison to the agency creatives (clients). Some of the larger agencies employ staff music producers who produce the sessions. The agency music producer communicates directly with the agency creatives.

Flyers and Newsletters

Some music companies distribute flyers and newsletters (generally through e-mail) informing agencies (and other potential clients) of their current activities. Continually update the company's website by adding the most recent television and radio commercials so that they can be seen and heard. Keep the company's image contemporary. The advertising business primarily mimics popular culture, and popular culture keeps morphing.

Marketing ideas are merely aids to draw attention to a music company. Musical excellence secures assignments. The best marketing aid is to have diverse video and audio reels that display inventive and exceptional work. It is also important to complete projects on schedule and to conduct business transactions in a professional manner. Advertising music is a business and must be conducted as such to retain clients.

Advertising

Some music companies purchase ads in trade magazines. Most often the ads focus on their latest commercials while projecting their company image. Some companies specialize in certain musical styles, while others retain a staff of composers and jingle writers; this projects an image of a full-service music house. The company should focus on its strengths.

Ironically (according to music company representatives to whom I have spoken), purchasing advertisements for music houses (in trade magazines) has not generally been effective. The consensus from the music companies is that advertising has rarely resulted in direct sales but has created awareness of their companies, helping to procure new relationships.

Public Relations Firms

Some companies hire public relations firms. It is their job to interest journalists and editors to publish articles about the music company; they also try to obtain publicity in additional mediums. The best exposure is in trade magazines such as *Advertising Age* (the ''bible'' of the advertising industry). Trade magazines publish the names of suppliers that have worked on specific commercials. For example, they will list the product, the advertising agency and producer, the copywriter, the art director, the editor, the composer, the music company, the director, and the name of the director's company. The information is usually published weekly. Potential employers read this information and contact suppliers they find of interest. Word of mouth results from public relations.

Company History

A short company history should contain a list of current and previous clients in addition to a short bio about each composer and/or jingle writer. This serves as an introduction to potential clients. Include a company bio when submitting demonstration reels.

Trademark Protection

A trademark is a symbol or a name that identifies a company or manufacturer and is registered with the government as a form of protection. Music houses often trademark their name and company logo. After establishing an image, they want their image protected so that other companies cannot infringe on their trademark and image.

The application process takes approximately 18 months. Information and application forms can be found on the Internet at www.uspto.gov. Attorneys specializing in intellectual property apply for and clear trademarks. Since it can be difficult to clear a trademark, it is best to hire an attorney.

Trademarks can be exceptionally valuable. For example, the Coke trademark is worth $69 billion (the shape of Coke's bottle, among other things, is trademarked); the Disney trademark is worth $32 billion. This is not to infer that a music house will have the same value, but after spending time and money to establish an image, it is best to be protected.

Agency Negotiations

When discussing business, reps normally contact agency producers. Producers generally request a detailed budget from music companies. Sometimes, agencies have a predetermined music budget and ask music companies to itemize their proposed budgets. When music houses submit budgets, there is generally a minimal negotiation until a mutually acceptable budget is agreed on. The agency proceeds by writing a detailed agreement outlining the exact terms of the assignment. The music company must sign the agreement before work can begin. The agreement is imperative for both sides because if a dispute arises, the terms are documented.

Negotiate the best possible budget. If the budget is too low to accomplish the creative objectives of the agency, tell the negotiators. Once a budget has been approved, it is very difficult to obtain additional funding.

Inform the creatives that for, say, budget A, the track will not contain certain elements (e.g., real strings as opposed to synthesized strings) but that for budget B the track will be produced in the manner in which the job has been creatively conceived.

A satisfactory compromise is generally agreed on. Always assure the agency that the final track will sound acceptable even if the requested budget is not approved. Inform the agency that some adjustments will be required, such as fewer musicians and singers, less mixing time, and so on.

Sometimes music companies negotiate a total price for an assignment. If an ''all-in'' budget is accepted by the agency, the music company is not usually required to submit a detailed budget because there will be no residual payments. If it is necessary for the agency (client) to pay residual payments (residuals), the agency must approve the number of musicians and singers in order to calculate the cost.

Budget

The budget is based on regions of the country where membership in unions is mandatory in order to work. These payments are included in the agency's overall budget that has to be approved by the client.

Traditionally, advertising agencies add a commission to the production costs (an average of 10 to 15 percent). Another business paradigm is also implemented. Agencies receive fees in place of percentages. Agencies' compensations are negotiable.

Some clients require that at least three qualified companies bid on each line item of a production budget. This includes the music, the director, the editor, and so on. If the suppliers are of equal creative ability, the lowest bid usually wins the assignment.

Right-to-Work States

Some states do not require union membership to work in certain industries. If nonunion musicians or singers work on union recording sessions, the law requires that their wages be the same as the union members. In reality, unions in most right-to-work states do not have much clout; therefore, music companies generally negotiate buyout fees. One fee encompasses the performer's participation, and there are no residual payments. The music company negotiates individual fees for each musician, singer, composer, and/or arranger that are deducted from a music company's gross budget.

In the United States, the majority of nonunion work is created in Dallas, Texas. Most radio identification jingles and a substantial number of commercials are recorded for regional and local advertising in Dallas because there are no residual payments required and session payments are negotiated. Clients can use the music for a predetermined period of time; occasionally, they purchase the rights in perpetuity.

Recording in right-to-work states is less costly than recording in union-controlled states. Fees and residual payments are based on the size of the markets; larger markets warrant higher creative fees.

Music Budget

Most music companies pay composers and arrangers based on a percentage of the creative fees received by the music company. For example, a composer or arranger might receive $33^1/_3$ or 40 percent of the fee received by the music company for composing and/or arranging commercials.

The music company usually deducts the portion of the budget that covers studio charges, engineering fees, and other direct fees because these charges are not considered part of the creative fee. A rep's commission is also deducted before arriving at the net creative fee.

The net income is determined after the charges have been deducted. This serves as the basis for determining the creative and arranging fees.

Composers encounter substantial expenses. To remain competitive, they must continually upgrade their equipment. Most computers have to be upgraded every two years. New software and hardware, which include synthesizers, samplers, samples, and effects units, are continually being developed; existing software and hardware must also be upgraded.

Demo Fee

The demo is the first step in the creative process. Most music companies submit several demos but are usually paid to submit only one. If several commercials require different scores, a demo fee is paid for each submission. A demo budget is usually not included when calculating the final budget. Demo fees are frequently deducted from the final budget of the company that is chosen to record the final production.

Demos are not simply demos anymore. Demos must sound like finished productions. In fact, some demos are not revised and are broadcast as final tracks.

Most music companies complain that demo fees are meager considering the work that has to be accomplished. Music companies almost always lose money producing demos. In essence, they pay to compete for jobs. Most companies are willing to accept the risk because the financial rewards can be substantial if they are awarded final projects.

> ♫ It is industry standard that if a demo is rejected, the music company retains the rights to the music. To be protected, make certain that these rights are stated in the contractual agreement with the agency.

There is almost always competition to win national commercials. Some music houses develop close relationships with creatives and agencies and are awarded jobs without competing. They still have to satisfy the creatives and the clients with the quality of their work, or additional companies will be hired to compete.

Creative Fee

A creative fee is a negotiable fee that is paid for an original composition. Fees for successful composers are usually higher than fees for composers with fewer successes. Most often, music companies do not charge excessive fees because of the potential income from residuals. (Residuals apply only to union jobs.)

Creative fees are often paid in increments. If there is a possibility that a commercial will be played nationally or regionally, the agency may first test it in one region. The first payment allows the agency to use the music only in the test market. The remainder of the fee is paid when the commercial is broadcast nationally or regionally. Additional fees are paid if commercials are broadcast in foreign territories.

Arranging Fee

The agency might only require an arrangement(s) of existing music. Agencies either own the music or negotiate licensing agreements with music publishers; the license allows them to rearrange existing music (e.g., a popular song). The music company charges an arranging fee (no creative fee) but sometimes charges a production fee that equals about one-half of the arranging fee. (Production fees are not considered standard and must be negotiated.)

Union scale governs arrangement fees. The scale is based on the number of measures and the size of the orchestra or combo. Most competent arrangers receive substantially more than union scale. The union requires an arranger to receive scale only on the musicians' contract. The remainder of the fee is paid directly by the music company and should be included in the itemized budget.

Only union scale is included on the contract because the agencies want to pay the minimum amount for pension and health benefits. (If the arranger's fee is higher than union scale, he or she submits an additional bill to the music company.) These benefits are based on a percentage of the arranger's fee. Higher fees increase the cost of pension and health benefits.

If a composer for a music company composed the original composition, the company will usually try to negotiate a clause in the agreement that states that the music company has the right to generate any additional arrangements of that music. This concession is not usually granted.

Costs of Musicians

Musicians—in states where union membership is mandatory—receive union scale for each recording session. (Some musicians receive double scale.) The following applies as well:

1. If musicians double their original parts or add new parts, additional payments are due.
2. If musicians play more than one instrument (called doubling), they receive additional compensation.
3. Health and pension benefits must be included when calculating the budget. The benefits are based on a percentage of each musician's wages.
4. Arrangers and/or orchestrators receive double scale.
5. Union scale for music copyists is based on the number of measures and number of parts copied.
6. If there is a possibility of overtime, estimate the cost and include it as a miscellaneous budget item.
7. Musicians who play a large instrument, such as a harp or double bass, are entitled to cartage fees, which pay for the transport of their instruments. The fees are listed in the American Federation of Musicians union agreement.
8. If there are more than a specified number of musicians, the union requires a contractor to be paid double scale. Contractors hire the musicians and usually fill out the union contract.
9. Session leaders receive double scale.
10. Conductors receive double scale.

Contracts are periodically renegotiated, so be aware of the most recent scales and other changes.

When recording a nonunion session, after establishing the performers' fees, detail their session duties. For example, singers must triple their parts, and a clarinet player is also expected to double on the flute. Even though the payments are not based on union scale, the performers will not perform unlimited services for one fee unless it is agreed on prior to a recording session.

Number of Singers and Cost

The number of singers must be specified (lead and background singers). If the singers overdub their parts or add new parts, additional payments will be due. Include health and pension benefits in the budget.

Cost of Engineer

Most recording engineers charge an hourly rate. Sometimes they agree to a flat fee with the condition that after they exceed an agreed-on number of hours, they receive additional compensation.

Studio Costs

Studio costs include studio time, hard-disk recording devices, video equipment, duplication costs, and so on. (It is rare to use tape.)

Studio time is charged on an hourly basis. (Include tax in the budget.) Always estimate additional studio time because creatives tend to request changes during sessions, and this can be time consuming.

Fees for Celebrities

If celebrities are hired to sing or play on a commercial, their fees can be costly. The agency negotiates the fees directly with their agent or manager. This fee is not included in the budget given by music companies.

Instrument Rentals

On occasion there is a need to rent instruments. Often they are unusual instruments that most players do not own, or they are very large instruments, such as timpani, harp, boo bams (percussion instrument), or balaphones (African xylophones). Call an instrument rental company and ask about prices so that the cost can be included in the budget. If the arranger decides to use additional instruments after the budget has been submitted, deduct the cost from the "miscellaneous" section of the budget.

Most professional studios rent instruments and equipment (as a courtesy to music houses) and charge the fee on the studio bill. Consult with the instrumentalist before renting an instrument. He or she might request a specific brand.

Payroll Companies

Handling fees (for talent and residuals) are included in most budgets. Sometimes the music company receives this fee, but most often external companies that specialize in performing this service manage the payments. Handling fees may include the preparation of union contracts, issuing checks to performers, the preparation of residual payment estimates, and budget estimates in addition to other services. Payroll companies handle payments for music companies and/or agencies. They receive a handling fee that is based on a percentage of the budget. Include the handling fee when calculating a budget. (This service is often not needed.)

If the music house is required to pay the talent, make certain to receive the payment from the client or agency prior to the recording session. Because of cash flow problems, when dealing with small agencies, arrange to be paid before paying the expenses. Refuse to begin work until payment is received since the music company will be responsible for all costs.

Most agencies submit a condensed contract, also called a heads-of-agreement letter, stating the agreed-on terms of an assignment. The terms of the agreement should be specific; if not, the music supplier could be held responsible for payments that were not agreed on during the basic negotiations. For instance, if a jingle is being recorded and the agency changes *one* lyric (one word) at the end of a session, overtime might occur. The music company should not be charged for the overtime and performer fees because the lyric change was not anticipated prior to the recording.

Always state the number of commercials and, in the case of jingles, the number of lyrics to be recorded (even if the backing track remains the same for each lyric). For instance, if one line of a lyric is changed, it is considered an additional version of the commercial (e.g., a city name, such as "in San Antonio" instead of "in Los Angeles," as stated in a prior version), and the singers must be paid for an additional commercial.

The American Federation of Musicians (AFM) allows a certain number of commercials to be recorded in one recording session. Thus, even though the singers might receive an additional payment because a lyric has changed, the musicians might not receive an extra session payment. However, when the commercial is broadcast, the session is listed as a separate commercial, allowing the musicians to receive residual payments for the additional commercial.

The terms of the Screen Actors Guild (SAG) agreement (the SAG represents singers and other performers) differ from the terms of the AFM (musicians) agreement. As mentioned, singers are paid for each commercial. Since union contracts change, always be aware of the most recent contractual revisions.

Most large agencies ask music houses to supply completed union contracts. The agencies (or a payroll company) pay the contracts. Check the bylaws of each union to determine the date a contract must be paid.

Late fees are applicable if payments are not received within the time frame stated in each union agreement. If music houses do not submit contracts in a timely manner, they will be responsible to pay the late fees; the agencies will not be fined. (The agencies deduct late fees from the final payment to the music companies.)

The unions require that all performers hired for a recording session be "in good standing." This means that the performers have paid their dues and that there are no supplementary problems that would hinder their eligibility to perform. The agencies or music companies may be fined if they do not verify each individual's status prior to a recording session.

The date of a recording session must be reported to the union prior to a session. The information required by the unions is the name of the advertising agency, the product name, and the date that the session will occur. If the session is not reported, the unions often fine the music company.

Unions

Musicians and/or singers recording in states that require union membership to perform on commercials must join one or more of the following unions: the AFM (musicians who perform on television and radio commercials), the SAG (singers who sing on television commercials), and the American Federation of Television and Radio Artists (AFTRA) (singers who sing on radio commercials).

Music houses in states that require union membership must be signatories to certain unions, or they cannot contract musicians and singers. The following applies as well:

1. Some states require union membership for performers to accept union jobs.
2. Union members may not accept nonunion jobs, under any circumstances, without prior permission from the union. For example, the unions might allow performers to work on public service commercials without receiving union scale.
3. Some states, called right-to-work states, do not require union membership to work. (Twenty-two U.S. states are right-to-work states.) Research the laws of the state you are working in.
4. Understand the terms of performers' unions and follow them exactly as stated. Sizable fines can be assessed for not complying with the rules.

The following information applies to the unions in the United States. Contact each organization or view their websites to gain in-depth information. Similar unions and performing-rights organizations exist in other countries. Become familiar with the organizations and unions in their countries.

Unions and Performing-Rights Societies

The following is a general overview of the main organizations and unions that directly affect composers, singers, actors, and announcers (performers) when participating in television and radio commercials.

It can be difficult to determine which union governs a specific job. There may be two unions involved with one job. For instance, a television commercial and a radio commercial require separate contracts with different unions. The scales and bylaws of the unions differ. When conditions are questionable, call the unions for information.

SAG

The following information was taken from the SAG website at www .sag.org. The SAG is a labor union affiliated with the AFL-CIO through the Associated Actors and Artists of America. Singers in major markets must join SAG in order to be eligible to perform on commercials. (SAG does not represent composers or musicians.)

All singers and instrumentalists who act or appear on-screen in commercials, films, music videos, television programs, industrial films, video games, and all new media formats must be members of the SAG.

Union-scale payments are dissimilar for singers and musicians who perform only on the recording and do not appear on-screen. (Musicians are represented from the AFM.) The singers' rates are based on performing as a soloist, a duo, or a group of singers of three or more. Doubling parts increases the payments. They receive residual payment (extended use) on a per-play basis, as compared with the AFM (musicians) reuse fees, which are based on 13-week cycles.

Definitions (www.sag.org)

The Producers signatory hereto and the Union confirm their mutual understanding and agreement that the term "commercials" as used herein and in all prior agreements between the parties, means and includes, and has always meant and included, motion pictures whether made on or by film, tape or otherwise and whether produced by means of motion picture cameras, electronic cameras or devices, tape devices or any combination of the foregoing, or any other means, methods or devices now used or which may hereafter be adopted. The foregoing provision shall be binding upon advertising agencies signatory hereto or to Letters of Adherence referred to in Section 56, Letters of Adherence, except only with respect to commercials made by means of electronic tape or any other electronic device produced for such advertising agencies by television stations or television networks using broadcasting studio facilities of such television stations or television networks.

Commercials are short advertising or commercial messages made as motion pictures, 3 minutes or less in length, and intended for showing over television. Advertising or commercial messages include any narration, dialogue, songs, jingles or other matter which depict or mention the advertiser's name, product or service. They include program openings and closings which mention the advertiser's name, product or service. Advertising and commercial messages over 3 minutes in length shall be subject to separate negotiations between the Union and Producer.

The term "commercials" also includes short advertising messages intended for showing on the Internet which would be treated as commercials if broadcast on television and which are capable of being used on television in the same form as on the Internet. If a dispute arises as to whether material used on the Internet qualifies as a commercial, as defined above, either party may submit the dispute to a joint committee established by the Joint Policy Committee and the Union. The joint committee shall consist of an equal number of persons appointed by the Joint Policy Committee and by the Union. If the joint committee fails to resolve the dispute within thirty days, either party may submit the dispute to arbitration.

Mission Statement (www.sag.org)

The Screen Actors Guild represents its members through: negotiation and enforcement of collective bargaining agreements which establish equitable levels of compensation, benefits, and working conditions for performers; the collection of compensation for exploitation of their recorded performances and protection against unauthorized use; and the preservation and expansion of work opportunities.

Joining Qualifications: A performer may become eligible for Screen Actors Guild membership under one of the following conditions:

1. Proof of SAG Employment
   A. Principal Performer Employment: Performers may join SAG upon proof of employment or prospective employment within two weeks or less by a SAG signatory company. Employment must be in a principal or speaking role in a SAG film, videotape, television program or commercial. Proof of such employment may be in the form of a signed contract, a payroll check or check stub, or a letter from the company (on company letterhead). The document proving employment must provide the following information: applicant's name and Social Security number, the

name of the product or the commercial (the product name), the salary paid in dollar amount, and the specific date(s) worked.

B. Background Players Employment: Performers may join SAG upon proof of employment as a SAG covered background player at full SAG rates and conditions for a MINIMUM of three workdays subsequent to March 25, 1990. Employment must be by a company signed to a SAG Background Players Agreement, and in a SAG film, videotape, television program or commercial. Proof of such employment must be in the form of a signed employment voucher (or time card), plus an original payroll check or check stub. Such documents must provide the same information listed in paragraph 1)A above.

AFTRA (www.aftra.com)

AFTRA is a labor union and affiliated with the AFL-CIO. AFTRA represents actors and other professional performers (singers), and broadcasters in live and taped television, radio, sound recordings, non-broadcast/industrial programming, and new technologies such as interactive programming and CD-ROMs.

Performers are permitted to perform their first job without joining the union. To be eligible to participate on subsequent jobs, they must join AFTRA within thirty days following the first job. Members pay an initiation fee plus yearly dues. The dues are calculated on the gross earnings of individual performers. AFTRA provides a pension plan plus additional benefits.

Residual payments (reuse payments) are based on per-use payments. Each time a commercial is broadcast singers receive additional payments. The reuse fees are calculated by using a formula, which is calculated using a geographical formula and also the frequency of airplay. To forecast residual payments, the media-buy must be known. This refers to the number of markets in which the commercial will be seen and how often it will be broadcast.

AFTRA members working on television recorded commercials work under agreements jointly negotiated by AFTRA and Screen Actors Guild (SAG) and the industry, represented by the Joint Policy Committee (JPC) on Broadcast Talent Union Relations of the Association of National Advertisers (ANA) and the American Association of Advertising Agencies (AAAA). Radio commercials are negotiated solely by AFTRA.

The current commercials contracts were negotiated and approved by AFTRA and SAG members in September 2003 and became effective October 30, 2003 for three years, expiring on October 29, 2006. In the summer of 2006, AFTRA and SAG negotiated a tentative two-year extension to the contracts to allow for a joint union-industry study of the developing and changing commercials market.

These agreements cover commercial work in both television and radio and address such issues as session, holding, foreign, theatrical/industrial and Internet fees; wild spot use fees and schedules, voice-over performers' and on-camera work on cable, as well as health and pension benefits. Throughout the year, AFTRA and SAG work together on various issues related to commercial work. In addition to a study, AFTRA, SAG, and the JPC agreed that:

- Along with advertisements that appear on TV, radio and the Internet, the agreement will also cover all commercials that appear in new media—for existing platforms such as cell phones and for future platforms yet to be developed.
- Actors will receive a six percent increase in basic compensation, and the contribution to both unions' pension and health plans will go from 14.3% to 14.8%. The agreement provides advertisers with more flexibility to edit commercials for the Internet and new media. (*Important note*: AFTRA and SAG would like to add the following clarification: If the advertisers wish to obtain broader Internet or new media editing rights, for commercials made initially for use on broadcast or cable television, then, in addition to the minimum use payments called for by the contract, they must bargain with the performer regarding the additional compensation to be paid for such editing rights. The extension agreement does not provide for a specific minimum payment as the basis of such bargaining.)
- A New Media Committee, comprised of representatives from both the unions and the industry, will be formed. This Committee will be empowered to make adjustments to the agreement to accommodate changing technologies and shifting paradigms within the commercials industry.
- Advertisers will receive a one-year waiver, which will allow advertisers to experiment with a shorter cycle of use in the new media and Internet areas.

AFTRA chief negotiator Mathis L. Dunn Jr., and SAG chief negotiator John McGuire issued the following joint statement: "Because of the tremendous growth of the Internet and digital technology, the unions have agreed to a two-year extension to conduct a comprehensive joint study that will allow us to determine whether existing pay structures should remain the same or be modified. This agreement also means that actors will have achieved increased opportunities for work and better wages and benefits. In a rapidly evolving media environment, our agreement demonstrates that performers and advertisers can work together to deal with change and build a stronger partnership that benefits us all." JPC chief negotiator Doug Wood issued the following statement: "This early collaborative effort between the unions and the industry is a balanced compromise, and provides the time needed to develop a comprehensive model that fairly compensates performers and ensures that advertisers receive a fair return on their investment. Today's call for accountability at all levels of business requires nothing less. I echo the comments of both John and Mathis that this break-through agreement was made possible by both sides working together and recognizing one another's critical needs going forward."

The results of the joint study will be considered in the next bargaining process surrounding the advertising industry's collective bargaining agreement with AFTRA/SAG. Nine consultants from the industry and academia were invited to respond to a request for proposal for the joint study on May 17. Since the early 1960s, AFTRA and SAG have jointly nego-tiated the collectively bargained recorded commercials contracts.

These agreements cover commercial work in both television and radio and address such issues as session, holding, foreign, theatrical/industrial, and Internet fees; wild spot use fees and schedules; voice-over performers and on-camera work on cable; and health and pension benefits. Through-out the year, AFTRA and SAG work together on various issues related to commercial work.

The following are the session rates charged by AFTRA for the partici-pation of actors, announcers, and singers in radio commercials. This Schedule of Minimum Fees should serve as a paradigm for rate schedules published by other performers' unions. (Visit the SAG and AFM websites to view their session fee schedules.)

2006–2008 Extension to the AFTRA Radio Recorded
Commercials Contract
Schedule of Minimum Fees

Paragraph 6: Minimum compensation, or "session fees"
6.B. Actor, announcer, solo, duo: $249.50
Group singer/speaker, 3–5: $183.80
6–8: $162.65
9+: $144.30
6.G. $275.70
Paragraph 9: Wild spots, 13-week use rates
A. Actors, announcers, solos, duos
1. Lineup of cities not including New York, Chicago, or Los Angeles
1 unit: $249.50
2–25 units, add per unit: $3.67

26 and each unit thereafter, add per unit: $2.76
2. Lineup of cities including one or more "major" city
New York City alone: $373.55
Chicago or Los Angeles alone: $338.80
Any 2 of the above alone: $455.60
All 3 of the above alone: $575.70
Additional units, add per unit: $2.76
B. Group singers
1. Lineup of cities not including New York, Chicago, or Los
  Angeles
3–5: 6–8 9+
1 unit: $183.80, $162.65, $144.30
2–25 units, add per unit: $1.91, $1.63, $1.44
26–60 units, add per unit: $1.63, $1.25, $1.25
61 and each unit thereafter, add per unit: $0.92, $0.80, $0.80
2. Lineup of cities including one or more "major" city
3–5, 6–8, 9+
Any 1 major alone: $203.15, $180.35, $160.10
1–35 units, add per unit: $1.63, $1.37, $1.31
36 and each unit thereafter, add per unit: 0.92, 0.80, 0.80
3–5, 6–8, 9+
Any 2 majors alone: $242.60, $186.15, $165.65
1–60 units, add per unit: $1.37, $1.37, $1.31
61 and each unit thereafter, add per unit: $0.92, $0.80, $0.80
3–5, 6–8, 9+
Any 3 majors alone: $270.30, $209.15, $186.15
1–60 units, add per unit: $1.37, $1.31
61 and each unit thereafter, add per unit: $0.92, $0.80, $0.80
Paragraph 10: Wild spots, 8-week use rates
A. Base fee (i.e., 1 unit, no "majors")
Actor, announcer, solo, duo: $249.50
Group singer/speaker, 3–5: $183.80
6–8: $162.65
9+: $144.30
B. Fees for use categories beyond the base fees above
Actors, announcers, solos, duos: 80% of 13-week use fee
Group singers—all: 95% of 13-week use fee
Paragraph 12: Dealer commercials
Actor, announcer: $674.70
Solo, duo: $535.20
Group singers, 3–5: $348.95
6–8: $279.20
9+: $174.50
Sound effects performers: $176.50

Paragraph 13: Network program commercials
1 week's use:
Actor, announcer, solo, duo: $422.15
Group singers: $316.80
4 weeks' use:
Actor, announcer, solo, duo: $684.90
Group singers, 3–5: $526.70
6–8: $471.00
9 + : $430.30
8 weeks' use:
Actor, announcer, solo, duo: $1,091.05
Group singers, 3–5: $839.45
6–8: $749.90
9 + : $672.05
13 weeks' use:
Actor, announcer, solo, duo: $1,353.85
Group singers, 3–5: $1,041.35
6–8: $931.10
9 + : $853.00
13 weeks' limited use:
26 uses
Actor, announcer, solo, duo: $677.00
Group singers, 3–5: $520.55
6–8: $465.50
9 + : $425.35
39 uses
Actor, announcer, solo, duo: $1,019.50
Group singers, 3–5: $713.85
6–8: $637.20
9 + : $578.90
13 weeks' use on across-the-board programs:
Actor, announcer, solo, duo: $1,417.70
Group singers, 3–5: $1,090.20
6–8: $974.95
9 + : $893.20
Paragraph 14: Regional network program commercials
13 weeks' use:
Actor, announcer, solo, duo: $817.00
Singing groups:
In cities including 1, 2, or all of the 3 major cities, 3–5: $817.00
6–8: $735.30
9 + : $661.30
In cities excluding the 3 major cities: $382.95
Paragraph 15: Local program uses
All performers: $271.15

Paragraph 17: Single-market commercials
Actor, announcer only (covers first 13-week cycle)
(60-minute session, per commercial): $171.95
Each additional 13-week cycle: $171.95
One year's prepaid use: $515.90
Singers only (5 commercials):
Solo, duo: $687.85
Group singers, 3–5: $534.70
6–8: $456.15
9+: $393.45
Additional 26 weeks' use beyond first year:
Solo, duo: $284.35
Group singers, 3–5: $220.30
6–8: $184.85
9+: $156.35
Paragraph 18: Demos, copy tests, Nonair commercials
Actor, announcer: $171.95
Additional quarter hour: $43.00
Solo/Duo (up to 4 commercials) : $173.50
Additional half hour or commercial: $43.40
Group singers: $113.45
Additional half hour or commercial: $28.35
Paragraph 20: Foreign use
Actor, announcer, solo, duo: $494.95
Group singer/speaker, 3–5: $287.10
6–8: $198.00
9+: $158.35
Paragraph 21: Contractor for group singers
When 3–8 singers are employed: $85.65
When 9 or more singers are employed: $137.00
Paragraph 22: Sound effects performers
A. Minimum fee for first hour: $191.85
Each hour beyond the first hour: $127.90
Paid in half-hour segments: $63.95
C. Dealer/sessions: $213.70
D. Use fees
Program or program and wild spot: $114.20
Wild spot only: $83.90
Dealer commercials: $176.50
E. Television use: $367.75
Paragraph 23: Editing and dubbing
Tags: $103.25
Tags—Local identifiable contact numbers:
Tags, 2–25: $103.25
Tags, 26–50: $74.10

Tags, 51 + : $40.45

Paragraph 24: Auditions

A. Auditions in excess of 1 hour—paid in half-hour units: $26.85

B. Third and subsequent calls, first hour: $53.75

Additional audition time, paid in half-hour units: $26.85

Paragraph 26: Ad-lib or creative session calls

Minimum fee for first hour: $223.40

Additional half-hour units: $111.70

Paragraph 32: Singers

32.A.3. Session fee: Solo/duo who multitrack: $275.70

Paragraph 66: Public service announcements

Actor, announcer: $564.45

Solos, duos: $586.15

Group singers, 3–5: $382.15

6–8: $305.70

9 + : $191.15

Health and retirement contribution:
14.8%

The AFM

The following information comes from the AFM website (www.afm.org). This organization is affiliated with the AFL-CIO.

With over 250 local unions throughout the United States and Canada, we are the largest union in the world, representing the interests of professional musicians.

The union represents musicians, contractors, music copyists, arrangers, orchestrators, vocalists, and conductors. Members file contracts for records, film, television and videotape, broadcast television, cable television, pay television, television and radio commercials, live events, industrial films, and other organized events. Except for the Commercial Announcements Agreement, there are no standard rates for the Internet as of yet. It is an all-inclusive union.

The AFM has local offices throughout the United States and Canada and an international office located in New York

♪♪ On October 17, 2007, the AFM signed a new two-year agreement that states that the union scale for jingles that are produced for the Internet will also apply jingles recorded for cell phones, iPods, MP3s, podcasts, and additional digital media. This new agreement is referred to as "new media." The scale, which is currently $110 per session, will increase to $115. In addition, a $32 fee will be paid for the first six months of initial use and $86.25 for each succeeding 52-week period. If the commercial was originally recorded for use for traditional television or radio, the fees will be $86.25 for each 52-week period. For more comprehensive information, view the AFM website.

City. Local offices handle all work within their jurisdiction but are governed by the rules of the national office. Union scale (minimum payment) differs depending on the type of work and the area of the country.

Members pay an initiation fee to join the union and then pay yearly dues plus work dues, which are based on a percentage of each payment received through the union. A percentage of all monies collected goes to the international office. For work performed under the Commercial Announcements Agreement, additional payments are due every 13-week cycle for the life of the commercial. Sometimes the same music used on the original spot(s) is dubbed into new commercials. In this event, each musician on the original session is entitled to additional payments.

Members receive pension benefits and are able to participate in additional benefits if they choose.

Performing-Rights Organizations: BMI, ASCAP, SESAC, and SoundExchange

Airplay of commercials generates performance royalties. Not all agencies allow composers to collect performance royalties. Most advertising agencies and their clients own the publishing rights to compositions written for their commercials; the writers' contracts are work-for-hire agreements, which means that composers assign their rights to the agency/client.

Broadcast Music Incorporated (BMI)

The following information is a quotation from the BMI website (www .bmi.com/home.asp):

BMI is an American performing rights organization that represents approximately 300,000 songwriters, composers and music publishers in all genres of music. The non-profit-making company, founded in 1940, collects license fees on behalf of those American creators it represents, as well as thousands of creators from around the world who choose BMI for representation in the United States. The license fees BMI collects for the "public performances" of its repertoire of approximately 4.5 million compositions—including radio airplay, broadcast and cable television carriage, Internet and live and recorded performances by all other users of music—are then distributed as royalties to the writers, composers and copyright holders it represents.

If a composer of a commercial is a member of BMI and the agency/client is willing to pay performance royalties, the commercial must be registered with BMI. BMI collects and distributes performance royalty income.

The American Society of Composers, Authors and Publishers (ASCAP)

The following is a quotation from the ASCAP website (http://ascap.com/index.html):

ASCAP is a membership association of more than 120,000 U.S. composers, songwriters and publishers of every kind of music and hundreds of thousands worldwide. ASCAP is the only U.S. performing rights organization created and controlled by composers, songwriters and music publishers, with a Board of Directors elected by and from the membership.

ASCAP protects the rights of its members by licensing and distributing royalties for the non-dramatic public performances of their copyrighted works. ASCAP's licensees encompass all who want to perform copyrighted music publicly. ASCAP makes giving and obtaining permission to perform music simple for both creators and users of music.

Work for Hire

Most agencies require composers or music houses to sign *work-for-hire* agreements. This means that the agency owns the compositions and/or arrangements in perpetuity and that the composers forfeit their rights to their compositions and/or arrangements. Unfortunately, when dealing with a large agency, this is a standard clause. A number of small agencies allow composers to keep the publishing rights primarily because the creative fees might be below standard fees and the retention of rights is viewed as a form of compensation. Some agencies allow composers to collect performance royalties; this is a point of negotiation and is worth pursuing.

Synchronization Licenses

Agencies are required to obtain *synchronization licenses* (also called sync licenses) to use existing music (e.g., popular records) for television commercials. It entitles them to synchronize music to visuals. Licenses for radio commercials are called *transcription licenses*. The license allows the licensor only the right to rerecord a song—not to use the master sound recording, which is owned by a record company or other rights holder. Obtaining the master sound recording rights requires a separate negotiation. Synchronization fees are negotiated; there are no standard rates. The popularity of a copyright and/or a sound recording and the extent to which an agency/client wants to license it determines its value.

Some composers who write commercials have written songs that have achieved commercial success (songs). It is not unusual for agencies to contact composers to license their songs (instrumentals) and adapt them for commercials. Approvals of the song editing (a 3-minute 30-second song has to be edited to 30 seconds), changing lyrics, and changing arrangements are some of the rights requested by agencies from composers and music publishers. Hire an experienced negotiator to negotiate synchronization and/or transcription licenses. Rights negotiations are complex and require an expert negotiator.

Synchronization and/or transcription fees are paid in addition to arranging and production fees paid to composers or music companies. Do not agree to one fee. Try to negotiate the exclusive right to do all subsequent arrangements of your song/instrumental for any commercial or commercial campaign using your music. This is a difficult concession to obtain but is worth negotiating.

Society of European Stage Authors and Composers (SESAC)

SESAC, the smallest of the three performing-rights organizations, is the only organization that is for profit. SESAC has a subdivision called SESAC Latina, which collects performance income for Spanish-language music. The following is a quotation from the SoundExchange website
(www.soundexchange.com):

SoundExchange is an independent, nonprofit performance rights organization that is designated by the U.S. Copyright Office to collect and distribute digital performance royalties for featured recording artists and sound recording copyright owners (usually a record label) when their sound recordings are performed on digital cable and satellite television music, Internet and satellite radio (such as XM and Sirius). SoundExchange currently represents over 3,000 record labels and over 20,000 artists. Its members include both signed and unsigned recording artists; small, medium and large independent record companies; and major label groups and artist-owned labels.

Managing a Music House

The following is an interview I conducted with John Russo, president of Russo/Grantham Productions, a commercial music house in New York City:

MZ: How does a young person start a music company?

Russo: Usually, it's extremely difficult to just hang up a shingle and declare yourself a music company and go out and solicit business successfully. Our business is known for having personal relationships, and it's very rare, if not impossible, to start off cold not knowing anybody as a potential client and winning business. Now, there are lots of different places to bring your work and try to get started. Usually the smallest of advertising agencies on a regional basis are your best bet—but it's the same as any other business—what comes first, the chicken or the egg? You need to get work to show people to get more work. If you have no work to show, you're virtually closed out of anyone giving you the opportunity to do work. My best advice is that if a person really feels as if they would like to be in their own company, they have no choice but to work for an established business first. In other words, you are going to have to do one, two, or three years of dues paying and work for an established company before you can even get a chance to understand how the business works. The business works a lot on relationship building. The first thing that I would think about is taking existing commercials right off the air and doing my own track. In other words, doing spec work. [John suggests that the composer call the agency and ask if she can do another music track to their commercial.] If you work in smaller markets, they might take you up on it. After that, what you would hope for if you have demonstrated enough capability is that they would give you a chance to do another spec track for a real job. In other words, to a storyboard or a rough cut. You will have to be doing a series of free demos and have to get familiar or somewhat acquainted with the producer on the job and/or the creatives, the copywriter or the art director, and best of all the creative director . . . there are a lot of people vying for a little work. You've got to be imaginative; you've got to be committed, very dedicated to the fact that you know you are going to have to prove yourself before you get a chance to do anything. Now, the flip side of that is that once you have been doing this body of spec work, you're creating your own reel. It's just an ongoing onslaught of making phone calls and diligence—you'll hopefully get an opportunity to work on a real job and have a chance of getting something on air at the time.

MZ: With whom do you negotiate at an advertising agency?

Russo: We deal primarily with the producer and/or the business affairs manager . . . you have to abide by a work-for-hire contract. In other words, the client will own all rights and entitlements to that piece of music. You're basically writing as a supplier—a vendor to this particular agency for this particular product, and you have to assign all right and title. It all comes down to what the budget is and usually it's for the United States and Canada. If the agency elects to use the work in Europe, Asia, or Mexico, or for additional medium rights, let's say radio or Internet, you could negotiate and include that within your budget.

MZ: Do you ever refuse to compete for a job?

Russo: Usually, you have to know the landscape of the job. If the creative assignment is something you know is not your strength—let's say, you're an orchestral writer and they want a pop jingle, it really won't make sense for you to write a pop jingle, if your strength is elsewhere because you're going to have a really hard time winning. Also, the demo fees never really cover the expenses involved in producing a demo. So, you're going to lose money, and you're going to have a very remote chance of winning.

MZ: When devising your budget, do you separate your demo fees from your studio and technical fees?

Russo: Absolutely . . . usually the writer that wins will get a split of 50-50 or 60-40 (40 for the writer) on the creative fee, plus that writer will try to sing on the commercial and participate as a musician on the commercial. So, they will get three avenues of compensation.

MZ: If the assignment is to write an arrangement of an existing composition, is there still a creative fee or only an arranging fee?

Russo: Usually, if there is [only] an arrangement involved, you are allowed to charge what is called a producer's fee. A producer's fee can be anywhere from a quarter to a third to a half of a creative fee, depending upon how much the producer has to work with the arranger.

MZ: How often do agencies allow you to charge a producer's fee?

Russo: Whenever there is an arranging job and there is no creative fee.

MZ: What do you do if the creatives are pushing the composer to almost plagiarize an existing composition?

Russo: I won't do the job. I have a strict policy about that. Lots of time agencies have a kind of idea about what they'd like and at times give us directions that have elements of songs preexisting in them. We don't mind having that as a direction finder but we do mind when an agency requests us to rip off, so to speak, that person's work, whoever it is. We have a policy where a musicologist is involved in assessing the work we've done to make sure that it has legal clearances. If an agency asks us to change something that is too reminiscent of the original work, we refuse to do it. You've got to stand your ground and say no because the agency, at times, will not be guided by prudence when they really have made up their mind about something they want and can't have. You have to give them as close to what you believe is safe and with a musicologist's blessing what is possible, but anything after that you have to decline.

MZ: I've seen contracts where the music house is responsible for plagiarism. What do you do to protect yourself from that responsibility?

Russo: Basically, what you have to do is have an indemnity clause in your contract that fits your comfort level. Indemnity clause means that you will be responsible for a track only up until what level of litigation you are in. In other words, when we sign an indemnity clause we like to include the phrase "finally sustained in a court of law," which means that we are not responsible for any possible infringement up until it's finally sustained, which means going up to the Supreme Court, if necessary. Honestly, the best way to stay clear of that is to know that you shouldn't be close to something to begin with.

MZ: Since demos cost the music company money, what percentage of the jobs do you have to "win" in order to make that investment prudent?

Russo: Typically, with a jingle demo, you are doing really good if you can win one in three. Typically, a company or person will win one of five or six, and that's a good company. It's not so much how good you are or how much better the next guy is—it's a question of whose track really seems to reach into the creative direction that's most endearing to the creatives. So it's a very subjective process, and you can't let it get you down if you lose a demo. You have to understand that you've done the best job you could and that, frankly, you have followed the assignment and you'd love to hear what won. On an underscore side, you need to win one of three or four to be able to stay in business. Jingles carry a premium in creative fees—triple that of an underscore—so you could afford to lose more underscores because they don't cost as much to make. Jingles, you have to really know that you're placing your bets, in that you don't want to be involved unless you know you have a really good chance of winning, which is a one in six, let's say—I mean anything more than five or six music companies I think is too scattered and honestly not necessarily a bona fide job. It may be more of a hunting expedition, and even if you won, would result in a final. So you could win and lose by being involved in the wrong job. Typically, we win over 50 percent of our demo submissions for underscores, and we win about one in four to one in three of our jingles.

MZ: On average, how many demos do you submit on a job?

Russo: On an average, we give a minimum of three and a maximum of five. We are trying to show that we are being sensitive to different aspects of the assignment, and we want to include as much as possible in the overall presentation.

MZ: Are there any words of advice that you would like to give to people who would like to manage a music house?

Russo: I would not shy away from the other side of the fence and try to work on the agency side. I think that for you to get to know the animal you are trying to wrestle with, you are better to know it from within than from the outside. My best advice would be that instead of trying to trudge up and down Madison Avenue looking for work as an outside supplier, I would rather put together a very nice résumé and some good thought put in introductory letters that really go to the point of how you would like to be involved as an employee and a part of the actual industry itself. This way, you can get a job as an assistant producer, you can get a job in business affairs, you can get a job as an administrator, you can get a job in contract law assisting—basically an apprentice-type situation—you could actually make some money rather than making no money, and you can learn the workings of the mechanics within an agency and actually take that as a three-prong initiative. Number one, you'll be earning; number two, you'll be learning; and number three, you'll be in a position to understand better how to create your best opportunity for yourself ongoing in a later stage of your career development.

MZ: How involved do you get in the creative part of the business?

Russo: I get involved to a point where I understand the overall scope of the assignment, the overall direction of the assignment, the overall budgetary allowances of the assignment, the schedule, and the players who are involved. After that, it is more my partner and the creative director who run the actual jingle creations or demo submissions. I have found that you can't be both things in this business and do them both well. In other words, my caveat is don't be an artist thinking that you're going to be an artist and a business affairs executive and vice versa. It's very hard to do sales and run a job from an administrative point of view when your job is already demanding from a creative point of view. So what happens is that one will suffer. Whichever that one is, is the one you don't pay enough attention to. So, if you don't do enough of your homework in making sure your work is excellent, then you are not going to get a next job because you are going to lose—and if you are spending too much time on the creative, you are not going to have a chance to get a leg up on what your next assignment is going to be because you are too busy doing the job you already have. So, there has to be a separate, divide-and-conquer-type message that one person cannot be all things to this business.

MZ: Is there any other advice you would like to give?

Russo: My best advice is to follow your heart. However you feel and whatever makes your soul want to be involved in the creative side, what is really the business of selling products is how you should approach what you do. We are in a unique position where we employ art to sell merchandise . . . it's as much a business point of view as it is creative.

Conclusion

It is prudent for composers to understand the business of advertising. It is wise to use experts, such as attorneys, accountants, and musicologists, to counsel composers and music companies. Remember the following:

- Adhere to all union rules.
- If there is a possibility of plagiarism, request that the agency employ the services of a musicologist.
- If you do not understand all terms of an agency contract, hire an attorney who specializes in the advertising industry.

Assignments

1. You have started a new music house that specializes in commercials. How are you going to market your new venture? Write a marketing plan.
2. Construct a budget for a local commercial. Determine average fees in the local market by calling local agencies and then proceed with writing a budget. Your budget must include musicians, singers, studio time, engineering fees, duplication fees, and so on.

14

Conclusion

Popular music reflects contemporary culture, as does most advertising. Composing for commercials is not necessarily a stepping-stone to composing music for films or television. It is a highly developed and specialized craft on its own. Advertising music serves several purposes:

- It helps to "sew" commercials together by creating the proper mood and emphasizing important information.
- A jingle is entertaining and delivers a client's message. Many composers specialize in writing jingles. The field is challenging and creative and should be studied as a separate subject; other composers specialize in underscoring and are generally excellent arrangers and orchestrators.

For students to gain the most from this book, they should purchase a computer music-sequencing program that contains digital audio and enables them to load video footage. In addition, it will be beneficial to own several synthesizers and samplers (virtual or hardware); this will allow them to produce adequate MIDI sounds or samples. *This craft can be learned only through practical experience.*

As exercises, tape commercials from television and radio and score them. Write down the dialogue and rerecord it with your voice. Load the new dialogue track into a computer music-sequencing program that runs in sync with the video. This is accomplished by using the video program such as Quicktime or another format. Turn off the sound on the original commercial and begin composing while listening to the new dialogue track and viewing the commercial simultaneously. This should become a routine procedure for practicing. (If you do not have a video capture card that enables you to load video into the computer program, it will be necessary to hire a video editor.)

Compose two or three completely different pieces, in a variety of styles, for each commercial.

Composing should always be approached from an emotional viewpoint rather than from an intellectual perspective. One's intellect should be used only to implement the mechanics of composing to film, analyzing the film, and the placement of music, called *spotting*. Composing music is a creative process. The following are quotes by Dale Johnson, a writer and creative director:

> "Music is often remembered after the words are gone."
> "The right music can be attention getting, motivating, and memorable."
> "Music is so powerful, it doesn't need words."
> "Music helps tell you what to feel and how to feel it."
> "Music can move people emotionally even when the advertising is rational."
> "Music reaches the emotional side of a person that no rational argument can."
> "Think how scary music can make you feel; that shows how music reaches deep inside you."
> "Music reaches into a person where nothing else can go."

Composing opportunities and the role of composers in commercials, corporate videos, the Internet, video games, and infomercials are continually expanding. As technology becomes less expensive, opportunities increase because the volume of work increases.

Composing is rewriting—there was only one Mozart!

Index

Note: Italic page numbers refer to illustrations.

About the Author

Michael Zager holds the Dorothy F. Schmidt Eminent Scholar Chair in Performing Arts and is a professor of music at Florida Atlantic University in Boca Raton, Florida. He previously taught at the Mannes College of Music, a division of New School University in New York City. He is a Fulbright Specialist (awarded by the Bureau of Education and Cultural Affairs of the Department of State and the Council for International Exchange of Scholars) and serves on the Board of Governors of the Florida Chapter of the Recording Academy (creator of the Grammy Awards). Some of Zager's original scores and original studio recordings of Whitney Houston, the Spinners, Luther Vandross, and the Michael Zager Band reside in the Rock and Roll Hall of Fame and Museum in Cleveland, Ohio. He is a graduate of the University of Miami and the Mannes College of Music.

Zager designed and directs the Commercial Music Program at Florida Atlantic University, which won an award for Best New Major from *Florida Leader* magazine in 2003. He has produced, composed, and/or arranged original music for a wide range of musical idioms, including commercials, albums, network television programs, and major motion pictures.

Zager has written more than 400 commercials for clients, including Dr Pepper, MCI, Masterlock, Cablevision, Buick, Acura, IBM, Schlitz Malt Liquor (sung by Kool and the Gang, the Spinners, .38 Special, and the Chi-lites), Bounce (sung by Whitney Houston), Crystal Light (sung by Raquel Welch), Budweiser, Crest, Kodak, Ivory Shampoo, Maxwell House Coffee, Clearasil, Lancôme, Volvo, Burger King, and Os-Cal (featuring Olympic gold medalist Peggy Fleming).

Zager has received numerous advertising awards for composing and/or arranging, including a Clio Award, three International Film Festival Awards, three Art Directors Club Awards, and a Mobius Advertising Award. For many years, his company produced the American Advertising Federation Hall of Achievement Awards.

Zager has produced Grammy Award–winning artists Whitney Houston, Cissy Houston, Peabo Bryson, Luther Vandross, Denise Williams, Jennifer Holliday, Joe Williams, Arturo Sandoval, Herb Alpert, Olatunji, and the Spinners. His tracks have been sampled by Jay-Z, 50 Cent, Missy Elliott, and others.

Zager's record awards for producing, composing, and/or arranging include 13 gold or platinum records; the Golden Boot Award (France); the Europe 1 Award (France); the Olé Award (Spain); two BMI Citations of Achievement awards (given for most-performed songs on radio in a given year); a Grammy Award nomination for "Cupid/I've Loved You for a Long Time" (performed by the Spinners); and a nomination for Producer of the Year, Golden Music Awards in Nashville. He produced Daniel Ray Edwards, who was nominated for Best New Artist, Golden Music Awards in Nashville; produced "You Win Again," which was nominated for Single of the Year, Golden Music Awards in Nashville; and nominated for Best Independent Record Label of the Year, Golden Music Awards in Nashville.

Zager's television awards include a Platinum Video Award for the ABC Television Network series *ABC FUNFIT with Mary Lou Retton* and a Daytime Emmy Award for *ABC FUNFIT with Mary Lou Retton*.

His book *Music Production: A Manual for Producers, Composers, Arrangers, and Students* is published by Scarecrow Press (2006).